MARIJUANAMERICA

One Man's Quest to Understand America's
Dysfunctional Love Affair with Weed

MARIJUANAMERICA

One Man's Quest to Understand America's
Dysfunctional Love Affair with Weed

ALFRED RYAN NERZ

Abrams Image, New York

Editor: David Cashion
Interior Designer: Christine Moog
Cover designer: John Gall
Production Manager: Erin Vandeveer

Cataloging-in-Publication Data has been applied for and may be
obtained from the Library of Congress.
ISBN: 978-1-4197-0408-6

Printed and bound in the U.S.A.
10 9 8 7 6 5 4 3 2 1

Abrams Image books are available at special discounts when purchased
in quantity for premiums and promotions as well as fundraising or
educational use. Special editions can also be created to specification.
For details, contact specialsales@abramsbooks.com or the address below.

The material contained in this book is presented only for artistic and informational
purposes. The publisher and the author do not advocate in any way illegal activity
of any kind. In the interest of maintaining the privacy of the individuals whose
stories are discussed herein, many names, places, dates, and other identifying
characteristics have been changed. The author and publisher specifically disclaim
any responsibly for any liability, legal consequences, loss or risk, personal or
otherwise, which is incurred as a consequence, directly or indirectly by reliance
on the information or advice provided in this book.

ABRAMS IMAGE
An imprint of ABRAMS
115 West 18th Street
New York, NY 10011
www.abramsbooks.com

For my grandfather, Clifford Perrine (9/21/1915 – 7/6/2012)

And for Fred, Ginny, and Tina

"I would especially tell you that this accursed hashish is a fiendishly perfidious substance."

"Here, then, is happiness!—it can be contained within an ordinary teaspoon!—happiness with all its rapture, childishness, and folly!"

—Charles Baudelaire, *The Poem of Hashish*

CONTENTS

10 **CHAPTER ONE**
THE LAMEST-LOOKING OUTLAW

24 **CHAPTER TWO**
THEM FIRST FEW KICKS ARE A KILLER

36 **CHAPTER THREE**
MAN ON A BOAT

48 **CHAPTER FOUR**
GOING TO CALIFORNIA

64 **CHAPTER FIVE**
INTERVIEW SNAFU

74 **CHAPTER SIX**
WEED 101

84 **CHAPTER SEVEN**
ENTER THE EMERALD TRIANGLE

114 **CHAPTER EIGHT**
CRAIG THE DEALER

130 **CHAPTER NINE**
SOMETHING POPPED IN MY BRAIN

142 **CHAPTER TEN**
WAITING FOR BUDDHA CHEESE

160 **CHAPTER ELEVEN**
GANJA LAND

180 **CHAPTER TWELVE**
BAD THINGS HAPPEN AT CHRISTMASTIME

196 **CHAPTER THIRTEEN**
ACKNOWLEDGING THE DOG

210 **CHAPTER FOURTEEN**
IT'S ALL HAPPENING

224 **CHAPTER FIFTEEN**
DRIVEN MAD

244 **EPILOGUE**
MARIJUANA ANONYMOUS

260 **CITATIONS**
268 **ACKNOWLEDGMENTS**
270 **AUTHOR BIO**

CHAPTER ONE

THE LAMEST-LOOKING OUTLAW

It's not until noon on Easter Sunday, thirty-three hours into this ill-advised cross-country mission, that it hits me: I must be the lamest-looking outlaw on the planet. The lumbar support attachment I've strapped to my seat is actually too supportive, pushing my belly out into a turgid ball that looks like early-stage pregnancy. My neck-support pillow is a shade of fuchsia that doesn't occur in nature, and so overstuffed that side-mirror checks require a full upper-body twist. Cruise control is set to sixty-six, one mile over the limit. My legs are crossed at the ankles, shorts unzipped, fly fully open, boxer briefs exposed by a shock of window-filtered sun, and I'm using a curious one-handed steering technique that involves holding the lap portion of the seat belt against the bottom half of the steering wheel.

I have devised this innovation to relieve the pressure on my bladder, which begs to be voided almost hourly. Actually, my driving schedule revolves entirely around my peeing schedule. In order to maximize hydration and driving efficiency, I've made a rule of one stop per large water bottle consumed. At the end of each bottle, when I grant myself the luxury of exiting the interstate, it's the most orgasmic old-man-style pee you can imagine, a minutes-long stream of startling velocity that yields audible groans of pleasure.

The point is: What started out as an adrenaline-fueled odyssey has become mundane and repetitive. I drive and I drive and I drive. The first day was tense, despite the calming scenery: northern California's snowy peaks, the pocked red rock formations of Nevada. That night, in a Salt Lake City hotel, I couldn't sleep because I kept compulsively checking on the rental car through the hotel room window. I rose early and got back on the road, snapping pictures of Wyoming's perpetual cow pasture. I made phone calls to people I hadn't talked to in months, always using the Bluetooth earpiece so five-o wouldn't get me on some petty cell phone/driving violation and start asking questions.

But today—my third day of travel—the scenery is all flat farmland. I'm starting to get restless, even a little crazy. I have been inventing inane car add-ons, like U-turn signals, to optimize the driving experience. I only brought two CDs—Lil Wayne's *Tha Carter III*, and *The Best of*

Bill Withers—and have so thoroughly memorized the latter that I shot a self-directed video singing "Use Me" with the camera balanced on the dashboard.

The real threat to my sanity, though, is FM radio. The lack of variety is appalling. There are at best a dozen songs in pop radio rotation. One of them—that Adele song with the chorus, "we could have had it all"—I can't listen to, because I keep picturing my ex-girlfriend singing it at me. I've got "S&M" down so cold I could perform it with Rihanna. The classic hits stations have been playing the same songs for a decade: I can feel it coming in the air tonight and, Why don't you come with me, little girl, on a magic carpet ride? The other stuff, from frothy conservative propaganda to save-the-lord mockumercials, I can only handle for a few minutes before nausea starts to set in.

It is in just this fragile state of profound boredom, driving east through Omaha, that I spot the state trooper. When I see the car skulking there on the left-side shoulder, my back stiffens against the lumbar support. I've seen dozens of cops by now, so the trauma of individual sightings isn't that big a deal. But something about this one feels different. Menacing. It's one of those barely marked all-black sedans that seems designed to look muscular and imposing. Just as the pang takes control of my stomach, the car pulls out of the shoulder and into the flow of traffic behind me.

No big deal. He probably clocked someone speeding. He'll pass me any second now. I flip on my turn signal and veer into the far right lane, as if maybe I can hide there. I turn down the radio, let go of the seat belt, put both hands on the steering wheel, and check the speedometer. What if the speed limit changed to fifty-five, now that I'm in city limits? Jesus! That was the one thing I promised myself: I would never go above the speed limit on this drive. I slow down to fifty-six and reset the cruise control.

He should have passed by now. Should I *not* have slowed down? I check my rearview, careful not to snap my head or make any darting, suspicious moves. Where is that car? Did it disappear? With a tightly controlled neck-swivel, I check the side mirror. There's the bastard, lurking in the lane to my left, about fifteen yards back, right in my blind spot.

I feel my hands white-knuckling on the steering wheel. *Keep cool. You're just driving.* But I know I'm not just driving. I did my research before I left, so I know the stakes here. Nebraska's laws are among the scariest of the twelve states I will go through: I'm looking at a $10,000 fine and a five-year prison sentence.

I realize I can't possibly calm down. But it's important to appear calm. I focus on down-shifting my breathing, which pulsates up from my lungs in hurried, shallow blurts. I try to inhale through my nose and exhale out my mouth, like in a yoga class. My shorts are still unzipped for bladder maintenance; no time to deal with that now. Eyes forward, no more mirror checking. This will all be over soon enough, for good or ill.

Am I just being paranoid? Maybe. But that car's vibe is ominous—like it doesn't like me. I know that, since I-80 is a main thoroughfare for this sort of thing, cops are on the lookout for certain types of drivers. I fit that type to a tee: male, between the ages of twenty and forty, driving a full-size rental car with a big trunk. And there's the most incriminating detail of all: the California license plate, flaunting the fact that my journey started in America's marijuana mecca.

Such a fucking rookie move! Why didn't I take the advice that Buddha Cheese gave me before I set off? Go straight to the Salt Lake City airport, drop off this conspicuous black car, then transfer the goods to a similar-sized car, preferably white, and with the more innocent-seeming Utah license plate. Then drive from Salt Lake to Chicago and do another transfer. "Keep your plate consistent to the region you're traveling in," I'd been told—advice that now seems devastatingly on-point.

But I thought my objection seemed reasonable. Transferring the goods in an airport rental car lot seemed more risky than driving straight through, especially since airports are one of five locations—along with sports arenas and international borders—in which authorities don't need probable cause for a search. Had I been able to fit all of the stuff into the massive suitcase and the even more voluminous duffel bag, a transfer might not have seemed so dicey. But it was a tight squeeze; I finally resorted to stuffing individual bags into every unoccupied nook. Transferring all of that to a different car in a public space just seemed reckless. But sadly, the real coffin nail was the advice of Roland, an admittedly unreliable weed grower. "Just come up with a story that originates in Cali," he said, "and stick to your guns."

My armpits are drenched. The fucker's still back there. I see Exit 419 and am tempted to take it, but exiting would be like an admission of guilt, right? To calm my spinning thoughts, I do a mental dry run for getting pulled over. I will flip on my signal and glide into the shoulder. I will look him in the eye and call him "officer." If he asks why I've driven here from California, I will hit him with my story: I am writing a sequel to my book about competitive eating. I'm traveling across the country, interviewing pro eaters and participating in restaurant challenges. Just did the Burritozilla Challenge out in San Jose, with Joey "Jaws" Chestnut, the hot dog champ. Now I'm on my way to the Fatty Challenge in Des Moines. Oh and hey look, there's a copy of my first book here in the backseat . . .

The more I rehearse, the more ridiculous I feel for having staked my freedom on such an absurd alibi. Plus, showing him the book feels like too hard of a sell. Especially since gesturing to it would draw attention to my real Achilles' heel here: all my luggage, sitting in the backseat. Two massive bags and assorted rubbish. There just isn't enough room in the trunk. The only plausible explanation I've got is that I am taking videos of each eating episode, so the trunk is filled with cameras and audiovisual equipment. Pretty weak, I know, but it's all I've got.

I see motion in the side mirror. Trooper's on the move. I see a hood, then a windshield, and I try to telepathically persuade him to pass. *Come on come on come on.* Instead he goes with a highly original driving move: He speeds up and then hovers beside me, window-to-window. I keep my eyes forward. Whatever this ball game is, I'll pretend it's not happening. I try to mask inward panic with the outward bearing of an earnest and focused driver, but there's a chance I just look fucking crazy. My peripheral vision picks up the glare off his tinted window and my mind's eye sees a mustachioed cop looking over, trying to crumple my composure with his evil Ray-Ban eye beams.

It's gonna be fine. I'm not breaking any traffic laws. They can't pull you over just for coming from California. I checked my turn signals in the hotel parking lot this morning. I showered and shaved. I'm wearing a collared shirt. I'm a normal guy. It's gonna be fine.

And you know what? I know my rights. I'll invoke the Fourth and Fifth Amendments, confess to nothing, and answer no incriminating questions. This trooper doesn't possess reasonable, articulable facts that I am involved in the commission of a crime. And if the cocksucker asks to look in the trunk, I'll refuse. He doesn't have a pinprick of a probable cause for a search. And if he threatens to bring out the sniffing dogs, I'll just say I don't have time for all that BS. I have a book assignment to eat a sandwich the size of an infant in just a few hours. If he insists, well, I know most courts will uphold that if a sniffing dog alerts to a suspicious scent, that's enough for probable cause. But I covered my tracks on the smell-abatement front. It's all triple vacuum-packed and rubbed in alcohol, and I've got air fresheners back there. So bring out the fucking dogs.

Just as I'm brimming with this bullshit bravado, the cop shoots past. My scrunched shoulders slacken. I take a hand off the steering wheel and exhale so hard I realize I must have been holding my breath. I can't shake the feeling that The Man is on to me, that he *knows*. But all he had to do was flip on the lights and falsely accuse me of speeding. It would have made his day and ruined my life. So why didn't he?

I am preparing to exit, even considering getting a hotel room for the day, when the cop reappears. *Really?* He's in the left shoulder just ahead of me, creeping along at fifteen miles per hour like it's his own personal prowling lane. I pass him, and he pulls out again. Within seconds he is right back on my tail, this time directly behind me. Game over. Part of me is petrified; another part is pissed. I mentally note the license plate number of a nearby SUV, in case I eventually need a witness to corroborate that I'm not speeding.

I decide on a new tactic: playing up the relaxed-driver vibe. For the first time I notice the radio is playing. It's one of a half-dozen half-tolerable songs on pop rotation, Cee-Lo's "Fuck You." I smile at the shared sentiment, then turn it up and start singing, careful to use the radio-friendly "Forget You" lyrics. I force my fingertips to tap against the wheel and try to convince myself of my own innocence. I'm just a writer living his material.

The cop pulls up beside me and goes with his now-patented window-to-window stalk. I can't take this anymore. I need to get out of this car. Like, right now. I flip on my turn signal, well in advance of—I swear I'm not making this up—exit 420.[1]

∗   ∗   ∗

The cruel irony of this trip is that I have no weed to actually *smoke*. It's all safely packed, and that is as it should be. But after all that, I would kill for a few puffs of a joint. Instead, I wriggle out a cigarette and suck it down in a crackhead frenzy. It's not enough. I decide to indulge in another vice I promised myself I wouldn't touch, not until I'm done driving at the end of each day: a drink. I see a Texas Roadhouse restaurant—a beer and a steak might take the edge off.

Just as I walk in the door, a cheerful country tune comes on. The entire waitstaff gathers in the central aisle and breaks into a grotesque, meticulously choreographed line dance. As the hostess ushers me down the aisle, they sing right into my face, flashing the kind of demented, saccharine smiles you sometimes see on cult victims. On the back of their T-shirts, it says: "I love my job!" I might normally find this episode amusing—a fun slice of American cultural anthropology. But under the circumstances, it's a special brand of torture that borders on horrific.

---

1 For those who missed the memo, 420 is the official number of all things weed. 4:20 is the time to get high during the day, and April 20 is the universal stoner holiday. There are a lot of theories as to how this came about. Hitler's birthday? The number of chemical components of THC? Police code for pot possession? The most widely accepted version is that a group of five teenage stoner buddies from Cali coined the term in 1971. Known as the Waldos for always leaning against the same wall at San Rafael High School, the group got word of a Coast Guard service member who could no longer tend to his marijuana grow near a local Coast Guard station. With a treasure map in hand, the Waldos staged a ganja hunt, meeting at the Louis Pasteur statue outside the school at 4:20 P.M. It quickly morphed into code for getting high. The Waldos claim they spread the 420 concept through their contact with the Grateful Dead and their Deadhead followers.

I sit down, order a tall Bud, and pull out Hunter S. Thompson's *Fear and Loathing in America: The Brutal Odyssey of an Outlaw Journalist.* The cover shot shows a brooding, paranoid-looking Thompson in the backseat of a car, arms crossed in a self-comforting way, clutching his trademark cigarette filter like it's his last grip on sanity.

I try to read but can't process the words. To my left a family of ten is having Easter lunch. The table's focal point is a radiant, wholesome-looking blonde teenage girl, encircled by a group of well-fed, conservatively dressed midwestern adults. I lean over and press my palms into my forehead. For the first time on this two-and-a-half-day expedition, I get sideswiped by a supremely rational—if downright obvious—question: *Why the hell am I doing this?*

One of the reasons, of course, is for the story. I wanted to get inside the narrative. I think about what Thompson said about marijuana: "It has been a source of joy and comfort to me for many years. And I think of it as a basic staple of life, along with beer and ice and grapefruits—and millions of Americans agree with me." I am among those millions. But I know millions of other Americans—decent, family-values types like this group sitting next to me—feel genuine fear and loathing . . . toward a plant.

I know 2010 was the second-biggest year for marijuana arrests in U.S. history. And I know 750,000 of those 853,000 arrests were for simple possession. It's obscene—a waste of time, money, and the lives of relatively innocent, nonviolent citizens. Ever since this project started, I have wanted to defy America's head-in-the-sand marijuana laws in some bold way, and I don't think it's too much of a stretch to call this drive a one-man protest march.

But let's not get too self-righteous here. The ugly truth is, my bottom line here is cash. I have $600 in the bank, thanks to my final unemployment check. I am essentially homeless. I have monthly loan payments and four maxed-out credit cards, for which I can no longer pay the minimums. For weeks I have been getting bihourly calls from maniacally persistent automated credit card nags. I decline the calls every time, because I have nothing to offer them. But they clog my voice mail with their creepy-perky robo-voices: "We are sorry we cannot speak to you personally. We appreciate your busy schedule . . ." And: "Hello, this is Great American Savings Bank, calling about a change in the status of your credit card account. It is important that you contact us . . ." This shit wears on you after a while. It chips away at your confidence and desiccates your soul.

But it's oddly fitting I've taken on this assignment to alleviate my debt, because I hold marijuana partially responsible for getting me into this fiscal mess. On a personal level, I feel genuine tenderness—even love—toward the plant. But our relationship has been complicated. It started out as a love affair, and we've remained pretty copacetic, but there was a point when pot turned against me.

Until college I was a classic "good kid," a three-sport athlete and a scholar. A firm believer in the American achievement ethos, I worked hard and expected to be rewarded with a lifetime of pats on the back. The world seemed to be pulling for me, and I wasn't going to let it down. In high school I almost never smoked but sometimes hung out socially with the stoner crowd. We seemed to share a delight in the absurdity of things. But I was a committed jock/nerd, and I'd heard pot was bad for your lung capacity and memory, so I steered clear.

Not until my sophomore year in college did I start smoking regularly. Becoming a part-time pothead coincided with a significant—and mostly positive—transformation of character. I quit hockey and pre-med, both of which were making me unhappy. I shaved my hair and started dressing less preppy, more alternative—raiding my dad's closets from the seventies and sporting vintage Salvation Army purchases. Instead of hanging out with the athletes and prep school kids who'd made me feel safe freshman year, I started spending time with a more arty and mischievous crowd. I signed up for classes in philosophy and Jewish mysticism. I fell in love with hip-hop, a realm in which marijuana and success seemed inextricably linked. I found myself hooking up more, with sexier and more intriguing women. And my former harried drive to succeed was supplanted by a Zen-like ability to observe the world with amused detachment. I loved it all and felt indebted to weed as a catalyst to my transition.

After I graduated, joining the Real World did nothing to moderate my habit. Marijuana became my closest confidant. In New York City, we went everywhere together. She was my spark plug, my painkiller, the drums to my saxophone. At 6:00 P.M., I would get released from my job (as an editorial assistant at a children's publishing company), take a few hits from the dugout[2], and launch into an adventure. I'd stalk down Sixth Ave. into Greenwich Village with my Walkman on, meet friends for happy hour, scribble story ideas in smoky dive bars, buy used books near NYU, watch street performers in Washington Square Park, spark fatties with friends on fire escapes. I took her with me to an endless flurry of events: gallery openings, readings, lavish corporate fetes, birthday parties. I'd step outside to smoke with a self-selecting group—friends and others along for the ride—only to find the cackling conversations more memorable than the events themselves. These huddled sidewalk crews looked diverse at first glance but shared certain characteristics—a desire for inner calm, and the shared sentiment that this was all basically a charade.

As twentysomethings, we were all pretty much lost—even the ones on the "right" track, the law school students and investment bankers. Weed was an ideal drug for sidestepping all that confusion. My solution was to stay high and keep moving, a perpetually smiling blur. For almost eight years New York City was a fucking blast, and marijuana was its perfect accompaniment. But in early 2005, I began to feel like I couldn't keep up this pace. Reality was catching up with me. I was sick of hustling random jobs—waiting tables, editing college essays, and conducting exit polls—to support my writing habit. Things weren't getting done, and the fun wasn't as fun as it used to be.

My relationship with weed started to feel dysfunctional. Smoking pot became less social, and more of a solitary prelude to just about everything. I started hiding my habit from my girlfriend, who said she felt distanced

---

2 The dugout is the most significant urban stealth stoner's device ever invented. It consists of a wooden container with two chambers: one for a metal pipe (usually shaped and painted like a fake cigarette), and another for a weed cache to dip the pipe into. If you smoke publicly and don't use a dugout, it's your own fault if you get arrested.

from me when I was high. I had developed an occasional high-pitched wheeze. I would smoke before writing, to summon the muse, only to scour my brain in vain for an elusive word, or rewrite a sentence a dozen times. I had gotten arrested for possession in Central Park, after graciously offering my lit pipe to an undercover officer. Back home for Christmas, I snuck away from my family and smoked—from a makeshift Coke can pipe—then covered up the smell with mints and sanitizing gel. Before boarding airplanes, I wrapped up tightly sealed bags of herb and stuffed them inside wide-mouthed shampoo bottles.

I started to wonder whether I was addicted. On the Marijuana Anonymous website, I answered "yes" to all twelve questions. I was no longer getting high to enjoy it, but simply to feel normal—whatever that meant. Weed was my way of coping with the sensory onslaught of urban life, and the chronic disappointment of adult life.

Things began to unravel. My girlfriend of five years, with whom I shared a Brooklyn apartment, moved away to go to med school. I was touring the country, announcing eating competitions and writing a book about it. While I was on the road, there was no pot but plenty of alcohol, and absurd adventures with competitive eaters, in the strip clubs and dive bars of places like Oklahoma City. My girlfriend and I grew distant and started breaking up, agonizingly slowly at first, then with melodramatic suddenness.

Weed amplifies reality. So when you're in a good place psychologically, getting high tends to make you happier. But as William Burroughs once said, "Marijuana is a sensitizer, and the results are not always pleasant. It makes a bad situation worse. Depression becomes despair, anxiety panic."

Looking back I realize I was depressed. All the signs were there. I withdrew socially, gained fifteen pounds, and was smoking weed three to five times a day. Getting high and being depressed fed off each other until they became one and the same, an endless feedback loop. Paranoia set in like a heavy, slow-moving cloud. I remember being sure I had contracted an STD, despite having no symptoms. At one point I called a buddy and apologized for a comment I had made weeks earlier, which I was sure had created an irreconcilable rift between us. When I finally finished my monologue, he confessed that he had no idea what I was talking about.

I also started spending. I bought clothes and books and a few vacations, throwing it all on my credit card. I got takeout sushi so often that the restaurant spontaneously gifted me a bottle of sake. By the standards of many Americans, it wasn't a luxurious lifestyle, but it was beyond my means. I ate and drank and smoked as much as I could, and paid whatever extortionate New York price I was charged. I'm not accusing weed of making me financially irresponsible. But it allowed me to create what they call in Marijuana Anonymous a "privately defined world," which bore little resemblance to reality. Being stoned allowed me to glaze over the tangible fact that more money was going out than coming in. And when the credit card bills arrived, I would just pay the minimum, pull out my $500 Volcano vaporizer, and get high again.

This sort of self-delusion eventually comes around to bite you in the ass. I finally woke up, in the spring of 2007, to the tune of $45,000 in credit card debt. I took the first job that came my way, a nine-to-five public relations gig for the International Federation of Competitive Eating. I cut down on my consumption and got high less frequently. Over a period of two years, I paid off half my debt. And I actually enjoyed having a proper job, grabbing my Starbucks in the morning and filing into a packed subway, then having a day's worth of tasks to keep my mischievousness at bay. But I have always struggled to maintain enthusiastic-employee status for long. So it was probably inevitable that I would get laid off, which happened soon after things went awry at an oyster-eating contest, in April of 2009.

Without thinking about why, I started researching marijuana. I realized I was having an internal battle regarding my favorite drug. I had always thought of myself as a productive stoner, but signs were pointing toward my being out of control. Was I addicted? Was it even possible to be addicted to marijuana? The more I researched, the more I realized my internal battle reflected an external one. America was hypocritical about weed. The pro-marijuana folks—NORML and *High Times* and all the blunted rappers—weren't willing to admit that the drug had downsides, that it held the real potential to fuck up your lungs, memory, and motivation. The anti-marijuana folks—while sipping wine—insisted that pot fried your brain, was more harmful than cigarettes, and was tarnishing the youth of America. There was no middle ground.

I started writing a book proposal about getting to the bottom of my own—and America's—hypocritical stance on weed. I had lots of questions: Why was America, year after year, among the highest per capita cannabis-consuming nations in the world?[3] Was there something about the superficial buzz and whir of contemporary American life that made marijuana its ideal psychospiritual antidote? Why were so many states following in the footsteps of California and creating medical marijuana laws that openly flouted federal law? Was it a miracle drug, as thousands of patients in the medical marijuana states had claimed? And if it was such an effective medicine and spiritual elixir, why did we continue to outlaw this plant, and what sort of underground culture had the war on weed created? Or were the prohibitionists right? Was weed actually dangerous and addictive, just another street drug turning otherwise productive citizens into jabbering, irresponsible potheads?

What sustained me while writing the proposal was a series of jobs—production on movie sets, writing for NPR—but most of all, unemployment checks. Which, as you might guess, won't sustain anyone in New York City for long. So even though I was a more restrained version of the depressed sybarite I had been a few years earlier, I started sliding into debt again, and . . . well, here I am, $35,000 in the hole again.

*   *   *

---

3   According to the 2012 United Nations World Drugs Report, the United States is fifth in the world in terms of prevalence of use as percentage of the population, with 14.1 percent. We trail only Palau (24.2 percent), Italy (14.6 percent), New Zealand (14.6 percent), and Nigeria (14.3 percent). But all four of these countries have significantly smaller populations—the closest, Nigeria, has a little more than half of America's population.

Back at Texas Roadhouse, I take a sip of my beer and look down at my steak entrée.[4] Turns out a "loaded" mashed potato means it's doused with shredded cheese, bacon bits, a golf-ball-sized dollop of butter, and a reservoir of sour cream. I feel a blast of bitterness at the duplicity of American culture. It's okay to drink alcohol until you're a blithering subhuman, to take Big Pharma–synthesized medications with worse side effects than the malady they claim to treat, to smoke cigarettes until you need a tracheotomy, or to biggie-size your trans-fats-laden fast food until you have arteries clogged like the Holland Tunnel at rush hour. But then we crack down like rabid militants on this peaceful plant? It just seems so juvenile. In the words of former Seattle police chief Norm Stamper: "Any law disobeyed by more than 100 million Americans[5] . . . is bad public policy."

4   Clearly I haven't learned my fiscal lesson, but I'd like to think these are extenuating circumstances.

5   This is the number of Americans who have tried marijuana at least once. Actually, statistics say it's closer to 130 million.

CHAPTER TWO
THEM FIRST FEW KICKS ARE A KILLER

But how did it come to this? How did I go from wanting to write about my own—and America's—hypocrisy regarding marijuana, to transporting a trunkful of it across the country? Where did this story begin, and what in God's name happened along the way?

I know where it began for me. In fact, I remember the precise moment when I decided to start doing this weed thing full-time. The scene: a parking lot in Indianapolis, winter of 1994. I was sitting shotgun in a purple Isuzu Rodeo. The master of ceremonies was Bill Budd, a teammate on my junior hockey team. After the loneliest, most confounding year of my life as a college freshman, I had decided to take a year off to figure shit out. One thing that needed figuring was whether to keep on being a jock—hence this questionable junior hockey stint, complete with an eighty-game, two hundred–practice season, a tribe of lovable puckheads for teammates, and a coach with the disposition of Heinrich Himmler.

Bill wasn't a complete puckhead. He was this tall, pale-skinned Coloradan creature with a robust imagination and a singular way of expressing himself. "You're not gonna believe how sickening this beat is." He was pulling a CD from its case, shaking his head. "These guys are fucking *lords*."

High praise. Bill slid the CD in the slot and pressed play. A delicious, laid-back hip-hop beat kicked in, with a surreal mélange of voices filling up the background. He packed a glass pipe with stinky, crystal-laden buds and passed it to me. I took a pull, exhaled a blast of smoke, and watched it curl up the windshield and roll back on itself like a wave. It crashed into me, and I broke into a coughing fit. Snapping out of that, I popped into a new reality. The Fourth Dimension. This stuff worked fast. The first round of lyrics seemed to come from far away. I pictured a guy with an Afro and baggy pants on the dusty surface of a distant planet, rapping into a headset: "Trapped in the cockpit, at forty thousand feet / The sky is the limit, but we supersede . . ."[1]

The second verse was sung by two guys at once, streaming into both ears from opposite speakers. I had somehow acquired the ability to focus on one instrument or voice without losing track of the rest of the song—

---

1 The song: "Pack the Pipe," by the Pharcyde.

like a TV's picture-in-picture function, only for hearing. Voices cascaded downward from everywhere at once, like choreographed waterfalls. The sound of someone choking echoed and became its own instrument. Beats wove together like some otherworldly tapestry, interspersed with childishly funny rhymes. It was a song about getting high, performed by artists who were (clearly) high when they recorded it, intended for a high audience, which sounded, somehow, like the sonic equivalent of what it feels like to be high.

Sure, it's a mundane moment. Two guys sitting in a car, smoking pot and listening to music. But that's the whole point. In that brief, banal instant, my perspective shifted from small-minded anxiety to pure transcendence. Looking back, I was at an impressionable stage—no longer content to spend my mind-life thinking about sports, worried about the future, bored and directionless. Introduce into that scenario a drug that has the ability to melt away earthly cares and replace them with total focus on, say, a single drum snare in the backbeat of a song. Or one fragmented but highly amusing thought. It was an escape, but the escape was inward. Not drowning out the world, like I imagine the effects of heroin to be, but fully embracing this one on fresh, new terms.

Turns out I'm not alone in having been seduced by weed through music—that's how America fell for the drug, too. Marijuana first seeped into the continental United States around 1900, as the cargo of Mexican peasants who migrated north over the Rio Grande into Texas border towns like Laredo and El Paso.

But the real spread of marijuana started in New Orleans. At the turn of the twentieth century, cultures collided in New Orleans's Storyville red light district, an early crucible of Southern diversity. In Storyville, black and Cajun "ladies of pleasure" mingled with white gentlemen. Dock laborers and field hands rubbed elbows with itinerant musicians in saloons. It was through this unique intermingling of cultures that marijuana cigarettes first reached the lips of artists playing America's newest contribution to the world of music: jazz.

These jazz musicians—including Jelly Roll Morton and a young Louis Armstrong—were primarily black, played exclusively in brothels and honky-tonks, and were no strangers to the artistic use of drugs. Alcohol blunted the senses, and opiates made musicians nod off, but marijuana—also called muggles, muta, gage, and Mary Warner—enhanced aural focus while softening the self-awareness that can inhibit an improvisational art like jazz. While jamming with Louis Armstrong, the great composer Hoagy Carmichael claimed marijuana elevated his playing to a new level, which felt almost like an out-of-body experience: "I had never heard the tune before, but full of smoke, I somehow couldn't miss a note of it. The muggles had carried me into another world. I was floating high around the room in a whirlpool of jazz. The rest of the night I have no memory of."

In 1917, the federal government shut down Storyville as part of a nationwide crackdown on red light districts. New Orleans banned marijuana in 1923, and the state of Louisiana followed suit in 1927. But it was too late—the magic weed's spell was cast. Jazz musicians traveled north up the Mississippi, joining the flight of black and migrant workers heading to cities like St. Louis, Chicago, and Kansas City. Jazz music traveled with them and became the new music of America, and eventually, the world. Their suitcases bore not just trumpets and horns, but marijuana joints as well.

It seems bizarre in retrospect to ban a weed that grew naturally on the roadsides of America, a domestic agricultural crop that had been used to make hemp twine, fabric, and the paper on which early drafts of the Declaration of Independence were printed. But because it was associated with foreigners and fringe musicians—Mexicans and blacks, respectively—it was only a matter of time before The Man would clamp down on weed. The precedent was already in place, as Chinese immigrants who poured in to service the California Gold Rush had already been demonized for introducing opium to the American populace.

In 1930, President Herbert Hoover appointed Harry J. Anslinger the first commissioner of the newly formed Federal Bureau of Narcotics (FBN). Anslinger, America's Darth Vader of Dope, was a horrifying-looking creature with an unnaturally large, square head and beady eyes. He likely developed his fixation on cannabis more out of pragmatism than genuine concern. Two years after his appointment, the FBN faced heavy budget cuts due to the onset of the Great Depression. Anslinger, who had initially been dismissive of a federal ban on marijuana, now decided to pin his hopes of a budget increase on exposing the drug as a burgeoning public menace. In his previous position as assistant commissioner of the U.S. Treasury Department's (alcohol) Prohibition Unit, he had learned that public outrage toward an enemy of the people was the best means of diverting money into a bureau's coffers.

Anslinger unleashed a relentlessly fear-based and racist publicity campaign against the "killer weed." He planted dozens of stories in the press about murders and rapes committed under the influence of marijuana, almost always by Mexican immigrants and blacks who had gotten high and transmogrified into "bestial demoniacs, filled with a mad lust to kill." The victims of these crimes were invariably white, and pictures of their mutilated bodies often accompanied the articles. Anslinger also spearheaded the production of several anti-weed movies, like *Marihuana*, released in 1935, with the unintentionally alluring tagline: *Weird orgies! Wild parties! Unleashed passions!* The most famous of these films was *Reefer Madness* (1936), a story of three teenagers whose lives are ruined by weed, which was partly financed by a church group and a distillery that was concerned about a loss of profits if marijuana grew more popular.

In 1937, after two years of secret planning, Anslinger's crony from the Treasury Department, chief counsel Herman Oliphant, drafted an anti-marijuana bill. In the preliminary Senate hearings, Dr. James Munch, a pharmacist from Temple University, claimed he had tried the drug (for scientific reasons, of course), and it had turned him into a *bat*. The only notable dissenting voice was that of Robert Woodward, legislative counsel to the American Medical Association (AMA). Woodward slammed Anslinger for using the word *marijuana* instead of *hemp* in the bill in order to dupe industrial hemp producers, and he questioned the legitimacy of the (mainly hearsay) evidence. He was dismissed outright by the committee chairman. When Anslinger got his chance at the podium, he didn't hesitate to drop lovely little xenophobic nuggets like this: "There are 100,000 total marijuana smokers in the U.S., and most of them are Negroes, Hispanics, Filipinos and entertainers. Their Satanic music, jazz and swing, results from marijuana usage. This marijuana causes white women to seek sexual relations with Negroes, entertainers and any others."

The bill, known as the Marihuana Tax Act of 1937, reached the floor of Congress late on Friday afternoon, when most congressmen had already left for the weekend. No vote was taken. Instead, a clerk simply counted the number of congressmen who walked by him. The bill passed and was signed into law by President Roosevelt on August 2, 1937, becoming the first federal legislation to control marijuana. The law didn't technically prohibit cannabis. But it raised a levy so steep—$100 per ounce every time the drug changed hands, in a time when a new Ford cost $200—that it effectively banned the legal sale and purchase of marijuana.

*   *   *

And yet, against all odds, seventy-five years after the passage of the Marihuana Tax Act, and after millions of marijuana arrests during the combined drug wars of presidents Nixon, Ford, Reagan, Bush, Clinton, Bush, and even Obama, weed somehow seems to be winning. More than a third of the U.S. population has admitted they've tried it, and a third of the states have legalized it for medical purposes. Our current president admits he not only smoked pot but inhaled it, and megamoguls like Ted Turner, Mike Bloomberg, and Steve Jobs (R.I.P.) have all enthusiastically hit the hookah.

The media now treats marijuana as commonplace. Smash-hit movies show characters smoking pot as if they were taking a sip of Cabernet,[2] and

---

2 In fact, there's an entire sub-genre of classic pot-smoking characters played by Hollywood A-List actors—Jeff Bridges in *The Big Lebowski*, Jack Nicholson in *Easy Rider*, Robert DeNiro in *Jackie Brown*, Brad Pitt in *True Romance*, and Sean Penn in *Fast Times at Ridgemont High*.

Showtime has based an entire TV series, *Weeds*, on the premise that marijuana is an integral part of American suburban life. Polls consistently show that over 70 percent of Americans support legalized medical marijuana, and a 2012 Rasmussen Reports poll found that 56 percent of Americans would support legalizing and regulating marijuana in a similar manner to alcohol and tobacco. In November of 2012, Colorado and Washington became the first states to legalize the recreational use of marijuana. If that doesn't qualify as a tipping point, how about the fact that weed is the country's top cash crop. According to a 2006 study, cannabis is valued at $35.8 billion per year, effectively bitch-slapping the combined value of two traditional American crops—corn ($23.3 billion) and wheat ($7.5 billion).

American politicians, who have been relatively mute on the subject since the Carter administration, are finally starting to have some balls regarding the red-eyed elephant in the room. In November of 2011, the governors of Washington and Rhode Island, Christine Gregoire and Lincoln Chafee, petitioned the DEA to allow doctors nationwide to legally prescribe medical marijuana. "Poll after poll shows an overwhelming majority of Americans now see medical marijuana as legitimate," said Gregoire, of Washington, where dispensaries had been distributing medical marijuana for thirteen years. Even ultra right-wing evangelical leader and former presidential candidate Pat Robertson has (inexplicably) come out in favor of legalizing marijuana. In March of 2012, Robertson said, "I really believe we should treat marijuana the way we treat beverage alcohol. I've never used marijuana and I don't intend to, but it's just one of those things that I think: this war on drugs just hasn't succeeded."

Despite all this apparent progress, the legalization movement continues to lurch forward in fits and starts. After having legalized medical marijuana in January of 2010, New Jersey officials are nearing their third year of delaying access to patients there. In August of 2011, a Michigan appeals court banned patient-to-patient marijuana sales, jeopardizing nearly five hundred dispensaries that had opened since 63 percent of voters had approved medicinal cannabis three years earlier. Some of the most vocal pro-marijuana politicians have either left office or been marginalized.

While in office former California Governator Arnold Schwarzenegger, who was filmed smoking a joint in the 1977 documentary *Pumping Iron,* was an outspoken proponent of taxing marijuana for recreational use. But he got caught schtupping the maid, so we won't hear from him for a while. Congressman Barney Frank has been a longtime supporter, co-sponsoring a 2008 bill attempting to curb federal penalties for marijuana possession. But he's retiring in 2013. Other than that you've got former New Mexico governor Gary Johnson and Texas congressman Ron Paul, both of whom admirably won't shut up about the subject, but aren't moving the ball much closer to the end zone.

Despite being the first American commander-in-chief to openly embrace his past pot use, President Obama has not yet proven to be the weed messiah many advocates had hoped. At the 2009 virtual town hall meeting, the most popular questions involved legalization; Obama dismissed them with a flip joke. At a 2011 town hall meeting in Minnesota, the President became uncharacteristically tongue-tied when asked if he could at least legalize medical marijuana. "Well, you know, a lot of states are making decisions about medical marijuana. As a controlled substance, the issue then is, you know, is it being prescribed by a doctor, as opposed to, you know ... well ... I'll ... I'll ... I'll ... I'll leave it at that." Leave it at ... *what?* We can only hope that, while sneaking out for one of his clandestine cigarette breaks in the White House Rose Garden, Obama will have an epiphany and remember how much he loved toking up back in his high school and college days.[3]

President Obama is caught up in a decades-old trend for politicians who are perceived to be liberal about marijuana: They take a hard-on-drugs stance to silence accusations of running a loose ship. Bill Clinton took so much flack for not inhaling that he became one of the most ruthless

3 In May of 2012, excerpts emerged from a book called *Barack Obama: The Story,* by David Maraniss, which detail Obama's marijuana habits as a youth. In high school he was a member of the "Choom Gang," with *choom* being a verb meaning "to smoke pakalolo," and with *pakalolo* meaning "weed" in Hawaiian. One of the Choom Gang's rituals, popularized by Barry, was "roof hits," where the gang would choom in a car with the windows rolled up. When the joint was gone, they tilted their heads back and sucked the last remnants of pakalolo smoke from the ceiling.

drug-warrior presidents in American history. New York City Mayor Michael Bloomberg, who has not been shy about having enjoyed marijuana personally, has overseen the arrest of more than four hundred thousand people for simple possession during his three terms in office. After a critical article by the *Village Voice* and mild public outrage, New York City Police Commissioner Ray Kelly released a memo in September of 2011 scolding his officers for using sneaky stop-and-frisk tactics. (This usually involves asking people to empty their pockets without telling them they can refuse, resulting in the coerced offense of "public display of marijuana.") Still, when the 2011 data was released, New York remained the marijuana arrest capital of the world with more than fifty thousand possession arrests, the second highest in the city's history.

American prisons now hold in excess of six million inmates, more than were stuck in Stalin's gulag prison system at its height. Since 1980, we have gone from having roughly equal percentages of prisoners as that of our European and Asian counterparts, to having seven to ten times more inmates on average today. What has changed in the last thirty years? The war on drugs—period. Drug convictions rose tenfold over 16 years, from 15 inmates per 100,000 adults in 1980 to 148 in 1996. Today, over half of America's federal inmates today are in prison on drug convictions.

Considering that polls show majority support for cannabis legalization, why isn't American law enforcement adapting to reflect the will of its citizens? We now arrest one American every thirty-eight seconds on marijuana charges. And we do so at a staggering cost in law-enforcement expenses, lost tax revenues, and profits for criminals. In 2007 alone, marijuana laws cost American taxpayers an estimated $42 billion in law enforcement costs and lost tax revenues. We could be using that money and jail real estate to imprison violent offenders. We could pay for more positive approaches to drugs, like substance abuse centers. And we might even be a step closer to resolving America's bottomless pit of debt.

Though the concept seemed like pure fantasy just a decade ago, I now believe the legalization of marijuana in the United States is imminent. It's only a matter of time, of an aging generation—who maintain an outdated stigma toward this plant—to die off, and of a few bold politicians to step up to the plate. I say this not because America is shifting into some leftist Fox-News nightmare of a nationwide commune, or in the other direction, into a radical libertarian Ron Paul–style version of laissez-faire government. America will legalize marijuana for the same reason the Dutch have created their quasi-legalized coffee shop culture: because cannabis is a weed that can be grown anywhere and thus cannot be contained. America will legalize marijuana for the same reason it has changed many of its other failed policies after years of hammering away at them: because it's practical. Or more to the point, we will legalize marijuana for the same reason I drove marijuana across the country: because it's profitable.

The idealist in me believes that legalization will be a good thing. On that historic day, I'll smoke a joint to celebrate no longer having to sneak around like a child, and the fact that marijuana growers will no longer be jailed for what is essentially gardening. Mexican drug cartel profits will shrink, and cash will flow into the coffers of American businesses no less legitimate than liquor stores. Ancillary businesses will develop—from marijuana tourism to the production of cannabis edibles and hemp fabric—that will help fill the cracks that our faltering economy has exposed. Millions of nonviolent marijuana prisoners will be released and gain access to jobs that utilize the very expertise for which they were imprisoned. And maybe some of the investment bankers and real estate hustlers who helped torpedo the world into economic recession will get high and become a little less greedy, or quit their jobs to explore the world with childlike wonder, or just generally learn to chill the fuck out.

But the realist in me knows that legalization won't solve many of the dilemmas about America's—or my own—relationship to weed. I'll have the exact same amount of access to the drug—which is to say, as much as I can afford, which is almost always more than enough. It won't change the reasons why pot smokers like me use the drug, or its effects on us afterward. Hundreds of thousands of my fellow Americans will still be getting high to blunt psychological pain, ease anxiety, or attempt to fill a spiritual void. Potheads will continue to cough and wheeze and lose shit and procrastinate. And though some weed virgins will enjoy the drug for the first time, many more will cling to their fears about the plant and opt for the familiar numbing intoxication of alcohol.

Just as Prohibition did little to stem the flow of alcohol into Americans' gullets, the repeal of Prohibition has done little to resolve the problems that alcohol abuse bestows upon our collective psyche. Which is why, when I think about the future of marijuana in this country, and in my own life, it is with a devil on one shoulder, and an angel on the other.

CHAPTER THREE
MAN ON A BOAT

Before I started moving drugs across state lines, my research started out much more innocently. Where and when it actually began is a bit nebulous, but perhaps it's best to start here: I'm on a boat with a man smoking a joint. It's a spectacular sun-breezy day in southeast Florida. The man smoking the joint is a successful stockbroker. He owns this boat. He is a regular guy—clean-shaven with short-cropped hair, wearing a T-shirt, shorts, and a pair of black Crocs. I would like to have a drag of his joint, but I can't. Technically, he is one of only four people in the United States of America that is allowed to smoke a joint here. And by here I mean the United States of America.

Make no mistake: The reason I can't smoke his joint has nothing to do with any personal moral concerns. It's just that he won't give it to me. And he shouldn't, because it was given to him as medicine by the U.S. federal government. Just to make sure, and because he seems to be relishing this joint so flagrantly, I ask the man if I could, under any circumstances, share it with him.

"No, you could never smoke mine," he explains. "To anyone who ever asks, 'Could I have any?' my answer is: 'You're undercover DEA.'"

"Got it," I say.

I steal a look at him, using my sunglasses as a shield. On closer scrutiny, maybe he isn't a regular guy. He does have some irregularities. He is short—5'5" at best—in a way that suggests stunted growth. His right ankle is wrapped, which draws your attention to his legs. And they are noticeably knock-kneed, with a peculiar bumpiness about them.

The man's name is Irvin Rosenfeld. He is telling me how it is that he came to look this way, and why he's allowed to smoke this joint. He says it started in Little League baseball. He was ten years old, playing shortstop.

"The ball was hit to me for the final out. I picked it up. Threw it to first. The first baseman caught the ball. We had won the game by one run . . . we're ten years old. You take your glove off and throw it in the air. Yay, we won!" Irv shoots me a pregnant look. "Only problem was . . . my whole arm was paralyzed. Couldn't move it."

"The arm that you just threw with?" I ask.

Irv nods. "Totally paralyzed. It didn't hurt, just wouldn't move."

By the time Irv's mom got him to the hospital across the street, he could feel his arm again. X-rays showed a jagged bone sticking out from Irv's wrist. The emergency room doctor misdiagnosed it, claiming he had most likely broken his wrist when he was a baby, and it had healed wrong. But Irv's mom had worked in a hospital before; it made no sense that a broken wrist would go unnoticed. She took Irv to an orthopedic surgeon, who said Irv's body felt wrong. "He took x-rays, and, sure enough, there were these knots everywhere on my body, okay? He said, 'This disorder, I've heard about it. I've seen it to a certain extent, but not like this. It's called multiple congenital cartilaginous extoses.'"

"That's a fun mouthful," I say.

But that's not the half of it. Irv says his other disorder, diagnosed later, is pseudopseudohypoparathyroidism—one of the longest words in the English language. Basically, the body makes normal parathyroid hormone but then doesn't use it. People with this malady have low calcium and high phosphate levels. And they tend to be short in stature.

At age ten Irv went to Boston Children's Hospital. Dr. William Green told Irv he had bone tumors throughout his body that would continue to grow as he grew. It was one of the worst cases he had ever seen. Irv had more than two hundred tumors, any of which could turn problematic—even malignant—at any point. The hard truth of the matter was that Irv might not outlive his teenage years. Dr. Green told Irv's parents that neither he nor they would have dominion over Irv's medical decisions.

"He turns to me and says, 'Irvin, you've got so many tumors in your body that would need surgery. And we can't operate that much; we just can't. You're gonna have to make all the decisions yourself, because we as doctors can understand and learn certain things, but we don't know how it feels. Your parents aren't gonna know that. *You're* the one.'"

Irv pauses dramatically and looks at me. Tropical-tourist music of the Jimmy Buffett variety is wafting over from a restaurant across from the marina. I try to empathize with a ten-year-old Irv: This must have been a terrifying feeling for a kid. At the same time, Irv seems to feel a retrospective aura of self-importance about his situation. Instead of being sad or embarrassed about his ailments, Irv seems to have taken the doctor's calling him "the one" as a point of pride, a sort of anointment.

The first surgery went smoothly. Irv's hand hurt while writing, so he asked for surgery. Dr. Waive, his local doctor in Portsmouth, Virginia, extracted the tumor, and Irv was back to playing baseball a month later. It wasn't until Irv turned thirteen that the seriousness of his condition became apparent. He came back from summer camp and went in for his monthly appointment.

"Doctor Waive does his X-rays, and all the sudden, he's looking at them, and he just goes, 'Holy shit.'" There was a tumor the size of a fist on Irv's upper calf, and it was growing inward toward a major growth center. "I had surgery two days later. And I was lucky I didn't lose the leg. And that took me years to come back from. I had to learn to walk again. I mean it was a very bad operation. And then each operation after that was almost that bad."

Chronic pain became Irv's daily companion. He was prescribed Demerol, Parafon Forte for muscle relaxation, and another pill for sleeping. But he didn't like the way they made him feel. When Irv was fourteen, Dr. Waive pulled his mother aside. "To be honest I don't like giving a young person this much painkillers," he said. "By chance do you have any alcohol in the house?"

Irv laughs. He says that "in the Jewish tradition, at least in southern Virginia," families would get together on Sunday and drink a shot of bourbon. Irv had been doing this since he was seven.[1] At fourteen, he started drinking bourbon as medicine. Dr. Waive explicitly suggested that, every night around midnight, he should make himself a drink, or two, or three. Whatever it took to get relief and sleep.

I shake my head. No doctor would make such a reckless suggestion today, in the skittish climate of multimillion-dollar lawsuits and HMO oversight. And yet few doctors would hesitate to dole out a prescription of potent, addictive painkillers.

---

1 I can only assume this tradition is exclusive to the Jews of southern Virginia.

Because of the pain and the surgeries—there would be six total—Irv started homeschooling part-time. He claims school officials encouraged this, out of fear that he might get hurt during school and sue the system. One day, during one of his rare appearances on campus, Irv ran into his principal. This was the late sixties, when drugs were becoming more prevalent.

"And I said, 'You know, it amazes me, all these kids talking about taking drugs. Why would a healthy person do drugs?'" The principal suggested Irv talk to the kids about it. "And that's how I came to invent the D.A.R.E. program," Irv says, referring to the now-international education program founded in 1983, whose goal is to prevent drug use, gang membership, and violence among students. To say Irv "invented" this program is a stretch—in that he had nothing to do with the actual creation of D.A.R.E.—but he was indeed an early student anti-drug warrior, the irony of which is not lost on him. "I would be speaking to kids my age at school, holding a baggie with prescription bottles in there, saying, 'Look what I have to take. Be thankful you're healthy. Don't do illegal drugs.'"

After graduation Irv enrolled at Miami-Dade Community College. Dr. Waive said the heat in southern Florida would ease the ache of Irv's tumors. Irv had met a young woman through a Jewish youth organization and arranged for her to be his roommate. On their second day together, she lit up a joint. Irv went ballistic. When she didn't comply with his order to put out the joint, he kicked her out. "I was not gonna have drugs in my apartment. Here I had Dilaudid, Quaaludes, Valium, all these heavy narcotics. But I was not gonna, you know, have *that.*"

But Irv was surrounded. This was the early seventies, when marijuana use was at a historical all-time high for the United States. A 1971 Gallup poll showed that over half of the nation's college students had tried marijuana. He couldn't escape it.

In the end Irv tried pot for the same reason many kids do—peer pressure. His apartment complex was full of college students. He would hang with them at the pool, but inevitably someone would suggest they go smoke pot. Irv would politely decline and slump back to his apartment. The taboo of doing an illegal drug was too heavy.

"After thirty days, I realized I wasn't making any friends and it was always because of marijuana." Irv takes a puff of his joint and exhales slowly. "And I thought, you know, these kids seem okay to me. It doesn't seem like it's harming them in any way. I'm gonna give in to peer pressure. I'm gonna try it. Okay, so I tried it. And it was garbage. Didn't get high, nothing."

Irv's newfound friends explained you don't always get high the first few times. Irv kept trying, sipping on bourbon while sharing a joint, hoping to feel something. It never worked, but then Irv didn't much care. He was making friends.

The sixth time he smoked, Irv played a game of chess, which lasted half an hour. He realized he hadn't sat for thirty minutes straight in almost five years. Sit ten, stand ten—that was his ritual. And it had been over six hours since he'd last taken narcotics. "And just then I hear, 'Hey, it's your turn!' And he handed me the garbage. I lit this garbage. And I thought: This is the only thing I've done differently. I've smoked this garbage. Hey, I wonder if there's any medical benefit to this garbage!"

Irv snapped into action. He called Dr. Waive and asked if he knew anything about marijuana as a medicine. The same man who had prescribed bourbon as an analgesic . . . was gobsmacked. He said he would look into it. Meanwhile, Irv called his family, and before long, they were all researching the then-novel concept of medical marijuana. "And lo and behold, that's when we discovered, it was a legal medicine in this country from 1860 to 1937. It was manufactured by major pharmaceutical companies, Merck and Eli Lilly and all of them."

He speaks truth. Before 1937, nearly every pharmaceutical company in America was manufacturing cannabis-based drugs. Parke-Davis had Utroval, Casadein, and a veterinary cannabis colic cure. Eli Lilly had a tincture marketed as an "anti-spasmodic, sedative, and narcotic," as well as Dr. Brown's Sedative Tablets, Neurosine and the One Day Cough Cure, a mixture of cannabis and balsam.[2] Pills of hashish coated with sugar were sold, as well as a mixture of snuff and marijuana, sold as an asthma cure.[3]

Though cannabis was historically used in America for a variety of disorders, Irv discovered it was primarily as a muscle relaxant and anti-inflammatory, both of which were applicable to his ailments. Irv decided to experiment on himself. He would go three weeks at a time, smoking marijuana daily. He found that he felt less pain and more alertness as his intake of Dilaudid and other medications decreased. Then he would take a week off. Within two days the pain would return and his narcotic intake would surge.

After conducting this experiment for four months in a row, Irv called his doctor. His dilemma: He was becoming a full-on pothead and was worried about getting busted. "I'm not a criminal," Irv told Dr. Waive. "I'm a patient. You can give me Dilaudid, but you can't give me cannabis."

Around this time Irv discovered a little known fact: The American government had a marijuana farm. Since 1968, the University of Mississippi has operated the only federally legal marijuana farm and production facility in the United States. The National Institute on Drug Abuse (NIDA) contracts with the university lab to grow, harvest, process, and ship marijuana to licensed facilities across the country for research purposes. The lab also collects samples of marijuana seized by police, to determine its potency and document national drug trends. The marijuana fields are surrounded by double fences and armed guards perched in towers.

Irv moved back to Virginia and started keeping data about how marijuana affected his symptoms. In 1976, Irv heard about Bob Randall, America's first legal medical marijuana patient. Randall had developed

---

2   There's a compelling history and image collection of these medicines online at www.antiquecannabisbook.com.

3   Using marijuana to treat asthma, while seemingly counterintuitive, actually has some basis in research and holistic tradition. Doctors such as Donald Tashkin have conceded that marijuana's active ingredient, THC, does have a modest bronchodilating effect. However, most doctors and researchers—Tashkin included—say that the long-term pulmonary effects of chronic cough and sputum production (from smoked cannabis) outweigh these positive effects.

glaucoma in his teens. In the early seventies, an ophthalmologist said Randall would be blind within a few years. He started using cannabis and noticed the "tricolored halos" he saw around lights at night would disappear after smoking. Marijuana eased the intraocular pressure that hampered his vision, and which would most likely lead to blindness. He started growing his own weed. Then he got busted.

Randall underwent testing to prove that no other glaucoma drug effectively halted the deterioration of his eyesight. He then used the "common law doctrine of necessity" to argue against his marijuana-cultivation charges, because the drug was a medical necessity. He won. The federal government started shipping him ten joints a day from the farm in Mississippi. He was the first legal medical marijuana smoker in the United States since 1937. But when he went public with his victory, the feds cut off his supply. Randall sued for reinstatement. Twenty-four hours after he filed the suit, federal agencies requested an out-of-court settlement that resulted in Randall gaining access to marijuana through a federal pharmacy near his home. By the time Randall died, of AIDS-related complications in 2001, he was still smoking government pot, and he could still see.

Irv met Bob Randall after a speech he gave at Old Dominion University. Randall started helping Irv create a compassionate care protocol to present to the federal government. They finished it in four months. Dr. Waive had recently died, so Irv had his new doctor, an endocrinologist named Dr. Goldman, sign it. They sent it off to the FDA and got stonewalled. It wasn't outright rejected; the FDA just claimed they were looking into other alternatives.

Three more years passed. By this point a lawsuit seemed like the only alternative. Irv sought counsel from his cousin, Donald Hornstein, a third-year law student at the University of Virginia. Intrigued by the idea, Hornstein approached one of his law professors, Richard Bonnie, who was the co-author of a book on marijuana prohibition. Bonnie thought it would be a good lesson for his students, who started putting a lawsuit together. Once it was prepared, they called the FDA to let them know a suit was forthcoming. This power play finally got the FDA's attention. Instead of prepping for battle, they decided to give Irv fifteen minutes to convince a committee of his case, at the FDA headquarters in Rockville, Maryland.

Irv called Bob Randall. Knowing it would be an open hearing, Bob decided to alert the media and advertise all over the building. "So when they turn you down, we'll have a record of all that," Bob explained.

Irv Rosenfeld's hearing with the FDA committee was scheduled for the first Tuesday in October of 1983. The room was full. All types had shown up—reporters, political types in bespoke suits, doctors in scrubs. The chairman thanked everyone, told Irv he had fifteen minutes, and slammed his gavel down.

As concisely as possibly, Irv told the committee the story he's been telling me: the six operations, all the narcotics, the homeschooling. And then, the revelation while playing chess: that this "garbage" helped his condition. And the ten-year study, which he claimed was monitored by Dr. Goldman, who concluded that cannabis enhanced the effects of Dilaudid, enabling Irv to take significantly less of this debilitating narcotic. All Irv had ever asked of his doctors was to do the best they could with what they knew. After all, Irv said, "they are just M.D.'s, not G.O.D.'s." If his doctor could give him all the potentially lethal and addictive pills he wanted, why couldn't he give him cannabis?

"And I saw it in the committee's face," Irv says. "This is a waste of time. But I'm doing my best. I said, 'Gentlemen, that's the end of my oral presentation. I'm open for any questions.'"

A guy in a white lab coat stood up. He said he was a visiting oncologist from Venezuela, and he didn't have a question so much as a statement. He was here studying pain treatments for cancer patients. He said the best medicine for pain in America was the same medicine they had in Venezuela—Dilaudid. And if Mr. Rosenfeld and his doctor have studied it, and marijuana enhances the effect of Dilaudid, but he doesn't have a steady supply, then this needs to be studied with a steady supply. The man sat down. The committee members looked stunned. The logic was irrefutable. And what possible agenda could an oncologist from Venezuela have?

"The chairman didn't say anything," Irv says. "So I said, 'Are there any more questions . . . or *statements*?'"

Irv gets a big kick out of this, busting out in raucous, self-satisfied laughter. The way Irv tells it, this mysterious Venezuelan was an angel sent from above, and the moment he sat down, it was clear that Irv had won. The chairman of the committee looked at the doctors to his left, then his right. They avoided his gaze. Without further discussion the chairman announced that he was speaking for the entire committee when he said he was confident Irv's protocol would be approved.

Flashbulbs snapped. A flurry of people patted Irv on the back. It was like a movie. Bob Randall and his wife, Alice, gave him hugs. Irv went out, found a pay phone and called Dr. Goldman, reminding him that, in case anyone called, it was *he* who had implemented the ten-year study with Dilaudid and cannabis. (Irv sort of fudged that part to the committee.) Irv got in his car, lit up a joint, and pounded on the steering wheel in jubilation.

The number of legal medical marijuana smokers had just doubled. Over the next few years, the government started to quasi-embrace the concept, calling it the Compassionate Investigational New Drug Program, or Compassionate IND. The program expanded to include some HIV-positive patients in the mid-1980s. But then applications to the program increased and—even though there were only thirty active patients at its peak—the George H.W. Bush administration shut the program down in 1992. Only four of the grandfathered-in patients are still around today, and Irv is the healthiest and most active among them.

A month and a half after the hearing, the federal government sent Irv a tin stuffed with three hundred rolled marijuana cigarettes. To this day he remains a walking symbol of the federal government's hypocrisy regarding the plant. As long as he lives and breathes and talks—and Irv likes to talk—he will serve as a reminder that the federal government has already admitted cannabis has medicinal uses. Yet the plant continues to be labeled a Schedule I substance under federal law, meaning it has "no accepted medical use." Meanwhile, the list of Schedule II substances—those with accepted medical use—include cocaine, opium, methamphetamine, and PCP. Considering that more than a third of the states have medical marijuana programs that openly disregard the drug's Schedule I status, the program is a tangible manifestation of the federal government's illogical stance on weed.

Since Irv has made it clear I won't get to sample his stash, I have to ask the obvious question. The word around the pothead campfire is that the fed's weed is basically schwag.[4]

"And is the marijuana good?" I ask.

"It's adequate. It works for me medically, and that's all that counts. I don't get high off marijuana anyway, okay?"

"Why? Is it just because you use so much?"

"My reason is my body needs it. And I'm using it up that way. Just like I took addicting doses of morphine, Dilaudid. Addicting doses. Okay? Never got addicted."

"Because your body . . ."

"My body was using it," he says. "My body was using it."

I'm having trouble wrapping my head around this. "So you've never felt what it feels like to be high?"

"No, there was one time. I had been without it for about a week . . . I had moved from Virginia down here to Florida. And my wife brought it to me at work. I smoked the joint, and all of a sudden I felt high. My wife looked at me and said, 'My God. Your eyes are glazing over.' This had never happened before. She said, 'Irvin, you're getting high.' I go, 'I know. I feel it!' You know?"

I nod. Of course I know.

"But I viewed it as, my body needed more medicine. I smoked more, and it went away. My eyes totally cleared up. The feeling totally went away."

Hmm. I suppose it makes sense that the cannabinoids would be utilized for healing instead of psychoactive purposes. But to smoke ten joints a day for decades and only get high once? I'm tempted to question Irv's sincerity, or his ability to perceive high-ness, or the quality of the product. Regardless,

---

4   *Schwag* is low-quality weed. What amuses me most about the prospect of government marijuana being garbage is that they analyze weed from criminal busts, so they would *know* their stuff is schwag.

I'm not going to pretend I can grasp this concept, but I'm still curious about what others think. "And have you had any incidences . . . socially, or with people at work, where they make comments or say that you're a bullshitter?"

"Oh sure. I've had people do that. I've had friends where I haven't been invited back to their house again. Even though I was outside, smoking. I wouldn't smoke inside the house. And I haven't been invited back. Even my own family. We have family get-togethers, and people will say, 'Who's gonna take Irvin?' Because of my smoke. My wife can't stand being around it, and we've been married thirty-seven years."

Irv starts telling me about a business idea he has, for a consulting company called High Integrity Business Solutions, when he gets distracted by someone at the gate of the marina.

"Oh wait. We gotta go," Irv says. "They're gonna lock us up."

I don't like the sound of that. Irv and I hop out of the boat and run to the gate. The man there is a representative of a foundation that, among other things, takes disabled children sailing. Irv happens to volunteer for this same organization. He tries to make conversation, but the guy is noticeably freaked out by the fact that he's smoking a giant spliff. Irv senses his discomfort and, irritated, tells the man that in all the interviews he does, he promotes the foundation. Irv says he wants to be a new kind of face for the medical marijuana community—one who wears suits and ties, not tie-dyed shirts and ponytails. The guy seems unconvinced.

Though I don't doubt Irv's claims about his medical reasons for using marijuana, I also sense he relishes the self-righteousness of his position, of being one of four American citizens who are allowed to smoke pot anywhere. He seems to enjoy being perceived as a rebel without having to pay any consequences for his rebelliousness. If he didn't feel this way, he probably wouldn't have had the persistence to fight the federal government for almost a decade.

The man sees I have a tape recorder and grows even more uncomfortable. He turns to me. "Well, whatever you write, please keep the foundation's name out of it," he says. "I'm trying to run a family business."

CHAPTER FOUR
GOING TO CALIFORNIA

Salivating while Irv Rosenfeld chain-smoked joints in the "non-compassionate" state of Florida has made me yearn for a trip to America's weed paradise. Ever since legislators passed Proposition 215 in 1996, California has become ground zero for liberalized marijuana policy in the United States. The ballot initiative was conceived by medicinal marijuana activist Dennis Peron, in memory of his lover, who had used cannabis to treat symptoms of AIDS. It was ostensibly meant to allow relief for patients with "serious" disorders, like nausea from chemotherapy, the wasting symptoms associated with AIDS, multiple sclerosis, or severe glaucoma. But the law allows doctors the wiggle room to "recommend"[1] marijuana use for patients who suffer from serious diseases or "any other illness for which marijuana provides relief." The ambiguously worded law and its follow-up law in 2003, the slightly less vague Senate Bill 420,[2] have paved the way for an ever-expanding system of distribution via hundreds of dispensaries statewide.

Though estimates vary widely (because California doesn't require residents to register as patients), there are likely more than 750,000 physician-sanctioned marijuana users in California, and approximately one thousand dispensaries openly distributing the drug. California doctors, protected by confidentiality privileges, recommend marijuana to relieve a wide array of ailments—everything from insomnia to post-traumatic stress disorder, with the most common diagnosis being "chronic pain." The result has been a massive production swell in what was already America's biggest pot-producing state. Drug policy analyst Jon Gettman claims that, in 2006, California grew more than twenty million marijuana plants at an estimated street value of $14 billion, easily outshining all other sectors of the state's sizable agricultural economy.

Just how easy is it to get a recommendation? On February 13, 2010, while vacationing in Los Angeles, I decided to find out. Ambling along the Venice Beach boardwalk, I was approached by a smiley, goateed guy carrying a sign that read, MEDICAL KUSH DOCTOR. I asked if I needed a

1   Peron and his fellow drafters avoided the word *prescribe* to circumvent any conflicts with federal law.

2   420!

California ID. "Not necessarily, dude," the guy said. "Just write down the address of your hotel. And say you've got migraines, or depression, or *whatever*." I walked up into a tiny makeshift office, where a secretary in short shorts said it would cost $150, and told me to fill out some forms. I wrote that I struggle with insomnia and anxiety (true), and that I had been prescribed Paxil for depression (false).

After paying my fee, I entered the doctor's office. Dr. Smithers was droll and schlumpy, with no affect, as if he had just smoked a bowl of his own self-recommendation. The office had no examining table, no inspirational posters—just one sad little taped-up anatomy chart. Dr. Smithers took my blood pressure and some stethoscope readings. He explained that I would be using sativas for my daytime blues and indica blends for my sleepless-ness at night. Only then did he ask about my symptoms. I said I was a writer, often isolated, incapable of turning my brain off at night, and had suffered bouts of depression. That sufficed.

He said not to drive within two hours after smoking, and to keep my stash in the trunk because police would need a warrant to search it. Then he signed a certificate that said, "This is to verify that Alfred Nerz would probably benefit from compassionate medical cannabis use, is recom-mended by me as satisfying the requirements of H & S Code 11362.5 and SB 420." Just forty-five minutes after I'd approached the so-called clinic, I had purchased a gram of L.A. Confidential and was puffing away at my medi-cine in the smokers lounge. When I opened the dispensary door and was submerged in a bath of lemon-yellow sun, with a beaming smile and not a speck of paranoia, it hit me that I could get used to this whole medical marijuana ballgame.

*   *   *

A year later, I returned to the West Coast—northern California this time. Having met Irv Rosenfeld, perhaps the nation's most visible consumer of medical marijuana, I wanted to powwow with Steve DeAngelo, the coun-try's best-known purveyor of medical marijuana. DeAngelo is the founder of Harborside Health Clinic, the world's largest dispensary, which serves more than a hundred thousand patients.

I had met Steve a few months earlier, after he spoke at the Marijuana Conference in New York City. The conference had been billed as "the first event covering the business, legal, health, and political issues surrounding the growing debate over marijuana." It was a surreal affair, held at the Hilton hotel in midtown Manhattan, and filled with serious, suit-wearing types eager to network with fellow cannabusinessmen. In the end I got to meet the likes of growing guru Ed Rosenthal and cannabis activist Dr. Lester Grinspoon, so it almost seemed worth the $600 price tag.

DeAngelo was treated like a celebrity. He was hard to miss—tall and thin, with his trademark shoulder-length Native American braids. After he spoke, people mobbed him with ideas and requests. I waited for an opening and pounced. Before he could squirm away, I handed him my card and said I was writing a book.

"You should talk to my publicist." He gave me a card and a perfunctory handshake, and then kept it moving.

My email correspondence with said publicist, Gaynell Rogers, started out with a mild reprimand. "The advocates of the cannabis movement may take issue with your title," she wrote. "They don't consider cannabis a drug, and they certainly don't view it as dysfunctional. You might want to consider separating medical cannabis from the recreational side of the industry." My knee-jerk reaction: The biggest *medical* marijuana dispensary in the world doesn't consider cannabis a *drug*? And hadn't I heard Steve DeAngelo make the case that *all* marijuana use was medicinal? As for her other quibble, of course they don't consider America's relationship to cannabis dysfunctional. They make millions off people who don't have to buy pot at some shady guy's apartment, and then go home and shut the blinds before they smoke it.

Attached to Gaynell's email was a document she had created for the edification of misinformed journalists like myself, entitled "New Terminology for the Medical Cannabis Industry." At the top of the document was a quote from DeAngelo himself: "Language defines thought. If we use our opponents' terminology in defining who and what we are, we are halfway to losing." Among the new euphemisms: cannabis, healing center, not-for-profit dispensary, caregivers, and patient-farmers. It presented an odd quandary: If I were to utter the word *weed* around the hallowed halls of Harborside, would I be persona non grata?

*   *   *

FEBRUARY 9, 2011

An hour before my interview at Harborside, I'm sitting on my buddy Nigel's couch in San Francisco, scribbling questions into a notebook. As I get up to pace the room for the umpteenth time, it occurs to me that I have drunk entirely too much coffee. Pot enthusiasts always talk about how much more addictive alcohol and tobacco are than weed, but I don't hear much chatter about coffee. America is chock-full of caffeine addicts, and the Starbucks-ization of the country hasn't hindered this trend one iota. And I don't know about you, but a couple cups of heavy joe can turn me into a jabbering, jittery lunatic.

The more substantive reason for my twitchiness is that I've been in a serious funk about my personal life. A few months ago, I moved into the apartment of my girlfriend of one year, Ida, and already our relationship has deteriorated almost to the breaking point. The day after my interview with Irv Rosenfeld, in a hotel room in Miami, we got into the most horrific fight I have ever had—with a man or a woman—in my life. My nerves have been shattered ever since. Couples counseling almost seems to be exacerbating things. When I'm emotionally overwrought like this, I fluctuate between mania—obsessive lip-biting and pacing—and near catatonic lethargy. In order to participate in life and get shit done, I often try to regulate mood and energy levels with substances like caffeine and, well, weed.

The devil inside says I *need* to get high right now, to counterbalance the caffeinated agitation, or at least to not outwardly seem as cracked-out as I feel. But I'm also deeply suspicious that actually I just *want* to get high, that I'm using this inner turmoil to rationalize an unhealthy habit. Regardless of

52

the motive, I do have a storied history with the coffee-weed combo dating back over a decade, to when I was writing teen romance novels. I found that this "hippie speedball" was often an effective cocktail for conjuring inspiration from nothing—a synthetic energy kick plus a chilled-out disposition. But that was for solitary writing. This is an interview that involves responding in real time to a changing flow of ideas. At some point this whole internal debate becomes moot, because the drawn-out deliberation about whether or not to get high has made doing it seem almost mandatory.

There's only one problem: I don't have any weed. I flew in the night before, and the trip seemed too significant to imperil it by flying with buds in tow. I also forgot to bring my medical marijuana recommendation, which probably wouldn't help because it turns out legitimate dispensaries won't accept my dodgy Kush Doctor certificate without proof of residence. Then it hits me: Nigel's roommate. He mentioned last night he was holding, and my selective memory would like to think he even said I could help myself. He is presumably at work—at a coffee shop, ironically enough—and people tend to hide their stash in predictable places.

As I speed walk back to his room, I have a flashback of how my old roommate in New York used to hide his stash—at first, to keep it out of plain view, and later on, to keep me from pillaging it. I barge into the room without knocking and immediately locate the general area I would hide it if this were my room—the shelf beside the bed. I open it, spot a red box, and pull off the lid. There's a blackened glass pipe, and the golden lid of a Mason jar, fairly glistening. . . . Damn I'm good.

I jog back to the living room and pack a bowl that's measured to level me out without going overboard. Just as I finish, my phone rings. It's Gaynell Rogers. She says she's double-booked my interview with a Discovery Channel TV crew who's following Steve for a documentary, and would I mind if they film it? I say no problem, and get off the phone as quick as possible before the conversation tests my stoned faux-professionalism. It's not until I hang up that it occurs to me: *Great. Now I'm gonna be zoot-suited on TV.*

Harborside Health Center almost looks like it's hiding. It's in a random industrial section, in the shadows off the Nimitz Freeway. There's no real signage—just the number "1840" on the side of a bland building that looks like it could house an accounting firm. Enshrouded by trees, the main entrance feels like it's at the back of the building. From what I've read about DeAngelo, this ambience of secluded anonymity is deliberate, a way of making patients feel protected.

While paying the cabbie a fee that's prorated to account for both eerie promptness and cluelessness regarding the destination, I am approached by a burly, goateed man wearing a Guinness T-shirt and shorts.

"Could you please shut down your laptop?" he asks. "We prefer not to have electronic devices on the premises."

"Oh," I say. "Okay."

Approaching the entrance I tell another guard I am Steve DeAngelo's media guest. He speaks into his walkie-talkie: "Guest coming in." I walk up the steps to a thick door, which buzzes open, revealing a metal detector. When it beeps disapprovingly, I look around, prepared for some sort of invasive baton search. I guess it's no surprise a place that stockpiles enough cash and cannabis to service a hundred thousand patients would know better than to skimp on security.

But once you're inside, Harborside has one of the most welcoming auras of any business establishment I have ever entered. A genial young woman with reddish black hair introduces herself as Dani and says Steve will be with me momentarily. A receptionist offers water. Everybody is smiling—not forced, look-pleasant-or-you'll-get-fired smiles, but genuine, I-have-a-cool-job smiles. To my right a full-figured woman in a wheelchair, who is flipping through a pamphlet, looks over and cheeses so big I wonder if I've walked into a smile-off. "Hello," she says. "Some of these coupons are expired. They have coupons, you know."

I watch patients file in. What surprises me isn't that they are diverse— women and men; twentysomethings and senior citizens; white, Asian, and

Latino—but that so many appear to need real medical attention. I count three wheelchairs. A lanky black man limps in with the help of a cane that doesn't appear to be a fashion accessory. After fifteen minutes Dani walks up. "Steve is ready to see you now."

The main room of the dispensary is a long, airy corridor with display cases and cash registers on the left-hand side, and a line of about fifteen patients. To my right is a nursery of cloned plants that are available for purchase, to start home grows. At the end of the corridor is a colossal polytheistic shrine—with Christian, Buddhist, Hindu, and other religious icons—intermingled with flowers and ornamental tapestries.

Dani leads me to a back office and introduces Steve. He is taller than I remembered but otherwise dressed in his go-to getup—fedora hat, earplug in the left lobe, face framed by braids, and braids framing a skinny tie. The Discovery Channel cameraman asks me to sign a waiver.

On the wall behind Steve, stripes of sunlight shimmer on a framed collage of articles about Harborside. Beneath that, shooting out from Steve's right shoulder, is an unsettling shadow of the carved wooden howling beast resting on the windowsill. This strikes me as so thoroughly awesome that I can't help wondering if I might have smoked more than technically necessary before I left.

"Okay," I say. "First off, what led you to becoming a cannabis reform activist at the age of sixteen?"

"So I grew up in Washington, D.C.," Steve says. "I was a young teenager in 1970 when I encountered cannabis for the first time. I knew immediately that it was a good plant, not a bad plant. And I knew that it was going to play a really important role in my life. I was like one of these people who finds out at a really young age what it is that they want to do, like a child prodigy who picks up a violin and starts playing it at eleven years old. For me, that was cannabis."

"You were thirteen?" I ask.

"I was thirteen years old when I first ingested cannabis." He pauses. "I smoked it then."

Then just say "when I smoked pot for the first time," I think. Steve says he came from a family of social activists. One of his earliest memories, as a five-year-old in 1963, was handing out sandwiches during Martin Luther King's March on Washington. Once he decided he loved cannabis and hated that it was illegal, it was a straightforward leap of logic to start fighting to change that.

It strains my imagination to conjure up such a childhood. "And did you get the sense that your parents had misgivings about you smoking weed, and your dedication to it?"

"My parents had profound misgivings. In fact, when I began to use cannabis, it sparked several years of conflict, which really ended in me leaving my mother's house, basically over the issue of cannabis . . . when I was fifteen years old."

Around this time Steve linked up with the Youth International Party, or Yippies, a countercultural movement made famous by the antics of hippie pranksters like Abbie Hoffman. They staged theatrical events to mock the status quo, including the first major marijuana smoke-in, which drew twenty-five thousand tokers to Washington, D.C., on July 4, 1970. Steve became a street activist—organizing teach-ins, lobbying campaigns, and performing street theater.

In his late teens, Steve became a nightclub manager and concert promoter. He helped renovate two aging movie theaters into live music venues. He organized free concerts for the National Organization for the Reform of Marijuana Laws (NORML), and executive produced two of their fund-raising music compilations, Hempilation I and II. Activism begat entrepreneurship, Steve explains, which begat more activism, until those two distinctions blurred. There is a term I would use for someone who operates this way, and I say this without judgment: Steve DeAngelo is a hustler. He puts it a different way. "I always liked the idea that I could fund my activist work with businesses that would keep me alive and provide jobs for my friends and comrades."

Steve was introduced to industrial hemp by his friend and fellow cannabis activist Jack Herer. "Jack showed up on the steps of my house in Washington, D.C., waving a tattered manuscript and saying, 'Steve! Steve!

I've got it, I've got it! They have to make it legal now.' And I said, 'Okay, Jack. Take a drag of this joint. Smoke this. Let me read it.'"

The manuscript was a rough draft for *The Emperor Wears No Clothes*. In a unique format that resembles a scrapbook, it's a disjointed collection of pro-cannabis essays accompanied by a patchwork of old articles, advertisements, and photos. The book details the links between cannabis and industrial hemp, and the alleged conspiracy to make both of them illegal. Providing a bottomless supply of trivia for self-righteous potheads—like how the first draft of the U.S. Constitution and Betsy Ross's first flag were both made of hemp—it has also been the object of much eye-rolling by prohibitionists.

The Emperor Wears No Clothes is decidedly biased, and not without its dubious claims. But it is also full of facts that had hitherto slipped through the cracks of popular history. Herer's assertion that the cannabis plant should be decriminalized because it's a proven source of renewable fuel, food, and medicine that can be grown in nearly every climate—all that seems valid. And his more provocative claim, that the Hearst and DuPont corporations helped instigate the law which made cannabis illegal, also seems to hold water.

Herer's book provides documents and quotes implying Hearst and DuPont saw hemp as a threat to their investments in timber and plastics, and that they knew in advance that the Marihuana Tax Act of 1937 would help increase their profits. It also documents that Hearst newspapers, in conjunction with FBN director Harry J. Anslinger, planted sensationalist anti-cannabis articles like those describing "marijuana-crazed negroes" going on killing sprees and raping white women. The book shows copies of some of these planted articles, with titles like "Marijuana Makes Fiends of Boys in 30 Days; Hasheesh Goads Users to Blood-Lust." In fact, as Herer points out, we have Anslinger and Hearst to thank for popularizing the term "marihuana"—then often spelled with an *h*—an obscure Mexican slang word which they co-opted because it sounded more threatening and foreign than *hemp*.

The Emperor has become one of the cannabis movement's most popular books, with 750,000 copies in print. On the back of the book's most recent edition is a bold wager, a "$100,000 Challenge to the World to Prove Us Wrong." The bet is that, in the exceedingly hypothetical future in which all fossil fuels and timber were banned, the only substance capable of picking up the slack would be hemp. I don't foresee anyone cashing in on this bet anytime soon, not only because it is pure fantasy, but because its author, the esteemed cannabis activist Jack Herer, died of complications due to a heart attack, in April of 2010.

But in 1986, Herer was very much alive, and he had a message for the world. After helping Jack get his book into publishable form, DeAngelo focused on promoting its message. First up: a traveling countercultural road show known as the Hemp Tour. Steve, Jack, and their band of merry stoners would roll into unsuspecting university towns to play music, discuss Jack's book, and screen *Hemp for Victory*, a film created by the U.S. Department of Agriculture, which encouraged farmers to grow hemp during World War II.

The tour also had a "Hemp Museum," which Steve admits was a gross overstatement of its contents. One of the few products he could find was hemp twine imported by the U.S. Navy in 1956. The Navy canceled the order, so three tons of it had been sitting in a Philadelphia warehouse for thirty years. Against all odds the twine became popular. Kids paid DeAngelo five to ten bucks for a ball of twine, often to make macramé jewelry, which became a grassroots fad. DeAngelo went from ordering boxes to palettes, until he sold out all three tons, effectively exhausting America's reserve of hemp twine. The search for more led Steve to its original manufacturer, in Hungary.

He spent the next decade traveling around Eastern Europe and the United States, buying hemp and making stuff out of it. In 1992, he started a company called Ecolution, which sold hemp products. By 1998, the company had twenty full-time employees and $3 million in annual sales. DeAngelo was making a solid living, all through cannabis, and his website gave him an outlet to extol the virtues of the plant.

"But in 1998," Steve says in a grim tone, "something happened that took me off of my normal trajectory." In the wake of California passing Proposition 215, DeAngelo and his cohorts drafted a similar medical marijuana initiative for Washington, D.C. Ballot Measure 59 passed by what DeAngelo claims was the largest margin of victory of any initiative in any state. This is tough to confirm because the U.S. Congress vetoed the initiative, demanding that the local board of elections count the votes but not announce the results.

"For years and years, people had said, okay, if you really believe in cannabis, pass a law and get it legalized. Well we did; we passed a law, and got it legalized, and Congress came in and stole it from us. So I pretty much decided the day I got that news that I had to leave Washington, D.C., and come out to California."

After successfully lobbying his family on the move, he sold his house and his company. By 2001, the DeAngelos had settled in the Bay Area. Steve realized there were basically two types of medical marijuana dispensaries. The first wave was started by cannabis activists who were "long on good intentions" but short on professionalism. These dispensaries were ultra-casual, with scant business equipment and untrained "budtenders."

"If you were lucky, it felt like going to someone's living room," Steve says. "But if you were unlucky, it felt like going to a soup kitchen."

Due to a lack of competition, most of these early dispensaries were profitable. This market vacuum led to the second wave of dispensaries, started by mercenaries with problematic backgrounds. Their owners were "comfortable operating in the shadow area," often with experience in pornography, gambling, or illicit drug distribution. DeAngelo says these facilities reflected the sensibilities of their proprietors. "They were often bristling with razor wire and bulletproof glass, and great big thugs with guns, who expected patients to line up obediently and purchase their medicine and get out without asking too many questions. It was just like, why did we pass the law? It felt like buying heroin in Alphabet City in New York!"

DeAngelo immersed himself in the scene, making a short documentary about the dispensaries. Slowly, his vision for a best-practice model dispensary "that would bring together the highest ideals of both activism and professionalism" began to crystallize. Finally, after a competitive application process, the city of Oakland approved DeAngelo's dispensary license in October of 2006.

"We got the license just over four and a half years ago, and in that period of time we've been, I think, quite successful in establishing that model of what we wanted to do."

*   *   *

Steve DeAngelo's success has come in the variety popularized by Teddy Roosevelt (or Kevin Costner's character in *Field of Dreams*, depending on your reference): Build it, and they will come. DeAngelo's approach was similar to that of another northern California businessman, Steve Jobs, whose achievements at Apple came not by creating the first personal computer or MP3 player, but by scrutinizing the competition and creating the most customer-friendly version of those devices. DeAngelo took his time, analyzed the other Bay Area dispensaries, talked to patients and insiders, and then created the biggest, safest, warmest, most scientifically advanced dispensary around.

Perhaps Harborside's most innovative breakthrough was its testing. When I toured the premises after my interview, I noticed that each cannabis strain—with names like Mango Sour Jack and Grand Daddy Purple—listed a specific percentage of not only THC, but also CBD (cannabidiol)[3] and CBN (cannabinol). Before he opened Harborside, DeAngelo decided to launch his own facility, Steep Hill Laboratories. After getting funding, Steve served as CEO until the lab was up and running; then he stepped down. The lab uses gas chromatography and mass spectrometry to test for percentage of cannabinoids, and also for the presence of toxic molds. Harborside claims it became the first dispensary, in November of 2008, to send all of its medicine to a lab for safety screening and potency

3 Cannabidiol, which is not psychoactive, has been linked in studies to relief of convulsion, inflammation, nausea, and anxiety, as well as to the inhibition of cell growth. A 2007 study by the California Pacific Medical Research Institute claimed CBD can help halt the spread of cancer. They said CBD works by blocking the activity of a gene called Id-1, which is believed to be responsible for the spread of cancer cells, or metastasis.

evaluation.[4] This breakthrough was, in DeAngelo's words, the "beginning of real public recognition for Harborside."

Public recognition, it turns out, would be the closest thing Steve DeAngelo has to a tragic flaw. In December of 2011, the documentary that was being filmed during our interview a year earlier aired on the Discovery Channel. *Weed Wars* offers an inside look at the day-to-day routine of Harborside employees like Steve; his brother and office manager, Andrew; Dave Wedding Dress, the dispensary's dress-wearing cofounder; and Terryn, a pothead budtender who started his own marijuana grow. The first episode focuses on Harborside's battle with Oakland's Business Tax Board of Review. Soon after Discovery wrapped filming, Harborside became the target of a much more intense battle, when the IRS cold-cocked them with a $2.5 million back-taxes bill.

Steve DeAngelo has a knack for branding and publicity. Just as the image of Jobs stalking the stage in a black turtleneck became synonymous with Apple's brand, the image of DeAngelo's silver braids framing his proselytizing mouth are now synonymous with the Harborside brand. The dispensary has a motto: "Out of the Shadows, Into the Light," which apparently includes the spotlight of near-limitless media attention. DeAngelo's biography on the website boasts that Harborside has been featured in news stories by the *New York Times*, the *Washington Post*, CNN, NPR, BBC, and media outlets from Canada, Japan, and Germany.

During our interview I addressed my discomfort with the way he and his publicist manipulate language. After he said he didn't like the "*M*-word" (marijuana) because of its racist origins, I told him about the scolding I got from Gaynell Rogers. Having worked as a publicist myself in the world of pro competitive eating, I am familiar with language control. Instead of using the "*V*-word" (vomit) to describe the often unpleasant consequences of an eating contest, we used euphemisms like "reversal of fortune." I explained to DeAngelo that, if you're talking to Joe Regular from Milwaukee

---

4 New cannabis labs have been springing up ever since, and testing—especially in Colorado's dispensaries—has become standard practice.

about "cannabis" and "healing centers," he's going to shake his head and say, "Come on, man—you're talking about smoking weed!"

DeAngelo said they were trying to change the way people think about cannabis, and people think in words. "This is why it's important to think about using different terminology in connection to this plant. Not to pull the wool over anybody's eyes, but because language is the way we define our thought processes." DeAngelo added that, from his perspective, all cannabis use is actually for medicinal or wellness purposes. He said patients often tell him they appreciate his work, but really they just like to get high. But when he asks these people to describe when and why they use, he says their motives aren't as recreational as they believe.

Here's the scenario: Joe Regs comes home from work. He's stressed. Doesn't want to chat with his wife or play with his kids. He's too wired, doesn't feel like eating dinner, and sure as hell doesn't feel like having sex. Then he smokes a joint. All of a sudden he's smiling, and pumped to play with Joe Junior. Dinner is delicious, and he's in the mood for sex, which turns out to be way more pleasurable than non-medicated sex. After that he's relaxed and tired, and he sleeps like a champ. When you analyze this scenario, according to DeAngelo, medical marijuana has taken the place of five prescription pills: anti-anxiety, anti-depressant, appetite stimulant, libido stimulant (Viagra?), and sleep medication. "And you compare the side effects of those pharmaceutical substances to the side effects for cannabis," Steve says. "It's like night and day. I mean the pharmaceutical side effects read like something out of a Stephen King novel. Severe rash. Stomach upset. Liver failure. Possible suicide! . . . And what are the side effects for cannabis? Maybe somebody will feel good. Or . . . hungry. Or a little bit horny. Or they might get a really good night's sleep."

It's a bit of a stretch, but I see his point. The problem is that the U.S. federal government doesn't. From their perspective, marijuana has no medicinal value, so Steve is not just categorically full of shit, but a big-time drug dealer to boot. And the FDA approves all these drugs that his cannabis is allegedly replacing. So when a slew of articles and a reality TV show put Harborside on blast, it's no surprise the feds take that as a provocation.

And when Harborside's Oakland tax bill of 5 percent comes out to a million bucks, meaning its annual income is around $22 million, the IRS sees dollar signs.

In accordance with the Catch-22 inherent to the state-vs.-federal-laws battle regarding cannabis, the IRS probe of Harborside exploits 280E, an obscure provision of the tax code, which prohibits those who sell controlled substances from claiming business expenses as a write-off. (Ironically, the only deduction Harborside could make under 280E is the cost of the marijuana itself.) The notion that the IRS can tax illegal drug dealers may seem absurd, but courts have ruled in favor of just that, including a U.S. Supreme Court ruling that California regulators cite to collect sales tax on medical marijuana. Hence the sudden insistence on $2.5 million in back taxes from the period before the IRS (with a nudge from the DEA, one can only assume) decided that Steve DeAngelo was not just some renegade entrepreneur but in fact the most publicized drug baron in America.

DeAngelo has been lobbying Congress to change 280E to exempt medical marijuana distributors. His pleas have thus far fallen on deaf ears. On July 10, 2012, federal authorities will file papers to seize Harborside, as well as its sister dispensary in San Jose. The U.S. Attorney for California's Northern District, Melinda Haag, will defend the action because Harborside has become a "superstore" that has been taking advantage of state laws. DeAngelo will respond by doing multiple media interviews, in which he will vow to keep both dispensaries open, contest the federal actions publicly, and "look forward to our day in court." One wonders if he wasn't deliberately inviting this public clash with the feds, at least on a subliminal level, when he signed on for a nationally televised reality show that exposed his wildly successful, federally illegal business. In the end that seemingly reckless decision may lead to his real endgame: the chance to bring the fight full circle, his entrepreneurial efforts dovetailing with his activism in grand fashion, not far from the Washington, D.C., streets where that activism began.

CHAPTER FIVE
INTERVIEW SNAFU

Two days after my interview with Steve DeAngelo, things start to go off the rails.

I am getting out of the shower when I hear someone shouting in Arabic. Hustling into the living room, I find my buddy Bilal, pacing and squawking into his phone. Arabic can be an unsettling language, but I sense from his tone that good things are afoot. He points at the television. CNN is showing crowds of Egyptians erupting in jubilation, shouting "*Allahu Akbar!*" Egypt's leader, Hosni Mubarak, has just stepped down after three decades of dictatorial dickishness. The resonance of this development is deepened by the fact that Bilal, who had flown in the evening before, is Egyptian American and just got back from visiting family in Cairo.

Beyond being an excellent partner in crime, Bilal is an intriguing stoner case study, not just for his sheer volume of consumption, but for the fact that he manages to both confirm and challenge the stoner stereotype. On one level he is intelligent and ambitious. He has a habit, when high, of launching into cerebral monologues that skip from subject to subject without segues.[1] On another level Bilal can be unreliable. He was just recently laid off from his high-paying job as a hedge fund manager, for reasons he is loath to discuss. As evidence of the sort of behavior you could expect from Bilal, he was actually supposed to arrive here in San Francisco a day earlier. When I called him a couple hours after his flight was due to land, he opted out of the call but texted back that he'd missed it.

Usually our collaborations involve the type of misadventures for which irresponsibility is an asset. But today I am depending on him. He is supposed to chauffeur me to my appointment with one of America's leading cannabis activists. I wait for a pause between the barrage of incoming phone calls.

"Bilal, you know I'm truly psyched for you and your liberated brethren." I smile. "But we've gotta get going soon."

"No problem, bro." His phone rings again. "Just a second . . ."

More shouting in Arabic. I should have known.

---

1 Just the night before, while having drinks with Nigel and his friends, a woman became entranced by Bilal's spout of esoteric knowledge, nicknaming him "Data."

Pulling into the parking lot of Oaksterdam University, I feel like a starry-eyed pre-frosh getting a first look at his new campus, which is actually kind of accurate. I have enrolled in the weekend-long Basic Seminar, slated to start the next morning. Oaksterdam is America's first cannabis college, featuring Basic Seminars, two-day Advanced Seminars, and semester-long courses. Based loosely on Cannabis College in Amsterdam, the classes focus on marijuana horticulture, edibles, and other ingestion methods, as well as the marijuana laws of America and California. The application process wasn't very rigorous: It involved faxing in a one-page sheet with my personal details and mailing a check for three hundred bucks.

I ask Bilal to take a photo of me on my new campus. Actually, I'm still in the parking lot, the adjacent wall of which has the college's name emblazoned in a green all-caps university font, half a block long. Next to it is the school seal—a send-up of Harvard's, but with the ivy replaced by marijuana leaves, and the motto VERITAS replaced with CANNABIS.

Bilal snaps the photo and starts cackling. Though most people probably wouldn't notice with a professional stoner like him, I can tell from the glazed eyes—he's high as giraffe nuts. On the drive over, he polished off most of a joint; I only took a few puffs because I wanted to stay on-point for this interview. I have loads of questions for today's subject, Richard Lee, the founder of Oaksterdam, and America's first aboveboard marijuana millionaire.

Lee's road to cannabis activism treads the boundaries of fiction in a way that eclipses even Steve DeAngelo's child-prodigy narrative. In 1990, while working as a lighting technician for rock concerts, Lee was setting up an Aerosmith show in New Jersey when he slipped on a catwalk. He was paralyzed from the waist down, sentenced to life in a wheelchair, and no longer able to ride his Harley or fly his beloved ultralight airplanes. The only thing that quelled the double whammy of back spasms and depression, he found, was herb. Because medicinal marijuana was illegal in his hometown of Houston, he was content to keep getting his prescription on the black market (which I imagine was readily accessible for a former Aerosmith roadie).

That changed when he got carjacked at gunpoint in 1992. The aloofness of Houston police, who showed up over an hour after his 911 call, pissed Lee off. The mere possibility that cops were wasting time on marijuana busts, instead of responding to more dangerous crimes, was too much for him to bear. He responded by opening a hemp-clothing store in Houston—which sold, among other things, DeAngelo's Ecolution goods—and becoming a pro-legalization spokesman.

When Lee showed up in Oakland in 1998, he had already established himself as a marijuana advocate. After working as an employee at the Oakland Cannabis Buyers' Cooperative, he opened his own dispensary, Coffeeshop Blue Sky. He then started transforming downtown Oakland from a district filled with vagrants and empty storefronts into a slew of cannabis-friendly businesses based on the model of Amsterdam's bustling "coffee shop" culture. At its height Lee's empire included Oaksterdam, two dispensaries, a memorabilia and T-shirt shop, a grow operation, and a magazine called *West Coast Cannabis*. Oaksterdam alone pulls in around $2 million per year, and the rest of Lee's businesses bring in another $3 million. Despite this apparent windfall, Lee says he pays around $1.5 million in fees and taxes, and his salary averages a modest $50,000.

Bilal and I struggle to find the university's entrance, which is next to a sandwich shop. The tip-off is the pungent waft of weed as we approach the door. I call Richard's assistant, Salwa, who meets us at the front desk. Unsure of Salwa's gender from our email exchanges, Bilal and I are pleasantly surprised to be greeted by an attractive young woman. I introduce Bilal as my assistant. He quickly establishes that Salwa is also Egyptian American. While they share a moment of solidarity in the elevator, I think about how quaint the fight for "cannabis freedom" must seem to an Egyptian battling for the baseline liberties that we as Americans take for granted.

We exit the elevator on the second floor and enter a vast, undecorated room with floor-to-ceiling tinted windows that reveal an expansive view of downtown Oakland. Next to a couch is a man in a wheelchair, positioned diagonally so that he's facing neither us nor the window, like some dark overlord pondering global domination. He shakes our hands without smiling. If he is trying to be intimidating, it's working. I fumble for small talk and take out my tape recorder. Bilal, sensing he should do something to justify his presence as my "assistant," offers to videotape the interview. Richard approves with a silent nod. I put the tape recorder away.

The interview starts off shakily. Richard responds to my first few questions with clipped responses and shrugs. Only when I start pressing him on Proposition 19, his recently failed ballot initiative to legalize recreational marijuana in California, does he start to take the interview seriously.

Prop 19, also known as the "Regulate, Control, and Tax Cannabis Act," was the first state initiative with a legitimate opportunity to legalize recreational cannabis. Lee put $1.5 million of his own money—his entire nest egg, he claims—into the signature drive to get the initiative on the ballot. Supporters said Prop 19 would bring in tax dollars to alleviate California's yawning budget deficit, while also cutting off funding to violent Mexican drug cartels. Lee started an advocacy group, "Yes on 19," which received funding from George Soros, several Facebook billionaires, and a host of other liberal-minded donors. But the campaign against the initiative, led by the "No on Proposition 19" opposition group, was equally fervent. In the end, Prop 19 became wildly divisive, with unlikely bedfellows like soccer moms and NorCal growers combining forces to oppose the initiative. Even Steve DeAngelo spoke out against it, claiming a midterm election wasn't a good time to bring out young voters and liberals. In the end it was defeated by a thin margin—53.5 percent voted no, 46.5 percent voted yes—and Richard Lee was delegated to the title of "former marijuana millionaire."

Lee shrugs off the defeat and vows to support another initiative as soon as the timing feels right. As the interview progresses, he becomes increasingly animated. In personal matters he can be dry and curt, but when it comes to the march toward cannabis legalization, he assumes the inspirational tone of a reverend. I'm happy we are getting this on video. After the interview Richard hits me with the bizarre request that I not use the footage for anything other than my own source material, ostensibly because he has not groomed for a videotaped interview. It sounds dubious but I agree.

In the end it doesn't matter. Because Bilal never pressed record.

Bilal's boneheaded move leads to a relevant question: How does marijuana use affect cognitive function?

Despite decades of research, it remains a question without an answer. That's partially because such studies are dependent on a smorgasbord of variables—the marijuana's potency, the subject's intelligence and tolerance, etc. But a more salient reason for the mixed results is that most of these studies—or the organizations funding them—have their own agendas, which skew the results. According to a leading researcher in the field, Harvard psychiatry professor Harrison Pope, "If there's one thing I've learned from studying marijuana for more than a decade, it's that proponents and opponents of the drug will put opposite spins on [their] findings . . . As a scientist, I'm struck by how passionately people hold opinions in both directions, no matter what the evidence says. The other striking thing is how little we actually know about the effects of a drug that has been smoked for thousands of years and been studied for decades."

Even science seems incapable of stripping emotion from the study of cannabis. One of the few sources I could find that seems to make a sincere attempt to synthesize the vast and contradictory pool of data on the subject (with a slight bias toward dispelling negative rumors about the drug) is the book *Marijuana Myths, Marijuana Facts: A Review of the Scientific Evidence.* The authors, Lynn Zimmer, Ph.D., and John Morgan, M.D., divided the cognitive data into two types: the "while high" studies, and the "long-term effects studies."

According to Zimmer and Morgan, the only thing we can say for sure is this: Getting high impairs short-term memory during the period of intoxication. They concluded that marijuana produces "immediate, temporary changes in thoughts, perceptions, and information processing." Here's the rundown: High people don't have a problem remembering things they learned before they got high. For example, stoned people and placebo smokers scored similarly when asked whether specific words were included in a list of words presented to them before they smoked. However, smoking pot does diminish people's ability to recall words, pictures, stories, or sounds presented earlier in the intoxicated period. A more specific fun fact about these short-term effects is that high subjects are inclined to "re-call" information that was not presented earlier. In other words the short-term effects of getting high not only involve forgetting things, but remembering things that never happened.

This could explain why Bilal insisted after the interview that he was certain he had filmed it in its entirety. But most potheads don't need studies to prove their subjective experiences—they know they do dimwitted shit while high. The most clichéd example is the stoned conversation that comes to a halt, followed by, "Wait, what were we just talking about?" On a personal level, my short-term memory lapses often result in small-scale compulsive behavior. I will walk into a room with the aim of grabbing something, then get there and realize I have no idea what I came in here for. (And some-times repeat this process a second and third time.) Or, because I don't trust my short-term memory while high, I will leave my apartment, then go back to make sure I locked the door . . . even though I *always* lock the door, on instinct. In these moments, there is a degree of self-doubt that rarely occurs while sober, an insecurity that things might go awry because you're high.

The more debilitating effects involve moments of complete inatten-tion to the task at hand. I've been known to throw my keys in the trash, find dishwashing detergent in the fridge, and interrupt conversations with something tangential or even wildly inappropriate. And though I have always been absentminded, the catalog of stuff I've lost during the stoner era is staggering. I once left one rollerblade on the subway (rendering the other one quite a bit less useful). In the mobile Bermuda Triangle that is New York taxicabs, I have, while high, lost two cell phones, five books, a gold bracelet (gift from girlfriend—awkward), a backpack full of personal items, and a scooter.[2] I have scattered enough umbrellas around the New York metropolitan area to shelter a village from a monsoon. It's really quite

2 After this latter episode, I miraculously remembered the cab driver's full name, which complicates the whole pothead-memory thing. Mohammed Mahmoud, you owe me a scooter.

pathetic. There should be a special insurance policy for stoners. The only real upside is that, later in life, my transition to Alzheimer's should be relatively stress-free.

But here's another perspective: Is it possible that memory loss is actually what getting high is all about? Maybe it's the price you pay for being in the moment. For me the primary allure of getting stoned lies in the momentary dissolution of worldly concerns—bills, insecurities, relationship and work woes—for complete absorption in, say, the captivating motion of a scurrying insect. We find ourselves engrossed in some previously overlooked detail, elevating an otherwise common insight and creating the sense that time has slowed considerably or even stopped.

In the book *On Drugs,* David Lenson says the perception shift that occurs when we get high transforms everyday objects into ideal versions of themselves: "A cup 'looks like' the Platonic Idea of a cup, a landscape looks like a landscape painting, a hamburger stands for all the trillions of hamburgers ever served, and so forth." With this in mind, isn't losing material things a small price to pay for the divine ability to recognize the sublime in the quotidian? I know I should be able to do this while sober, but the fact is, I often don't, not without my magical elixir of amusement.

Actually, short-term memory loss may be a crucial link between cannabis and creativity. According to author Jonah Lehrer, getting high "diffuses attention," which basically means you're not able to maintain focus on one thing for an extended period of time. This "lantern theory of attention" accounts for marijuana's greatest asset and biggest weakness at once. On one hand getting high causes that hackneyed Cheech & Chong–like drifty mind state of not being totally *with* it. On the other hand, research shows humans are more susceptible to receiving perspective-altering epiphanies when not totally focused. During such relaxed states of mind, when one's attention is more spread out, we are able to access what are called "remote associations" in the right hemisphere of the brain. This can lead to profound leaps of creative logic that are otherwise inaccessible to the non-altered brain. Or in the immortal words of dope-smuggling legend Howard Marks, "Forgetfulness is the catalytic germ of spontaneous creativity."

Or maybe it just feels like we're more creative when we're baked. When I asked Dr. Margaret Haney, a cannabis researcher at Columbia University, about marijuana's effects on creativity, she said one of her colleagues was studying that very phenomenon. And though the results aren't yet conclusive, her colleague has noticed an interesting pattern. She said 50 percent of respondents believed getting high affected their creativity. Then these same subjects took a test that measures creativity, both while sober and stoned. Afterward many said they thought they had performed better while high. They were wrong. "So it was more their perception of their creativity being enhanced occurred, without their creativity literally being enhanced," Dr. Haney explained.

Regardless, marijuana's hindrance of short-term memory might have applications beyond boosting creativity, in the treatment of post-traumatic stress disorder (PTSD). A growing number of American veterans returning from our wars in the Middle East claim that weed's combined effect of memory loss and anxiety relief makes it an ideal remedy for the haunting memories and sleeplessness that plague PTSD sufferers.[3] When I asked Dr. Haney about this, she said she knew of animal studies that showed cannabinoids helped with the extinction of fearful stimuli: "If it could help extinguish the association people have . . . say, if there's a loud noise, and they associate it with a bomb and their over-intense response to that—if they could extinguish that relationship a little bit, I could see that helping."

Wait, what were we talking about? Right, memory. So the bad and good news is your short-term memory will take a hit when you smoke pot. But according to Dr. Haney, if you have been smoking marijuana for a long time, you become "tolerant to a lot of the cognitive disruption that would occur in a nondependent person." The other good news is that, if you quit smoking for a month, your memory will return to normal. In Dr. Pope's study about cognitive changes caused by heavy marijuana use, he found no lasting effects twenty-eight days after quitting. His tests of intelligence,

3   In July of 2011, researchers sent a proposal to the federal government asking permission to purchase medical marijuana (from the same University of Mississippi pot farm where Irv Rosenfeld gets his supply) for studying the effects on fifty combat veterans who haven't responded to other treatments. After an initial approval from the FDA, the Health and Human Services Department has stymied the study indefinitely.

attention, learning, and memory resulted in lower scores for heavy smokers than nonsmokers on days zero, one, and seven. But on day twenty-eight, the potheads scored the same as the squares.

So we've got that going for us. But is there a cumulative effect on the brains of long-term stoners like Bilal? It might depend on how early you start. A decades-long study of New Zealanders claims that those who smoked pot heavily as teenagers turned out to be demonstrably dumber as adults. Adolescents who got high at least four days per week lost an average of eight IQ points between the ages of thirteen and thirty-eight, a pattern not seen among people who began smoking heavily only in adulthood.

As for adults who start smoking later in life, Zimmer and Morgan unearthed a boatload of studies on this, all with contradictory conclusions. In articles published in the early 1970s, psychologist M. I. Soueif described "significant cognitive deficits" in Egyptian prisoners with a history of cannabis use. (So maybe there's some weakness in the Egyptian brain that explains Bilal's brain fart?) Other studies of the same era in Jamaica, Greece, and Costa Rica found no difference in cognitive measures between long-term cannabis users and nonusers. A 1985 study showed that long-term cannabis users were slower than sober-ites to complete one test out of fourteen. But when subjects were instructed to perform that task as quickly as possible, there was no difference between users and nonusers. In a cognitive study of ten American Rastafarians who smoked ganja multiple times a day for an average of 7.4 years, researchers found nothing unusual in the group's scores compared to national samples. If *Rastas* aren't showing signs of cognitive impairment, it's tough to take the prohibitionist palaver about weed causing permanent brain damage all that seriously.

CHAPTER SIX
WEED 101

Bilal's arrival coincides with a steep decline in journalistic responsibility. I awaken the next morning with a brutal hangover. Dim visions of the evening before include two new female friends cackling in the living room, and our host, Nigel, telling us to please keep it down. Nigel is, to use his own British slang, a "diamond geezer"—a great guy—so I feel genuine guilt. But you have to live while you're alive and get on with things. It's been over a month since I've been able to calm my brain and laugh freely, so a headache now and an apology later seem like fair consequences. After showering and readying my school supplies for the first day at Oaksterdam, I walk outside to where our rental car should be. It's gone. A sign nearby explains why: no parking for non-residents. Violators will be towed at owner's expense. Bilal and I are violators.

After a pricey cab ride I pick up my student ID and a thick binder at the Oaksterdam front desk. On the second floor a hallway lined with class photos of past alumni leads to a large, low-ceilinged classroom, which has the feel of a former office space. Thirty-odd foldout tables face a podium, upon which rests a slender dais covered by a cloth Oaksterdam logo.

I step right into "Legal 101: An Overview of Medical Marijuana Law." The teacher is Kali S. Grech, a criminal defense attorney. She begins by outlining America's federal marijuana laws—a grim way to start the day.

Grech says federal sentencing is "very serious." Possession of more than one kilo (2.2 pounds) of marijuana carries a sentence of six months to a year. And if the feds catch you moving serious weight, you can pretty much grab your ankles. Thanks to the Anti-Drug Abuse Act of 1986, enacted into law at the height of Reagan's War on Drugs, weed kingpins get mandatory minimum[1] sentences, of which at least 85 percent must be served. If you're caught with 100 plants or 100 kilos (220 pounds) of processed marijuana, you'll get a minimum mandatory sentence of 5 years. If you're caught with 1,000 plants or 1,000 kilos of weed, the mandatory minimum is 10 years.

---

1 A mandatory minimum sentence means that if someone is convicted of a certain crime, it is mandatory for the judge to give that person a minimum of however many years the law stipulates. The judge can opt for a longer sentence, but not a shorter one.

If you have a prior felony drug conviction, those sentences are doubled. Two priors and you get life.[2]

I take a moment to check out my classmates. They look like working-class Americans, the type of folks you'd see at any given Applebee's on a Tuesday night. Nearly everyone has on baggy jeans with a sweatshirt or a button-down. I count thirty-two students—twelve women and twenty guys. Four black, the rest white. Average age: around forty. Two women in their early sixties sit together in the back, looking the part of an aging lesbian couple. Stationed in the teacher's-pet position up front is the guy I will call Sergeant Bilko, burly with a buzz cut and a perma-smile. A tall black man sits in the front row's far left corner, nodding his head passionately throughout the lecture, as if the professor is channeling divine wisdom.

Grech says the Obama administration's hands-off approach to medical marijuana was established by a Justice Department memo written on October 19, 2009. The Ogden Memo, as it's now known, has been a perpetual topic of conversation in the American cannabis community since Deputy Attorney General David Ogden sent it out to select state attorney generals. It said medical marijuana patients and their "caregivers" who operate in "clear and unambiguous compliance with existing state law" would not be targeted by federal law enforcement officials. This might seem like no big deal, but for states anxious about implementing medical marijuana laws, it was the go-ahead they'd been waiting for. Officials in Maine and New Mexico quickly moved to license dispensaries. In the first eight years since Colorado voted to legalize medical marijuana, in 2000, only two thousand identification cards had been issued for the program. In 2009, that number grew to sixty thousand.

What Grech does not say—because there is no way for her to gauge its significance just yet—is that the Obama administration has recently made a crucial change that will effectively reverse the Ogden Memo. A month before this class, for reasons I can't begin to guess at, President Obama appointed Michele Leonhart as the head of the Drug Enforcement Agency. *Renominated* is the more precise term, as Leonhart—an avowed medical

2 According to Allen St. Pierre, the executive director of NORML, sixty to eighty people are currently serving life sentences for marijuana charges.

marijuana opponent—had been head of the DEA under George W. Bush.

Just weeks after her appointment was confirmed, her agency released a revised version of "The DEA Position on Marijuana." With headings like "SMOKED MARIJUANA IS NOT MEDICINE," it suggested the DEA would be backtracking to the Bush-era policy of intolerance toward medical marijuana. Earlier that week I had asked Steve DeAngelo what he thought about Leonhart's appointment. He said that, though she "holds unscientific and emotional, irrational views on" medical marijuana, he didn't think it would affect the situation in California.

He was wrong. In fact, the war has already started. Just two weeks prior to this class, on February 1, 2011, U.S. District Attorney Melinda Haag sent out a letter to John Russo, an attorney for the city of Oakland. City officials were considering licensing four industrial-scale indoor medical marijuana–growing facilities. Russo had contacted Haag to determine what the federal response might be if they moved forward. She responded with a stern warning, now known as the Haag Memo. After reminding Mr. Russo that cannabis is a Schedule I controlled substance, she added that prosecuting drug trafficking organizations "is a core priority of the Department." As for the four industrial grows, Haag said the Justice Department "is carefully considering civil and criminal legal remedies regarding those who seek to set up industrial marijuana growing warehouses in Oakland." City officials abandoned the plans, which might have single-handedly erased Oakland's deficit of $31 million.

But the federal crackdown had only just begun. Over the course of 2011, Haag will shutter a handful of California dispensaries, including the state's oldest, Marin Alliance for Medical Marijuana.[3] On October 13, Haag will send drug agents armed with battering rams, chain saws, and machine guns to the Northstone Organics marijuana garden near Ukiah. They will handcuff the owner, Matthew Cohen, snatch computers and testing equipment, then cut down the ninety-nine plants he grows under direct supervision of the county sheriff.

3   The Marin Alliance was owned by Lynnette Shaw, a cannabis activist who ran for California lieutenant governor in 2006, garnering 130,000 votes after an endorsement from Willie Nelson.

And of course Haag won't leave Richard Lee out. The IRS will audit him for fiscal year 2010 and slap him with an exorbitant penalty similar to the one levied against Harborside. In October Haag will order the landlord of Lee's dispensary to evict him or face criminal prosecution. Lee will respond by reopening the store a few days later, three doors down from the original dispensary. At the opening of the new shop, employees will hand out fliers that read: "Thank you for your support. Together we will survive the attack. Long live Oaksterdam."

Not that long, actually. Just over a year from now, on April 2, 2012, dozens of agents from three agencies—the DEA, the IRS, and the U.S. Marshals—will use battering rams and power saws to bust open the doors of Oaksterdam University. As they carry bags from Lee's dispensary, a mob of protesters will heckle the agents, openly smoking joints and banging on government vehicles. Neill Franklin, a former cop and the head of Law Enforcement Against Prohibition (LEAP), estimates the total taxpayer cost of the raid and follow-up investigation at $250,000. Meanwhile, just a few blocks away, a gunman will murder seven people at Oikos University.

Within the week Oaksterdam will suspend the majority of its classes, and Lee will publicly announce that he's bankrupt and, in the face of a possible federal tax indictment, will relinquish ownership of all of his businesses. "I think with my legal issues, it's the best thing," Lee will tell the press. "I've been on the front lines for twenty years. I think I've done my duty, and it's time for other people to take over."

In the end Richard Lee will be the sacrificial lamb of a symbolic publicity battle. Considering all the billions of dollars in quasi-legal marijuana being grown, distributed, and ingested in California, the federal government knows these busts aren't putting a dent in the industry. Logically it would make more sense to bust shady "dispensaries" like the Kush Doctor who sold me a semi-bogus "recommendation" in L.A. Or the outlaw megagrowers and distributors in rural northern California, who use the lenient laws to make millions by taking weed across state lines, where profit margins are significantly higher. But those people are hard to find, and the public relations coup of busting the Kush Doctor would be minimal.

The point of making busts on Harborside, Oaksterdam, and the Marin Alliance—the dispensaries most concerned with paying taxes and abiding by state and local laws—is that they have been *publicly* flouting federal laws. They have made a mockery of the feds by creating respectable, profitable businesses, like a trade school that educates students about how to succeed in the marijuana industry. The surface-level message of these busts to medical marijuana entrepreneurs is pure intimidation. The message to voters is that the Obama administration isn't a bunch of patchouli-stinking hippies turning a blind eye to America's moral decay. The message to some of the most mercenary special-interest lobbying groups—Big Pharma, the prison industrial complex, tobacco, etc.—is that the feds will give small-time dispensaries a pass, but the powerful businesses who threaten the status quo will feel their wrath. The message to Mexican drug cartels is that the federal government continues to make space for their product in the American market. And the deeper message to medical marijuana industry insiders is that, as long as you stay underground and don't get too much attention, if you don't pay taxes or create the remotest pretense of a successful, legitimate business, there will always be an opportunity to make money off marijuana in America.

*   *   *

Jesus is this hangover merciless. I feel like I've been microwaved, all the moisture leached from my body. If there is a case to be made in the debate between the detrimental effects of marijuana vs. alcohol—beyond the more tangible zero vs. a hundred thousand American deaths per year attributed to those substances—we need look no further than the hangover. Getting high might lead to the condition I've termed "vacuum brain," that empty-headed feeling about three hours after smoking that's akin to a friend overstaying his welcome. But that's nothing compared to the full-body siege and punishing headache of a hangover.[4]

4   It should also be noted that the combination of marijuana and Alka-Seltzer is a remarkably effective hangover cure.

Hoping to regain my focus, I open my Oaksterdam binder and flip to the "Legal" section. It has some interesting tidbits. For example, the statute of limitations on most crimes in the Controlled Substances Act is five years. And in most judicial districts, you can be prosecuted for a felony just for using a phone "to facilitate the purchase of marijuana." I try in vain to think of an instance when I have purchased marijuana *without* using a phone.

I flip the page. A section called "Dealing with the Police" instructs you to always use the "Magic Words" during run-ins with the fuzz: "I am going to remain silent. I want to see a lawyer." If they ask to search anything—your house, car, backpack, pockets, anal cavity, etc.—you are to use the "Magic Words 2": "I do not consent to this search." The basic theme of this section is expressed by what they call the Golden Rule: "Never trust a cop." This is my kind of college.

I look up from the binder. On cue Grech says the main problem for growers is "shady cops, not informants." Do not steal energy, she adds, because that's a federal offense. Don't send weed in the mail—seizures due to U.S. mail K-9 units are common. And even though you might feel the need to defend your valuable crops, you can't have guns at your house if you're cultivating.

A hand goes up. To my right is a white dude in a hoodie for whom I have created the backstory of ex-pro skateboarder turned rogue grower. "What about a Taser?" he asks. I instinctively assume he's joking, but his grim expression says otherwise. It occurs to me that even "legal" growers might actually have good reason to arm themselves against thieves and scoundrels.

Next class: Horticulture 101. Turns out it's easy to grow great marijuana indoors. All you need is light, water, and weed. That, and an electrician to set up your digital ballast, a growing medium like rock wool, a charcoal filter to get rid of the smell, neem oil and other pesticides to get rid of the spider mites, a humidifier, a carbon dioxide tank, fans to circulate the carbon dioxide and strengthen the plant tissue, two-gallon pots, drainage tubs, Mylar sheets to reflect the light, and constant supervision. Oh, and those plants need to come from clones or seeds with proven genetic histories of creating killer pot. And that water needs to be pH balanced to 6.0 and juiced with all kinds of nutrients and fertilizers and N-P-K (nitrogen-phosphorus-potassium). And if you want to maximize your yield, those lights need to be thousand-watt sodium halide bulbs the size of your thigh. And those monstrosities will be hot as Hades, so you'll probably need an air conditioner or some sort of cooling system. And all those gadgets running at once will quadruple your electricity bill, which might lift some eyebrows down at the electric company, so you'll want to find a good lawyer.

There are so many intricacies to cannabis cultivation that Professor Erenata has to rush through them at a breakneck pace to cram in an abridged version in the two-hour class period. I pity the fool who gets into the growing game without doing some research first. American marijuana enthusiasts have become spoiled connoisseurs. The increase in horticultural knowledge that began in Amsterdam and northern California has, through the Internet and *High Times* and grow bibles by experts like Jorge Cervantes, created a market that demands cannabis as beautiful and fragrant as a stargazer lily, with a THC concentration potent enough to take you to Phase Two after just a few puffs. Growing that type of marijuana without getting busted requires a delicate blend of artistry, scientific knowledge, patience, paranoia, and luck.

The last class of the day is called "Methods of Ingestion: Extracts 101." Professor Gilmore teaches us all the ways to make and consume cannabis in its non-smokable forms. This includes making hash, which he says is a great way to turn your leftover leaves and less handsome buds, or "trim," into something useful and profitable. Making hash is basically a way of separating the trichomes—those little THC-packed, crystal-laden hair-like outgrowths—from the rest of the vegetative matter.

There are several ways to make hash. You can rub the plant material on a screen so that only the trichome heads pass through it. You can make cold water or bubble hash by putting excess weed in a washing machine with cold water and letting the trichomes (which aren't soluble in water) separate from the plant material. "It's like cleaning your clothes and collecting the dirt," Gilmore says. He teaches us how to make tinctures, which basically involves soaking weed or hash in strong alcohol, like Everclear. You can also make capsules by heating pot in oil and pouring the resulting cannabis oil into capsules.

"These are great for dosing at work," Gilmore says, as I imagine a collective cringe from employers everywhere.

Gilmore tells us about one of the newer methods of weed ingestion: vaporization, a rather magical technique that I've been using for almost five years. Out of concern for my respiratory health and a total lack of concern for my fiscal well-being, I purchased the Mercedes-Benz of weed vaporizers, the Volcano. It was created by Storz & Bickel, who I like to imagine as two mechanically inclined German potheads who sat down and vowed, "Vee vill create zee perfect veed smoking muh-sheen."

The original, non-digital Volcano retails for over five hundred bucks, but this is more than just a glorified bong. It's a metallic, eight-inch-tall, conical device with a knob and two buttons, like some 1950s time-travel mechanism. You plug it in and wait five minutes for it to reach the desired temperature. Then you attach a marijuana-filled bowl to the Volcano's peak and turn on a fan, which blows vapor into a cylindrical balloon that inflates to whatever size you want. The Volcano heats the herb just enough so that it boils off the cannabinoids, but not enough to spark combustion and release more noxious gases. Then you simply attach a nozzle to the balloon and suck in the vapor. If it sounds almost sexual, that's because it is.

I'm not suggesting that people rush out and splurge on a Volcano, but pot smokers would be wise to take their respiratory health seriously. The effects of smoked marijuana on respiratory function are heavily disputed and widely misunderstood. An inordinate number of pot smokers insist, while coughing, that it has no negative effects. Prohibitionists insist smoking weed causes lung cancer. Research says they're both wrong.

The effects of smoked cannabis on the respiratory system are almost as confusing and counterintuitive as America's hypocritical stance on the drug. One of the most prolific scholars in this field is Dr. Donald Tashkin of UCLA, who has been conducting studies since 1983. In terms of lung cancer, here's what he's found: Marijuana smoke contains several known carcinogens. It deposits more tar than tobacco smoke, and that tar produces more chemicals linked to lung cancer. Yet Tashkin's subjects—more than twenty thousand heavy marijuana users—showed no increase in the risk of developing lung cancer. Tashkin's educated guess for why this is the case is that THC causes aging cells to die off before they become cancerous, but he would readily admit that he really doesn't know why.

In terms of bronchitis, though, the outlook for pot smokers isn't so rosy. Marijuana-only smokers report fewer bronchitis symptoms than tobacco smokers, but the rest is bad news. The common symptoms experienced by heavy marijuana smokers includes chronic cough, wheezing, and increased production of sputum—a lovely synonym for that already lovely term, phlegm. During heavy periods of marijuana consumption, even when I wasn't smoking cigarettes, I've noticed this sputum buildup, and it's not pleasant. If you want to get into the polysyllabic medicalese beneath this, well, bronchoscopies show that heavy marijuana smoking causes edema and angiogenesis in the airways, which in turn causes squamous metaplasia, where the cilia are replaced with mucus-secreting surface epithelial cells. Or in layman's terms, smoking weed turns the hairs that line your airways into nasty little mucus-squirters.

Beyond introducing us to such revolting imagery and fun new vocabulary, Tashkin's research also dismantles a long-held myth. Because marijuana smokers tend to hold smoke in their lungs longer than tobacco smokers do, they deposit more dangerous materials with each inhalation. (They also tend to smoke less than tobacco smokers, so the number of inhalations is less.) But here's the thing: The stupidest ritual among marijuana smokers is inhaling deeply and holding the smoke in your lungs for those extra few seconds. This deposits more dangerous crap in your chest, while barely increasing the psychoactive effects. So if you're among the scores of pot smokers who go with this ritual, no matter how convinced you are that those violent coughing fits are getting you higher, you might want to reconsider that move.

CHAPTER SEVEN
ENTER THE EMERALD TRIANGLE

It's Valentine's Day and everything rational says I should head back to New York. My plane ticket says it; my reservation at a romantic restaurant in Brooklyn says it; my conservative notion that everything-will-be-fine, you-can-work-this-out says it. But the nagging sense that my relationship is on the wane, unanimously confirmed by Nigel and Bilal and a half-dozen other close friends and family members, is saying something quite different. And the knowledge that New York will be literally and figuratively frigid, while here—in the nation's most marijuana-obsessed region at the most marijuana-obsessed moment in American history—it's temperate and calming, is really making me question this flight home.

Compounding all that is the nagging feeling that I am playing my research too safe. Talking to activists and going to cannabis college has its place, but I want to go deeper. I know that, just north of here, thousands of people are living on the fringes of society, avoiding publicity and writers like me, making a living off this plant and profiting off the contradictions between state and federal marijuana laws. In California as well as the rest of America, the vast majority of weed culture is happening secretly—in sealed-off basements, or on remote mountainside grows. But I'm so close to that story, I can almost smell it. After some cajoling from Bilal and a final, melodramatic phone call to Ida, I cancel my flight.

We drive north from San Fran with no particular destination in mind, only the murky hope of finding a marijuana-related adventure in or around Humboldt County, the fabled hotbed of American cannabis horticulture. The scenery on Highway 1 does its best to justify our impulsive voyage. We weave through lanky redwoods that extend up into the ether, far beyond our windshield view. With striated bark and dense knots like swollen ankles, the trees look like animated creatures. I open the window half-expecting them to talk to us, like those trees in the Wizard of Oz. With no advance warning, this grand canopy ends and is replaced by an entirely new ecosystem: shrub-lined cliffs sloping down to a distant shoreline. Mini rock islands jut out from the sea like massive breasts. The ebb and flow of the surf is a wavering whisper, the misty air above it indistinguishable from the clouds. We pull over at a lookout point, follow a path out into the thick vapor, smoke a joint, and hover above the Pacific Ocean like a couple of perched birds.

After a fitful night of sleep in a Fort Bragg hotel room, I wake up early with a jolt of inspiration. We're in Mendocino County—the epicenter of the Emerald Triangle, ground zero for the Green Rush! It's time to get involved, time to make the call I've been putting off since we left the Bay Area, due to the very real possibility that it could go unanswered. Time to call the only link I have to the shady underworld of northern California marijuana operators. Time to roll the dice and see if we're going to get an insider entrée into an epic weed adventure, or be forced to troll the hills of Humboldt in the blind hope that we'll stumble upon "American marijuana culture," which might come in the form of a shotgun-wielding sociopath.

It's time to call Buddha Cheese.

I made contact with him through a mutual friend, Joaquin, who said technically his name is Mike, but that doesn't begin to capture his magnitude. They all call him The Mikey, or Buddha Cheese. Beyond describing him as a midlevel kingpin who grows and distributes marijuana across the country, Joaquin otherwise made The Mikey sound like a fictional character: "He's a fucking force of nature, man. He's got crazy amounts of energy and severe attention deficit disorder. The guy is super-smart, and he has a good heart, but he is the most reckless, irresponsible human being I have ever met." As an example of what I could expect, Joaquin told me the story about when The Mikey boasted, while drunk at a party, about having $300,000 buried in his yard. When he woke up in a ditch several hours later, three hundred thousand dollars poorer and with a severe machete wound to the back of his head, he calmly got up and walked to the hospital.

"But you can't kill Buddha Cheese," Joaquin said. "You can only hope to contain him."

I have been tracking The Mikey for two months now—to Louisiana, Rhode Island, North Carolina, California, Thailand. I know that he's vetted my trustworthiness not only through Joaquin, but three other friends. I also know there is about a 30 percent chance that he has lost or discarded his phone, a 15 percent chance he will pick up, a 3 percent chance that he will be in our vicinity, and a 0 percent chance of leaving a voice mail. (The Mikey uses many phones and never sets up voice mail.) I dial the number and, miraculously, as if to confirm that there's a Higher Power with a twisted sense of humor, he picks up on the first ring.

"Mikey! It's Ryan, man. What you up to, kid?"

"*Heyyy buddddy*. I'm driving all over NorCal, picking up all my babies, hundreds of babies.[1] It's crazy, crazy . . . it's all happening! Where are you?"

"We're in Fort Bragg, at some hotel by the ocean."

"Damn, that's not far from us."

"So let's meet up then."

"Hmm. Yeah, yeah, that might work . . . There's just so much happening. I gotta roll up to Humboldt and get more babies, stop by my boy's place and get some flow,[2] and I don't even know where I'm gonna be at any given moment."

"I hear you . . ." I trail off, hoping he doesn't hear the disappointment in my voice. I've been eager to hang with the legendary Buddha Cheese in this environment ever since I met him a few months ago at a jazz bar in New York City. He's elusive; you have to catch him while you can. Which means this has to happen now.

"Come on, man!" I say. "Let's make the dream come true. Just pick a place and a time, and we'll come to you."

"All right, yeah, okay," Mikey says. "So you wanna see the game, how it all works?"

"Of course!"

"How many people you have with you?"

"Just one—my boy Bilal. He's cool. We can meet up beforehand on neutral ground or whatever, if you wanna meet him and make sure you're comfortable."

The Mikey ignores my offer. "Drive up to Circadia. There's this brew pub on the main strip. We'll meet you there in like an hour. We go there all the time . . . it's our spot."

1   "Babies" is his term for marijuana plant clones, which he plans to use in his upcoming grow.

2   Flow = cash.

"Sounds good. See you soon."

I hang up and smile. "It's *on*." Bilal gives me a high five.

We drive through the pissing rain, drinking Budweiser road sodas and smoking joints, listening to classical music on the only available station. I call The Mikey from a Taco Bell to say we are about twenty minutes away. There is a schedule change—he'll be there in four hours. Not a shocker; I know Buddha Cheese occupies his own space-time continuum. "Oh, and keep a low profile in Circadia," he adds. "I'll introduce you to everyone."

Circadia is a gloomy little town but still the biggest we have seen in miles. Its main street is flanked by strip malls, run-down motels, auto parts stores, and hydroponic grow supply shops. Billboards advertise a product that normally doesn't merit such prominent advertising real estate: turkey oven bags, which are used to store and cure weed in large quantities. We visit one of the many grow stores, but the cashier and customers seem edgy, eyeing us suspiciously. We look like out-of-towners, maybe even narks. Emotionally drained and beaten down by the rain, we get a hotel room.

The term *fleabag motel* doesn't begin to capture the sordidness of the Redwood Inn. For forty bucks a night we get an eight-by-ten room with a queen-sized bed, a discolored comforter with amoeba-shaped stains, a tiny cube of a television, a door that neither shuts nor locks, and an air conditioner that belches out dusty, carcinogenic air. After a five-hour wait and several restless attempts to nap, we call The Mikey. He's already there, he says, at the bar.

We find him standing in the back, beneath an overhang. He is dressed in cargo shorts, a gray sweatshirt, and flip-flops. Just over six feet tall and rangy, good looking but not strikingly so. His manicured stubble and wool Irish cap are the only outward hints he may not be the vintage American boy-next-door type.

I sense immediately that Buddha Cheese is tense. When I met him in New York, he was a virtual vortex of positive energy. Sitting at the front of the bar, facing the jazz band, he raved about his huge outdoor grow operation and even huger distribution network, cackling and intermittently poking me in the shoulder for emphasis. I had asked him flat out if he was on cocaine; it seemed impossible he could be that exuberant without the aid of some stimulant. But he insisted he wasn't and kept talking so loudly the bass player shot him disgusted looks.

Mikey's affect couldn't be more different today—strained smiles, jittery gestures, constantly checking his iPhone. I sense his tension is somehow related to his companion, whom I will call Puck. Though I've never had a clear vision of how a northern California weed distributor would look and act, Puck owns the part. He is short and roguishly handsome, unshaven and unshowered, dressed in a hoodie, baggy hippie pajamas, and a fedora. Smells like cigarettes and dirt, and so brimming with barely contained energy you are half-waiting for him to detonate. He has the fixated stare of a pure sociopath, and bulbous lips that look like misplaced labia. And there are tics, little head quivers and spontaneous out-loud blurts of nonsense—a dash of Asperger's and a sprinkle of Tourette's—which somehow makes him more endearing.

Two more dudes show up. There is Armand—Brazilian, bearded, chill. Buddha Cheese introduces him as his "chef and facilitator." And then there's Noah—Puck's right-hand man, and a growing expert. Looks like a field scientist, tall and bearded with sensitive, intelligent eyes. It's obvious from their interactions that Mikey and Puck are the alpha males—they make the deals, take the risks, and handle the cash. Noah and Armand are betas. They cook, drive, maintain the plants, provide company, and take orders.

We have dinner and a round of organic beer. The tension is heavy. Puck keeps whispering into Buddha Cheese's ear. Noah sits next to me and waxes scientific. He talks about using mycorrhizal inoculants on the roots of the cannabis plants, and running a hydroelectric GM alternator out of his house, from a creek a hundred feet above it, by just using the velocity of gravity. I nod and feign curiosity in an attempt to veil total confusion.

I ask The Mikey if he wants to go outside for a smoke. A beefy mountain man with a tangled beard follows us out. Once outside he sidles over to tell a joke about turkey baster bags. The setup: A rep from Reynolds Wrap comes to Mendo and asks the local grocery store owner why they sell so many more turkey bags here than elsewhere.

"Dunno," the guy says. "We never sell any turkeys."

This gets a laugh, and even Mikey seems to momentarily lighten up. But after our smoke, he abruptly says he has to head up to Humboldt. It's a four-hour drive and it's already snowing up there. I ask if we should come; he obliquely makes it clear we shouldn't. Maybe we can meet him tomorrow instead? Mikey says something about coming down, then going back up again. It's all very vague. Maybe it would be better for us to hang with Puck and Noah tonight, he suggests, to go check out their spread. "You're in good hands with them," Mikey says.

I'm not convinced of this. But we have come too far to retreat now, and anything is better than an evening in the Redwood Inn. Buddha Cheese tosses a couple of hundreds on the table, and we all leave. When we are safely seated in our rental car, Bilal pauses before putting the keys in the ignition. "What have we gotten ourselves into, bro?"

*   *   *

There is no subtle way to describe my first impression of Puck's bachelor lair: It reeks of dog shit. The barking is deafening. He flips the light on, revealing the source of it all. Thirteen caged pit bulls line the perimeter of his family room.

Puck circumnavigates the room, addressing the dogs while opening their cages. They pop out, one at a time, the constant barking replaced by a tap dance of clawed feet on linoleum. A few trot up to investigate me. I like dogs but am capable of being intimidated by a pit bull. I tentatively bend down to pet one of them.

"Don't worry," Puck says. "They're human friendly." He opens the back door and watches them file outside.

Noah gets on Facebook, which is being streamed onto a flat screen TV in the corner of the living room. The kitchen has all the bachelor pad trademarks—dishes strewn about, a central table covered with mail and randomness. Apropos of nothing, Puck starts telling us about the marijuana business.

Like Buddha Cheese, he's both a grower and distributor. He makes his most consistent money being a middleman—buying ganja in bulk from local growers and transporting it to buyers in other states where the profit margin is high. Most of his deals are in the neighborhood of a hundred pounds, but he has moved as much as five hundred at a time. The hardest part about the gig isn't the weed but the cash. What do you do with three hundred grand in cash? You can only deposit like nine thousand at a time.[3] Puck reinvests it, he says, in more deals. He has no idea how much cash he has at any given moment because it's always in circulation. For example, he just put $500,000 into a real estate deal with his cousin. When the construction is done, his cousin will "gift" the real estate to him. I can't help but think, *I hope you trust your cousin.*

Puck says the Cali market was best back in '97, right after Prop 215 passed. Thirty-five hundred dollars per pound was the going rate then. These days there are so many heads[4] in the game, and so many who are passable growers but abysmal hustlers, that the price is plummeting. "You get some jackass selling a pound for fifteen hundred to a guy on the East Coast, and he ruins it for everyone else. Next time you try to deal with that guy, he's like, 'Well, Johnny fucking Jackass over here gave it to me for fifteen.'"

Certain strains still bring in dependable cheddar, though. With OG Kush, for example, you can still count on around $2,800 per pound. If you're a decent negotiator and grower, and you're selling a hundred pounds at a time, there's still a fantastic profit margin there.

"You guys are modern moonshiners," I say.

Puck nods. "Exactly."

Puck is a local, and his reputation around these parts is solid as cement. "I'm the only one in this area who can get weed on consignment. If I say I'm gonna get them twenty-five per pound in advance, that's what I'll get them."

3   The Bank Secrecy Act of 1970, which was designed to prevent money laundering, requires financial institutions to report deposits of more than $10,000 (daily aggregate amount) to the federal government.

4   A "head" is a member of a particular drug subculture. The term originated in the hippie heyday of the late sixties. For the purposes of this book, it means someone working in the marijuana industry.

But there are risks. You lose shipments. Puck lays out a hypothetical scenario that's clearly based on reality. "You could lose money when some kid who's delivering a load for you, he gets in a fight with his girlfriend, and she calls the cops on him." Puck shrugs. "I don't know this fucking kid. I met him once, seemed nice to me."

Puck opens the cabinet beneath his sink. It's filled with piles of turkey bags. He tosses one on the table. "That's a pound of Blue Dream." He pulls out another. "That's Kush." And another. "That's Big Buddha Cheese." And another. "I don't know what the fuck that is."

Bilal's face lights up. "Yo man, I know you just brought this out to show us what you do and all that . . . but can we buy some off of you?"

"Yeah, yeah . . ." Puck dismisses him with a flip of his hand and walks off into a back room. I can't tell if he thinks selling Bilal a bag would be too small-time for him, or if he just isn't comfortable enough with us yet to make a money transaction. Bilal and I look at the bags and then each other, incredulous. I pick up a bag and push my face into it, absorbing the skunky, earthy smell. I have never seen this much marijuana in my life. And I have never really thought about how light buds are—a pound is a lot of weed. Puck walks back into the room carrying a box, which he dumps on the floor. It's filled with buds and stems.

"This is all trash," he says.

They don't look bad to me. But Puck says they all have mold, or are just of middling quality. Bilal shakes his head. "Man, I could break this up and get at least five G's out of it in New York."

"Yeah," Puck says. "Sometimes we take these bags into town and go up to teenagers and say, 'You smoke weed? Here, this is for you.' And the kids just about shit their pants."

Puck tells us how he got into the weed game. When he was just out of high school, he started working at his parents' grocery. His stepfather promised him $30,000 at the end of the year if he increased profits and productivity. Puck worked his ass off and increased profits by 60 percent. At the end of the year, his stepdad said he didn't have the money he had promised, and instead gave him seven pounds of just-harvested weed—still moist, and untrimmed. Puck figured out how to trim and cure the pot, then took it to Sacramento. Once he got there, he didn't know where to go, so he went to a head shop. He saw a guy there who was well dressed and had a certain shady gravitas—seemed like he might be an operator. Puck waited until he went outside and asked him if he wanted to buy. Puck showed him the goods. The guy said he had to call his associate, who would come with the money.

When the associate showed up, he pulled out a gun and pressed it to Puck's temple. Game over. An entire year's worth of work down the drain. Puck says he was like, *Fuck this, slaving for peanuts.* He would quit working at the grocery and start making loot, in the most profitable game in town. And here he is a decade later, doing just that.[5]

While we chat Puck is in perpetual motion, always working. He drops a few nuggets in front of Bilal, who rolls a joint. Then he cleans the entire house, stopping by every few minutes to explain the finer points of pit bull genetics and behavior. The pervading theme is impossible to forget: *Pit bulls are not man-aggressive. They are man-friendly but dog-aggressive.* He says he can't put his alpha males in the same room, and all his dogs would get aggressive in the presence of other dogs. This is because they were bred to fight. The humans are the ones who trained them, led them into the ring, fed them, told them when the fight was over, etc. Puck is adamant about this and he clearly feels seething contempt for owners who train their pit bulls to be aggressive to humans. They fuck it up for all the other pit bull trainers.

Puck tells a story about a pit bull he used to own. This particular dog was not trained by him; they took it off someone who didn't want it. It's a short story: "One day this dog snapped at a visitor." Puck's eyes widen, and he makes a dramatic neck tic. "So I took him outside and shot him in the back of the head."

"No shit?" I say. "Wow."

I get the sense Puck told me this story to comfort me, but the opposite

5 This logic strikes me as counterintuitive. My response would most likely be, *Fuck this. I'm gonna go to college, or get a bartending job.* I decide to keep this perspective to myself.

could also be true. Regardless, I make a mental note: Not only does Puck have thirteen pit bulls; he also has a gun.

Bilal lights the joint and passes it to me. Strangely enough, neither Puck nor Noah smoke weed anymore. Puck just seems bored by it, due to overexposure. Noah says he used to be an incorrigible pothead. He was an insomniac, and he would roll three joints every night before bed. He would smoke one, fall asleep, then wake up over the course of the night and ultimately finish the other two. But now that he doesn't smoke, he can actually go out socially and have coherent conversations. I ask if they were into any other drugs. Puck leans forward and pries back his lip. His side and back teeth are blackened from decay. "I used to be addicted to Rock Star Energy Drink. Look what it did. Dentist told me I had to stop."

I ask Puck and Noah about the locals. Do people know what they do and look down on them for being outlaws? "No way," Puck says. "They love us. We tip well, and we treat everyone with respect." They say the younger people—like the guys that gather at the brew pub—know what they do. Most of them are heads too. I ask what the women are like. "Incestual," Puck says, explaining that if you hook up with a local girl, you'll find out next week she's been hooking up with another grower/distributor.

I mention that people around here seem distrustful and avoid eye contact, especially if you look like an outsider. They agree. People are paranoid about feds, robbers, and all varieties of sketchy bastards. Which is why Puck and Noah deliberately keep a low profile—no fancy cars or clothes, always look a little disheveled and unshaven. They see young bucks acting a fool, driving around in tricked-out trucks with sparkling rims. "That's the kinda shit'll get you arrested," Puck says.

He asks if we want to go see their grow operation. Of course we do. Puck leans into the kitchen counter. "You guys aren't cops, are you?"

"Absolutely not," I say.

"We're definitely not cops." Bilal chuckles. "Trust me."

We grab Dizzy, a black pit bull with a neck the size of my head, and pile into an old, customized van. Driving separately isn't an option; they don't want us to be able to find the grow on our own. Puck drives the van like a Porsche, sixty miles per hour on back roads, blasting death metal the whole way. Bilal sits up front, absorbing another pit bull monologue. I feel for him—the cacophony of Puck's rant mixed with angry guitar groans is unsettling even in the way-back seat, where I am situated next to Noah and Dizzy. Noah is dropping knowledge—about how LED lights actually work for indoor grows, how he adds tryptophan for extra kick when he's growing 'shrooms, and about DMT, the drug that gives you a fifteen-minute-long hallucinogenic rush peppered with indescribable visions. "I try to smoke DMT at least twice a month, to keep my head clear and focused on what's really important."

Noah says a lot of folks in the game use their proceeds to fund their real passions. His is glassblowing, and he's proud of his work. "I come from salt-of-the-earth, middle-class folk. I believe in hard work. I am an artisan, so I believe in craft. I believe in taking my craft to the absolute limit, through discipline and education. And I believe in elevating myself and mankind through my work."

We arrive at the grow site, which has a security gate. "Yeah, we're in a gated community here," Puck jokes. It's dark and snowy. We trudge through the mud to the grower's quarters, which is basically a raised platform with a tarp over it. Noah lives here for months at a time during grow season. Puck shines the lantern on the inside of the tent. It's open on both ends, with a couple of makeshift beds and a table.

Behind the tent are a generator and a pump for funneling nutrient-rich water to the plants. We walk around it and start heading down a steep hill. In plaid pants and slip-on Chuck Taylor–style sneakers, I'm a bit fashion forward for the farming environment. I keep sliding down the hill. Puck says they positioned it on this hillside because it's a southward-facing slope, which maximizes exposure to sunlight. The hill has thirty-six circular plots, about four feet in diameter. By harvest time the plants will grow to around ten feet tall—marijuana *trees*, essentially, whose trunks will be strained to the tipping point by the denseness of their buds.

Security is also a factor in their geographic positioning. Non-marijuana trees shelter the grow on both sides, so it would be hard to notice if they "get flown" by drug-enforcement helicopters. Noah says they'll soon take their medicinal marijuana recommendations and permits, have them blown up at Kinko's, and post them on a placard facing the sky, so helicopters can see from above that they're legit and paying taxes.

When cops stop by, which is not uncommon, Noah calmly greets them. He says pot farmers around here know their rights. He stops any official at the gate and explains that they are in compliance with local laws. Unless they have a warrant, he politely declines access. If they do he reads it thoroughly. Often it will have the wrong address—partially because there are so many growers around—and he just tells them to go away. Puck says one time a neighbor called the cops on them. But they accidentally went to the property of another neighbor—a friendly older woman who was also a grower. She got busted, and they felt bad. But you can tell they didn't feel *that* bad. The incompetence of The Man amuses them, and it's especially entertaining that accidentally stumbling on the wrong house in this environment could still lead to a bust.

We drive back to the house. Noah asks us if we want to do DMT. He says dimethyltriptamine, or DMT, is the primary psychoactive in ayahuasca, a brew made of vines and shrubs from the Amazon rainforest. For centuries Amazonian Indians have been drinking ayahuasca to attain a trancelike state that they believe cleanses the body and mind, allowing them to commune with spirits. Part of me wonders if this is a test to see if we are willing to involuntarily incriminate ourselves with this unknown drug. But I'm feeling nihilistic and eager to step outside my consciousness, so I'm up for it regardless.

"Sure," I say. "Let's do it."

Noah lights some candles and pulls out a butterfly-shaped glass pipe that he blew himself. He packs it with weed, sprinkles crystal pellets of DMT on top, and sparks the bowl. After the first hit, my vision is already distorted. His fingers are dissolving and the pipe has a green vibrating halo around it. When I inhale again, the default world starts slipping away at an astonishing clip. It's scary—a surge of panic strikes as I surrender control of my mind. The third hit is a real struggle, not just physically, but because I'm not sure I want to push this any further. I motion to Noah that that's *it*. All connections to conventional reality have been obliterated.

I lie back on the couch and close my eyes. The first wave is charged with negative emotions and heavy on visual imagery. This new world is animated, painted in primary colors and filled with ever-morphing squiggles. It's like a concentrated dream, which takes a dark turn. Distorted faces laugh in disgust as they whisk by. Something tells me I created these demons, but now they are in control. I hear myself laugh—was that out loud?—in an attempt to defy them.

Disregarding Noah's advice, I open my eyes. Bad idea. Everything is glowing and pulsating. Bilal is staring at me like I'm some riveting museum exhibit. Puck is sitting in a chair next to the window, sucking on a cigarette, body curled up in a snakey position, looking at me sideways in an ominous way. I shut my eyes again.

Now the visions are more lifelike. I find myself in a sort of boxing ring. My opponent—a colorful creature that's more human than demon—and I are circling each other. It looks irate. We keep circling. I don't want to be here. Then, a revelation: Just step out of the ring! I can navigate the dream. And just like that, with a blast of willpower, the world changes. Trees and people and neighborhoods start shooting out from me. I've gone from negative to positive. There is a sense of total Zen interconnectedness. My breath is in sync with the respiration of all life, and a feeling of sweeping benevolence overcomes me that sounds maudlin to describe but is incredibly powerful to experience.

Then it's over. The comedown is quick. It gets incrementally less trippy and then it stops. I open my eyes and smile.

"How was it?" Bilal asks.

"Amazing," I say.

His turn now. Bilal takes four hits and starts coughing. After a few minutes he opens his eyes and looks at me. There's real panic there. Immediately after he's done, Bilal says we should be getting back to the hotel now. Which is suspicious, because no one wants to get back to the Redwood Inn.

We buy a smorgasbord of herb—Big Buddha Cheese, Sour Diesel, and Dairy Queen—smoke a final cigarette on the porch, say thanks, and get into the car. Driving away, we can't stop laughing and shaking our heads.

I ask about his trip. He says he had a vision that Puck and Noah were brain-frying us and planned to tie us up and turn us into pit bull food. The line between reality and paranoia feels thin in this realm. We keep retelling the story of what just happened as if it was decades ago, or all just a bizarre dream. And I still wonder if maybe it was.

*   *   *

We have driven back to San Francisco through Napa Valley, been wowed by red wine and sun-splashed vineyards, showered, shaved, cooked dinner with Nigel and his dynamite six-year-old daughter, and are just beginning to regain some semblance of civility when Buddha Cheese sends me a text. Come up to Green Canyon, he says.

Bilal and I are torn but agree to toss our stuff in the rental and head north. We make it to the designated strip mall parking lot in Green Canyon by nine. Outside the car it's a gloomy diarrhea of wet snow. Bilal has hit The Wall. We have traded the creature comforts of the city for the no-man's-land of waiting in a parked car for an unreliable drug dealer.

"This sucks, bro," Bilal says.

I agree but I'm keeping the faith that things will not-suck soon. After a half hour a white truck pulls up and parks nearby. I walk up to it. It's Buddha Cheese but he's on the phone. Finally, he looks up and opens his window.

"Ready to rock?"

I can tell he's in a better mood this time. He says we're supposed to meet someone named Roxanne here and walks across the parking lot. When he returns he outlines the plan. Bilal will drive with Roxanne, because she doesn't want to drive up on "The Hill," where the terrain is snowy and treacherous. I will ride with Mikey in the truck. The rental car stays in the parking lot, because the chance of it getting stuck on The Hill is high. I'm reluctant to separate ourselves from our only means of escape if something untoward pops off, but the last thing we need is a rental car stuck on an outlaw's ranch in the middle of nowhere.

We drive several miles outside of town, turn right, and begin a steep climb. The Hill, it turns out, is a mountain. Paved road turns to pothole-pocked gravel, winding ever upward. Mikey lights a joint and, triple-tasking, puffs at it while sending texts, using his knee to steer. Reggae is blasting. A few minutes into our ascent, fat snowflakes start to fall.

"We're above the snowline now," The Mikey says. "Have you heard about the Donner Party, those explorers who got stuck in the snow and ate each other?"

"Of course."

"That happened right near here, a few mountains over. Crazy, right?"

"Yeah," I say. "Crazy."

Not the most comforting nugget of trivia. I am tempted to check his geographical accuracy, but my phone isn't getting any bars.

Buddha Cheese points up ahead. "If we kept going straight here, we would get to my house. I own the house at the bottom of The Hill, where I stay, and a shack for the growers at the top of the property. That's where we keep the babies. Wow, look, the boys are doing their job . . . the chain is up. Go out and move that, would you?" A chain is linked to two metal poles, with a sign in the middle: KEEP OUT. PRIVATE PROPERTY. I trudge through the snow, unlatch it, and lay the chain on the road. This road is even steeper now, with more potholes, and the occasional tree branch felled by accumulated snow. The rental car wouldn't have had a chance.

Beyond a wide-open space at the crest of the hill, we see a building too big to call a shack but too shabby to call a house. The final run-up to this shack-house is so precipitous Mikey has to beach the truck near a lumber pile a hundred yards downhill. We grab beer, groceries, grow supplies, and fuel tanks, which run the generator and are thus our surest defense from ending up like the Donner Party.

Trekking up the hill, I see two puppies coming to greet us, making hops that send up puffs of snow. Winded, I take a break and check out the shanty—two stories tall, with five front-facing windows and brownish gray wood siding. The front of the cottage is on stilts that strain to keep it level. A makeshift ladder with a missing rung leads to a front door of sorts, which evidently goes unused.

Mikey shines his flashlight on the side entrance, revealing outdoor shelves holding bleach, lighter fluid, and candles—all covered by snow. A soggy wooden step leads to a door that was probably once white. The pups—more pit bulls, of course—are leaping about, covering our jeans with muddy paw prints.

"Yeah, buddy!" Mikey leans over to pet the dogs. He points to a white-and-caramel bundle of furry muscle. "The brown one's Stash." The other one is a pink-nosed pup with a color scheme that's the inverse of a Holstein cow, black with white splotches. "And this is Gypsy. She's a good little bitch. Aren't you, Gypsy?"

A guy wearing matching beige canvas Carhartt jacket and pants walks out of the shack. He looks like a more rugged version of The Dude from *The Big Lebowski*. Mikey introduces him as Bull.

"How my babies doin'?" Mikey asks.

"Good," Bull says. "We had a little spider-mite issue, but . . ."

"You put neem oil on them?"

"Yesss."

"Is it too humid up there?"

"Nooo."

"I'll be the judge of that. Come on."

We walk through the shack on a dusty floor, past a washer and dryer covered with clothes, a refrigerator, a gas stove, and a sink littered with dirty dishes. A claustrophobic kitchen is followed by a living room with a glowing furnace. The table is clogged with empty soda cans, ashtrays, and parcels filled with stacks of cash. We walk up a small set of winding stairs to the second floor.

When Mikey opens the door to a room off to our right, light pours out. Hundreds of baby marijuana plants are arranged in rows along the floor, illuminated by hanging lights. Fans blow their leaves, which wave at us invitingly. This is the origin of what Mike says will be a million-dollar harvest, come November.

I used to think the weed I smoked started as a seed. And all cannabis plants do, if you trace them back far enough. But most growers in places like NorCal start with clones. The first step to cloning is cutting a branch tip off a "mother plant" and rooting it. This reduces the time it takes the plant to mature, ensures that the offspring will be female, and that the quality of buds will be roughly that of the mother plant. Growers who start from seeds can root out the males at around four to eight weeks, when the males form little balls where the branches converge at the stem, almost like testicles between the legs. But compared to cloning, this sexing process wastes valuable time, energy, and space.

The ideal growing environment is one of extreme sexual frustration. Male plants aren't just useless; they can fuck up your whole ball game. Unless you have an incompetent dealer or an undiscriminating palate, you will only ever smoke the flowers of female cannabis plants.[6] As long as no male plants are in the vicinity, female plants will remain unpollinated,[7] and their flowers—called calyxes—will continue to develop THC-laden, sticky trichomes in a last-ditch effort to attract insects carrying male pollen. If you can maintain all of the major requirements—water, nutrients, appropriate temperature, carbon dioxide, light, and sufficient space—and stave off pests and pathogens, then female plants will grow like exactly what they are . . . weeds. They will put all their energy into producing new calyxes, instead of making seeds. They will be so desperate to get laid that they resort to making the densest and most beautiful flowers that nature can conjure, and that money can buy.

Speaking of sexual frustration, it's a relief to finally have some female energy around. It's been a sausage-fest for days. Not that Roxanne is a girlie

6   Male flowers and leaves do contain THC, but a much smaller amount than their female counterparts.

7   Unpollinated female plants are also known as "sinsemilla," meaning "without seeds" in Spanish.

girl. Svelte and tallish, with wavy blond hair and sparkling, mischievous eyes, she comes upstairs while we're inspecting the clones. Her style is sort of Burning Man rural princess—a hipster sweater, fingerless gloves, and the only cool-looking fanny pack on the market. It's leather with snap-able pouches and a main compartment that, when she unzips it, reveals dozens of hundred-dollar bills. When Bilal and I ask to snap photos of her gangsta fanny pack, Roxanne laughs in the most self-satisfied way.

Roxanne is a queenpin in her own right. In fact she's been in the California weed game longer than The Mikey and claims she was his main contact when he first moved his operation from the East Coast to Cali. They were a couple for a few months, but the chemistry was all wrong. Now they are business associates, which means constantly negotiating prices, comparing recent transactions, and bickering like an old married couple. Roxanne keeps complaining she got Mikey started in the game, and now he's taking over. "You're leaving me in the cold dark dust!" I hear her saying as we walk back down the stairs.

Bull passes me a joint—a Bob Marley–sized fattie with no tobacco or filter. Joints are in constant circulation; the shack is an embarrassment of riches. Two quart-sized Mason jars are stuffed with Mikey's "head stash," the stockpile a grower keeps after harvest for his personal use. This cache is full of "littles," the smaller buds that are less picturesque and thus less profitable, but just as high quality. On the table I notice three droppers filled with sewage-colored cannabis tincture, and two jars filled with dozens of half-inch-thick hash pucks. If we run out of food and supplies up here, at least we'll die stoned to the gills.

Moving onto our fourth joint, I think, Why am I still smoking? I have reached a plateau of maximum highness that can't be transcended, and being this zooted under these circumstances makes me acutely self-aware of my conflicting emotions. On one hand I don't know these people and have no idea where I am. My phone is dead. We are stuck on the top of a mountain in a dirty, claustrophobic shanty, surrounded by weed, pit bulls, and vacuum-sealed bags of cash. And although the marijuana part is technically legal in northern California, the illicitly shipped bundles of cash underscore the fact that these folks probably aren't supplying much weed to dispensaries. Because that's not where the money is.

On the other hand, I feel oddly secure. If the authorities have the gumption to raid this remote of a locale during a blinding snowstorm, they can have us. And it's sort of cozy up here, snuggling up to the kerosene heater and rubbing Stash's furry ears. I'm far away from my relationship and debt issues. And though I can't hear their banter over the incessant *whomp* of dubstep music, watching the wild gesticulations and dramatic eye rolls of Buddha Cheese and Roxanne makes me feel like I'm stuck in some plotless indie film.

Mikey takes a call. Roxanne turns her attention to Bilal and me. She is reveling in the fact that we're outsiders awed by their hippie-hustler lifestyle, and now wants to up the ante. She holds up a little vial. "You guys *have* to try this."

I squint. It looks like cloves. "What is it?"

"Sassafras," Roxanne says. "Amazing. It's like Ecstasy, only natural."

"How do you take it?" Bilal asks.

"Just pop a couple twigs in your beer." Roxanne drops a sliver in her Corona and takes a sip. "Like that."

She shakes a few brown nuggets into my hand. I pop them into my beer and watch them float to the bottom. Here's to our second obscure psychotropic mind-blast in as many days! I have friends who like drugs, but these people take psychedelic exploration to another level. Maybe they are so inured to being stoned on premium-quality marijuana, it's only natural for them to seek out new mind-altering frontiers. That almost sounds like a confirmation of the gateway theory—that marijuana leads to harder drugs—but in actuality I think the type of people who are drawn to tweaking their consciousness will find a way to do it, one way or another.

"Cheers, everyone," Bilal says.

A half hour later, we start to set sail. The effect is pure positivity—a serotonin surge with no obvious downside. Roxanne is right: Sassafras has all the good parts of Ecstasy without the chemical, speedy restlessness. Bilal and I go outside for a cigarette and are rendered speechless by our surroundings, light-years from New York. There's a full moon in the sky, and all that that entails—insomnia, insanity, lycanthropy—seems wholly possible. When we come back in, Buddha Cheese has turned down the lights and Bull has turned up the dubstep. Any residual trace of anxious claustrophobia is washed away by a brain-cleansing sensation of bottomless happiness. Bilal and Roxanne and I are content to dance in our tiny plots between the couch and the heater, laughing occasionally at some cosmic, telepathically transmitted joke.

If you accept that intoxication is a fundamental human desire—from the spinning-'til-you're-dizzy games of children, to the happy hour drinkers, to the religious ecstasy-seekers of so many cultures—then you have to wonder if there isn't something good (or at least natural) about this basic impulse. Is it so irrational to think that plants like sassafras and cannabis would evolve into substances that psychologically benefit the animals that consume them? If certain plants have helped heal our bodies for centuries, is it such a leap of logic that they could help heal our psyches as well?

I don't have any hard evidence on this. All I know is the feeling I get from sassafras is why I sometimes like to do drugs, and why millions of others do too, and why a *war* on drugs with the goal of eradicating drug use is inherently a losing proposition. Because drugs can make you feel good, and some of the best drugs are made from plants that grow in the earth. Though they also have a dark side, these intoxicating plants can help you step outside the daily onslaught of text messages and work concerns and Internet searches and all that worldly, soul-numbing stuff, and into the acquisition of a fresh new state of mind.

*　　　　　　　　　*　　　　　　　　　*

I wake up clinging to a warm body. My mind shuffles through the possibilities. If it's Roxanne, I have made a tactical error, because she clearly has an unwritten friends-with-benefits contract with Buddha Cheese, and it's essential I maintain his trust. If it is any of the guys, well, it would be a testament to the power of sassafras that my boundless love of humanity under its influence somehow rendered me bisexual. But on closer inspection, the body feels smaller and hairier than any human should rightly be. Pretty sure I'm spooning a pit bull.

In another context this might be cause for alarm. But it's arctic cold in here; the heater must have shut off during the night. And considering that the only uncovered part of my body—my ass—is a good fifteen degrees lower than that of its frontal counterpart, I feel real gratitude for this furry little heating pad. But there's always room for improvement. Without a second thought, I pick up Gypsy's radiant body and transfer her to my caboose.

I try to jolt my brain back into consciousness. What happened last night? The table next to the bed is full of helpful hints—empty wine and beer bottles, half-smoked joints, a cannabis tincture dropper bathing in a puddle of its own juices.

The night comes back to me in a slide show of mental snapshots. I remember opening the front door and watching the full moon light up the falling snow like spent fireworks. Bilal and I looking at the outhouse and laughing about the thought of being eaten alive by a bobcat while dropping a deuce. Buddha Cheese turning off the music and insisting we tour the property. Bilal in a furry cap that made him look like an Uzbek goatherder. Snow clumps dumping off bent tree boughs. Seeing not one but three plots for marijuana grows and thinking, *This place is huge.* Mikey's rhapsodic monologue about what this will all look like come October: ten-foot-tall ganja bushes covered with buds the size of your fist! And then back at the shack, feeling so empty-headed and bone-cold I just couldn't do it anymore.

I sit up and look over at my sofa-bed companion, Bilal. Beneath us is a giant pink fur carpet Buddha Cheese must have added for warmth. We look like a gay homeless couple who raided the dumpsters behind IKEA.

"Dude, are you awake?" I ask.

"I am now," Bilal says.

"Is Stash with you?"

"Yeah. This dog is so fucking warm, man!"

We hear the side door open and the stomp of feet. Bull walks in holding a lit joint. "Ready for wake-and-bake?"

"I am," Bilal says.

He hands over the joint. "Breakfast is coming too. I got five free steaks with my tire purchase the other day. I call it the Long Island Special . . ."

God bless Bull's survivalist instincts, but he has no morning voice. His bluster awakens Roxanne and Mikey, who clearly hooked up last night.

Roxanne saunters in. "Jesus, look at you two. One night of sassafras and you're reduced to bestiality."

"I love it!" Buddha Cheese pops into the room with Kramer-like spasticity, his hands down his pants. The rest of us look exactly as we should—dead-eyed and hungover—but The Mikey is like a case study in attention deficit disorder, pacing the floor, texting manically, bouncing upstairs to check on the babies, telling stories, barking orders at Bull, berating Roxanne for her lack of professionalism, and just generally putting on a show.

When he finally sits down, Buddha Cheese wants to talk about dogs. All the pot farms in northern California have dogs, he says, for security and companionship. There are even roving bands of stray-dog "security teams" that prowl the mountains looking for work during the harvest season. At the beginning of their harvest last year a big black pit bull and a mutt showed up at their grow.

"I said, 'Take those dogs away!'" Mikey says. "'Someone's gonna come looking for 'em. And all of the guys were like, 'But they're so *cooool.*'"

His underlings drove the dogs seven miles away and dumped them. They found their way back in three hours. The workers hid them in a shed. When Mikey discovered them a few weeks later his defenses were weakened. They stayed on through the harvest, when—like most seasonal migrant workers—they sensed they were no longer useful and disappeared.

Buddha Cheese goes back to fiddling with his phone. I have learned that you either engage him or lose him, so I ask about the layout of his farm. "From my vague memories of the tour last night," I say, "you've got ambitious plans."

The Mikey sets his phone down and grabs a scrap of paper. He draws a map of The Hill. There will be three separate grow plots, he says, plus a greenhouse, a small orchard of bing cherry trees, geodesic domes for workers to sleep in, a community bath dome, the shack we're in, the storage shack nearby, and the house at the bottom of The Hill. He just bought a Bobcat to improve efficiency, and by harvest time, there will be about twenty workers living here.

"And is this going to be legal?" I ask. "How many plants can you legally grow in this county?"

"The socially accepted guidelines around here are thirty-six plants." He explains that, technically, the limit per each patient in this county is six mature plants, or twelve immature plants, plus eight ounces of dried bud. In fact, these are the guidelines for the entire state, as outlined by the cheekily named SB 420.

Though much of the state has adopted these guidelines, individual cities and counties are allowed to enact higher—but not lower—limits than the state standard. In Mendocino County, patients used to have a 99-plant limit; now it's 25. The city of Fort Bragg allows indoor growing within a 100-square-foot space. Oakland has a 72-plant indoor growing limit. These ordinances change frequently, and it's not uncommon for them to change in the middle of a grower's season, rendering their current grow illegal. All of this is further complicated by a state supreme court ruling, *People v. Kelly* (2010), which says the state government can't impose any legal limits on the amount of marijuana users can grow or possess. And in all counties and cities, growing marijuana is always illegal under federal law. All told it's a complete and utter legal clusterfuck.

"Okay, so thirty-six plants then," I say. "But I thought you said last night you were going to have thirty-two plants per garden. Isn't that ninety-six?"

Buddha Cheese laughs. He says two of those gardens are on the edge of the property, close to the neighbors, so it will take some work for helicopters to figure it out. And you can get around the limits by just making your co-op bigger.

Though I'm not convinced Buddha Cheese cares about the laws, he is right about this. One of California's medical marijuana loopholes is that you can build cooperatives with other patients. These collectives can scale the limits to the number of members, and only a few cities seem to place finite limits on membership. So if you are allowed six plants per collective member, and you have thirty members, that's 180 plants. If you have 99 members and each one is allowed 99 plants, you could ostensibly have a legal grow the size of Rhode Island.

The Mikey says his plan is to grow as close to 99 plants as he can manage, and then collect the appropriate number of co-op members once his operation is up and running. He didn't choose that limit arbitrarily. Growing more than a hundred plants risks a five-year mandatory minimum sentence under federal law. Meanwhile, the state and county laws are a crapshoot. Many "legal" patients have been raided and arrested for a variety of reasons: neighbors' complaints, dubious recommendations, or for just growing amounts that local police deem excessive. Once patients have been charged—and not infrequently, their plants and cash seized—it's up to the courts to decide the legitimacy of their "medical" claim.

But Mikey doesn't want to talk about regulations. He just assumes he won't get busted. He wants to talk about growing. In this area of northern California growing weed is a decades-old occupation. From summer into spring it has an almost optimal climate and mean temperature—between seventy and eighty-five degrees—for growing cannabis.

Buddha Cheese may have the instincts of a common criminal, but his grasp of horticulture is fairly sophisticated. He and his crew keep the plants indoors for much of the vegetative stage, he explains, battling plant-enemies while they are still in a contained environment. The whole process is organic, so spider mites can't be fought with insecticide. Instead, Mikey employs predators like ladybugs.

During the vegetation and early flowering stages, the crew on The Hill will feed the plants compost tea, a liquid version of compost that's packed with beneficial fungi and bacteria. To induce early flowering, they use a light deprivation technique. Without "light dep" marijuana will naturally start flowering when there's less than twelve hours of sunlight in a day. Instead, as the flowering stage nears, Mikey's growing crew pulls a lightproof cover over their greenhouse from 7:00 P.M. to 7:00 A.M. daily, triggering the plant's natural 12/12 light cycle early.[8] This tricks the plants into budding more than a month before the days are short enough for the plants to flower on their own, saving time, effort, expense, and risk.

Bilal takes a puff of a joint and passes it to me. He says he had a grow operation in college, but it didn't begin to compare to this level of refinement. He just took the lights from his fish tank and set them up as grow lights, then got seeds online from Marc Emery Direct. "I mean, I gave them some nutrients, but it wasn't very advanced. I used to dance for my babies! I'd be like, 'Yeah, come on! Grow, grow!'"

Despite the crude technique, Bilal says he made plenty of loot off the batch as a college student, keeping the best buds for himself and selling the dregs to naïve freshmen. I ask Buddha Cheese what kind of profit he'll be looking at for his grow. He does the math in his head. "So we'll have ninety-six plants. If all goes well, that should yield about four hundred pounds. Let's say four twenty. And then we sell each pound at twenty-five, or let's say twenty-eight. So all said, without expenses . . ."

I'm punching numbers into my cell phone calculator. He is estimating a yield of almost four and a half pounds per plant, which seems inflated. But if he uses these heavy-duty horticultural techniques, it wouldn't be unheard of in this climate. I punch it in, and my eyes pop at his estimated gross: $1.17 million.

"But then you've got all your costs," Mikey continues. "And you're paying workers a pound of weed a month, so shave that off. And then you've got shipping costs, which is $350 a pound."

"How do you ship it?" I ask.

"Trucking company. We just put it in a crate, package it like produce or any other cargo. Or sometimes I just have people do it in a rental car. That's even cheaper . . . like two, two fifty."

"Interesting."

8 A related word for this concept is *zeitgeber*, a German word that literally translates as "time-giver" or "synchronizer." A *zeitgeber* is an external cue that synchronizes an organism's internal clock to the earth's twenty-four-hour cycle of light and darkness.

"Or if it's a small amount, like ten pounds or less, I'll just ship it." He points his phone at me for emphasis. "Always United States Postal Service, never FedEx."

Mikey's phone rings. He speaks in clipped blips of coded language. I go back to calculating. Subtracting workers' salaries and shipping costs (and omitting costs like a mortgage, supplies, food, and maintenance), the estimated profit for one grow: $900,000.

I look at the parcels on the table, stuffed with stacks of bills. Over on the bookshelf is another stack. They have been sitting around all night, in plain view. Once again I wonder if we are being tested, to see if we're trustworthy. Or is he so jaded by the presence of cash that he barely notices?

"I'm just curious," I say, to no one in particular. "How much money is in these parcels?"

The Mikey covers his phone with his hand. "About eighty grand."

Roxanne shakes her head. "Yeah, the money's great. But I'm getting tired. I'm trying to put someone else in my position. I'm just gonna manage, which will be less money. When you're doing it all yourself you can't take anything else on, like yoga or whatever. Dealing with people and money gets stressful. Putting a hundred thousand dollars into a deal and then waiting a month to get a return from someone you're not even sure you trust . . . that's stressful."

"I could see that," I say.

"Okay, okay." Buddha Cheese is almost whispering into his phone. "I'll see you there . . . call you on the way. Yep, bye." He tosses the phone on the sofa. "Boom! Another pickup, in Humboldt . . ."

"With who?" Roxanne asks.

"Not important," Mikey snaps. He turns to me. "Off to Humboldt tomorrow. Or whenever. That's all I do is travel these hills, kid."

This devolves into a shit-talking session between Bonnie and Clyde. They mute their voices so I only catch snippets. Roxanne focuses on the amazing deals she's gotten for different strains, while Mikey keeps admonishing her for talking too much on the phone, despite the fact that I just heard him make a deal on the phone.

While they spar Bull gets his own project underway: making butane hash. This is one of the methods we didn't learn about at Oaksterdam. It's technically illegal, because making concentrates with solvents can be dangerous. But once it's made, it's indistinguishable from other hash and thus legal. Bull doesn't give a shit either way. He's already created a home-made hash-extraction mechanism, with materials he got for forty bucks at Home Depot.

Bull sits Indian style on the floor, packing shake into the mechanism: a steel pipe with a spigot on the bottom end and an adapter at the top, which is duct-taped to keep it from freeze-burning Bull's hands. He pops off the lid of a butane can, sticks it into the adapter, and releases the butane. After a few minutes, the spigot starts squirting out pea green liquid, which evokes all sorts of bodily function analogies.

"Ohhh shit," we coo in unison.

Bull pulls the can off and replaces it with another one. Now the liquid is really pouring out—a whirlpool of trichome soup.

"That happens so fast," I say. "It's such an efficient process."

"That's chemistry for you, bro," says Bilal.

I survey the scene. Mikey is on the couch in a T-shirt and a cotton bracelet, wrapped in a dirty blanket. Roxanne stands next to him, in a gray hoodie and black yoga pants, tapping at her cell phone. Stash is between them, licking himself. Everyone is wearing socks. Jay-Z's "American Dreamin'" is playing in the background.

The extraction is done. Bilal holds a kettle of hot water, and Bull goes in search of a bowl to put it in.

"So what are we doing now?" I ask.

"Evaporating all the butane out," Bull says. He puts the glass bowl inside a plastic bowl that's filled with steaming water. The glass bowl looks too delicate for such a radical temperature change. I bend down to check out the furiously bubbling resin stew. It looks volatile, almost angry. Something doesn't feel right. The liquid is vanishing at an alarming rate. "Wow, it evaporates so fast!" I say.

On cue, the bowl explodes.

"Oh, FUCK!" Bull shouts. Smoke mushrooms. As it clears I see dozens of glass shards floating in a pool of burbling green schmagma.

"Whooah!" Buddha Cheese shouts. "A-ho-ho-ho-hooooo!"

"You all right?" I ask.

"Not entirely," Bull says. "Well actually, I'm okay."

"Pull the glass out," Mikey says.

"No, we're gonna scoop it, like crack!" Bull says, rushing into the kitchen. I decide not to probe into his familiarity with the crack-scooping process. He reemerges and starts spooning the goo into a coffee mug.

"It's like baby food!" Bilal says.

Bull laughs skittishly. "That was a little more excitement than I was hoping for. But we still collected the oil."

The chuckling continues, but the hash eruption episode has tainted the tranquility of the morning. It's pouring snow outside. The flame in the heater is dimming; we don't have much fuel left. After cleaning up the mess, Bull says we should probably get off The Hill soon, go into town, and get supplies. Bilal starts packing his bag.

The only person who's not in a hurry is Buddha Cheese. He dismisses Bull's call to action, taps out text messages, then starts tutoring me on some of the strains he'll be growing this year.

"I'm just doin' Blue Dream and Train Wreck this year," he says. Train Wreck is a pure sativa, while Blue Dream is a hybrid of the two main varieties of the cannabis plant, sativa and indica. It's a cross between the Blueberry and Haze strains, and combines the heady, energetic vibe of a sativa with the mellow, full-body relaxation of an indica. This latter variety is known to cause "couch lock," from which Buddha Cheese currently seems to be suffering.

"Wow," Mikey says, looking at his phone. "Looks like we're supposed to get four to eight inches of snow today, and another twelve tonight."

"Which is why we should get going," Bull says.

"I'm ready," Bilal adds.

But the more we press, the more recalcitrant Buddha Cheese gets. His new conversational topic is how badly he has to take a shit, without making any obvious moves toward making that dream come true. I'm getting hungry, and we're running low on food. The Donner Party anxiety is taking hold. I start running my hands through my hair obsessively, as if searching for ticks. Knowing I'll likely come back up here at some point for further research, I make a mental note to make sure I have an exit plan next time. Bilal and I go outside to smoke a cigarette we don't really want and commiserate in private.

"This has been awesome," Bilal says between puffs. "But we gotta get the fuck out of here. It's like a hostage situation."

We go back inside. Mikey looks up from his couch perch. "Hey, you guys should come back for the official opening of the gardens. Next full moon, like March 18."

An hour creeps by. Understanding that it's counterproductive to prod him, everyone stops mentioning the obvious fact that we're all waiting for Buddha Cheese.

"When you have an outhouse," he says, "and you used to shit three times a day, you'll shit one time a day."

"Right, right," I say.

"We used to have a ninja bucket out back, for late-night shits. You never know if there's gonna be predators up at the outhouse."

This continues until Mikey either senses he's pushed us too far, or he just has to answer the call of nature. He picks up a magazine and ambles out to the outhouse. Another half hour crawls by, another inch of snow accumulates.

"Whooh!" Mikey says, when he strolls back in. "That was magical."

"Awesome," Bull says. "Can we go now?"

"Of course," says Buddha Cheese. "What are we waiting for?"

CHAPTER EIGHT
CRAIG THE DEALER

Much of the marijuana grown by northern California farmers like Buddha Cheese is not consumed by Californians. It's transported to dealers and distributors in other states, where the demand for high-quality weed far exceeds the local supply. One such place is the city I've lived in for a decade, New York City, which has a population of eight million and an unknown stoner population in the hundreds of thousands.

On my personal roster at this point in my NYC pot-smoking career, I have three dealers. After many years of market research they have risen to my upper echelon for possessing consistent greenery of the highest quality, for which they charge exorbitant prices. All of them are hip, artistically in-clined guys who have established lives outside of the weed world. But only one of them, Craig,[1] is willing to talk, and to readily admit that his source is in northern California. Which is why I find myself back in Brooklyn, in a smoky, cramped apartment, trying to find out what it's like on the other end of the California supply line—no pit bulls or mountain shanties, just a regular weed dealer slinging quarter-ounce baggies to a steady stream of angst-riddled New Yorkers.

"So what's the worst part of your job?" I ask.

"The worst part is, you have to do a lot of small talk," Craig says. "They'll be like, 'Oh, so blah blah blah.' And it's like, 'Yeah, really?'"

He shakes his head in disgust, as if the mere thought of these trifling exchanges has caused him genuine trauma. I didn't see this coming. The hardest part of being a weed dealer in New York City: all the excruciating small talk.

"They're not really like your real friends," Craig says. "It's ill, 'cause you got different people with different energy. I know 'em, but I don't hang out with them. You know what I'm sayin'? Most of my clients are females, who come to the house. Females and teachers."

Craig explains that he's not sure how he got so many female and teacher clients, but he thinks it has to do with his gentle giant vibe. Craig is a tall, schlumpy black guy who seems to accidentally take up more space than he means to. He dresses casually—in shorts and hip-hop-inflected

---

1 I'm guessing he chose "Craig" as his nom de guerre because it's the name of Ice Cube's character in the movie *Friday*.

T-shirts, not droopy jeans and sports jerseys. Over time, due to his affable mien and quality product, he accumulated female clients through word of mouth. "They're like, 'He's easy, he's real chill,'" Craig says. "Girls, they get ripped off and shit. Guys'll be tryin' to holla at 'em and shit, and then they will rip 'em off or whatever."

Craig passes me the blunt. I'm back to that mind-state of feeling like I *need* to get high. Coming back to New York has been a heavy-handed bitch slap of reality after the living daydream that was northern California. Going AWOL on Valentine's Day hasn't done much for the reestablishment of trust that Ida and I have been grasping at since the Miami Incident.

Having moved out of my apartment and into hers three months prior, my existence there feels temporary. Most of my possessions remain closed off in a side room, almost like an in-house storage unit. We can't compromise on how to integrate my stuff with hers. Meanwhile, we sit on the couch together, watching TV but not touching, and never kissing. There is a feeling that we're on the fence, waiting for some force beyond ourselves to push us over to one side or the other.

I'm perpetually on edge—uncomfortable in my own apartment, doubting my decision to lay it all on the line with Ida, and working insanity-inducing nocturnal hours at NPR. Adding to this tension is my growing discontentment with New York—the unforgiving weather, the expensive everything, the needlessly aggressive people. I will always love this city, but even the most loyal New Yorkers have their moments (predominantly in the winter) when they wonder why the fuck they subject themselves to this punishing lifestyle. I take a deep pull on the joint, hoping to erase thoughts like this and shift my psyche toward the positive.

For his part Craig is taking self-medication to a much more literal extreme. Though he's chill by nature, the concoction in his Styrofoam cup is certainly accentuating that inclination. For those unfamiliar with the pastime of "sippin' sizzurp," let me provide some background. The delights of "drank" or "lean," aka prescription cough syrup, usually containing codeine and promethazine and often mixed with a soft drink and/or Jolly Rancher candies, were allegedly popularized by DJ Screw, a hip-hop producer from Houston, Texas.

DJ Screw became regionally famous in the Southern indie hip-hop scene for making mixtapes of tracks that he "chopped and screwed," his signature style of slowing down beats until they sound warbled and psychedelic. Many fans thought the sluggish sound was meant to simulate the lethargic effects of lean, but DJ Screw, aka Robert Davis Jr., told *Rap Pages* magazine in 1995 that his sound was actually inspired by marijuana: "When you smoking weed listening to music, you can't bob your head to nothing fast." Though some outsiders were bewildered by the screwed sound, scores of Southern hip-hop heads would line up outside his record shop, Screwed Up Records and Tapes, to buy ten-dollar copies of his "Screw-tapes."

When DJ Screw died in 2000, fans and friends claimed his tireless work ethic, fueled by fast food and drank, is what did him in. But when the autopsy confirmed the cause was an overdose of codeine (though Valium and PCP were also found in his blood), he became the namesake martyr of a music genre and lifestyle that was just starting to attain mainstream success. Three 6 Mafia had just released a single, "Sippin' on Some Syrup," which introduced the term *purple drank* to a nationwide audience. Since then, rappers like Eminem, Kanye West, Ludacris, A$AP Rocky, and Drake have all recorded sizzurp-inspired tracks. Lil' Wayne has repeatedly acknowledged his love of lean, and in the video for the song "Duffle Bag Boy" he carries a Styrofoam cup with "R.I.P. DJ Screw" written on it.

It's appropriate to mention DJ Screw in this setting, not just because Craig's trashcan is filled with empty prescription cough syrup bottles, but because he also represents Houston. He grew up there, and the H-town hip-hop scene is where he started dabbling in dealing herb. Craig says he smoked for the first time when he was fifteen years old, in 1994, while visiting his cousin in Los Angeles. They hung out with his cousin's friend, who already had a hip-hop recording contract as a fifteen-year-old. Despite being too young to have a license, he drove a new Lexus.

"He had a top-notch studio," Craig says. "And he wanted to be like a gangsta. So he had all these fuckin' rappers, like Long Beach rappers, comin' to his crib. That's when I started smokin'."

When Craig got back to Houston, he smoked a few times with friends and was appalled by the poor quality. "This shit was totally different weed," he says. One of his boys said he wanted the good shit, the Chronic, so Craig had his people out West ship him some. Craig says he only sold small amounts, mainly to friends. But he was in art school, so weed was "lightly tolerated." This might be an understatement, considering he remembers selling weed to a teacher at "the fuckin' union shit." I don't know if this means a student union, a teachers union, or a class reunion, but as with Craig's other fragments of slurred gibberish, I nod and go with it.

I mention that I started smoking around this time too, in the early- to mid-nineties, and that hip-hop played a big part in me getting into ganja. In fact, I have a theory—highly speculative and, frankly, unprovable—that hip-hop's migration toward the mainstream in the early nineties played a significant role in the surge of youthful marijuana use during that period. In 1992, after the decade-long arrest and propaganda assault of Reagan's War on Drugs, overall marijuana use dropped to its lowest point in decades, to 4 percent. Past use among high school seniors declined from a peak of around 50 percent in 1978 to a low of 20 percent in 1997. But by 1997, that trend had made a startling reversal, skyrocketing back up to almost 40 percent.

This begs the question: Did Dr. Dre start an American pot epidemic? I mean: Is it pure coincidence that the steepest rise in youthful marijuana use in recent American history coincided with the swelling popularity of weed-centric hip-hop? In December of 1992, eight months after the L.A. riots, Dr. Dre dropped *The Chronic*, introducing the world's coolest pothead, Snoop Dogg, and showing the world that the good people of Compton and Long Beach knew how to have a good time.[2] The title was a reference to high-grade ganja, and the cover design was a mock-up of Zig Zag rolling papers. The album sold more than three million copies and is considered by many rap fans to be among the best-produced hip-hop albums of all time.

But it wasn't just *The Chronic*. The early nineties was a coming-out party for weeded hip-hop. A year before Dre dropped his masterpiece,

2   It was no coincidence that cocaine and crack had proven to be decidedly *not* a good time, after almost a decade of ravaging the inner cities with addiction and violence.

Cypress Hill, a blunted Cuban American hip-hop band from L.A., put out their self-titled debut album. With songs like "Stoned Is the Way We Walk," it went double platinum. Just a month before *The Chronic* came out, another L.A. band, the Pharcyde, put out a trippy album, *Bizarre Ride II*, with tracks about decidedly un-gangsta themes, like being dissed by a girl ("Passin' Me By"), smoking weed ("Pack the Pipe"), and telling yo mama jokes ("Ya Mama"). On every track pot was the fuel for a gang of self-deprecating class clowns to let loose on a microphone.

Moving toward the mid-nineties, dozens of now-classic hip-hop albums appeared in rapid succession. It seemed like all the heavy hitters were smoking blunts, and the result was more imaginative, introspective material. The Wu-Tang Clan started hip-hop's East Coast renaissance in '93, smoking trees and spitting about martial arts, numerology, and life on the mythologized streets of Shaolin (Staten Island). In '94 Nasty Nas, a street philosopher from Queensbridge projects, dropped his blunted ghetto manifesto, *Illmatic*. And the Notorious B.I.G. went triple platinum with *Ready to Die* that same year, telling dark semiautobiographical tales about rising up from the Brooklyn street corners, with lyrics like "I let my tape rock 'til my tape popped/Smokin' weed and Bambu,[3] sippin' on Private Stock." I couldn't relate to Biggie's upbringing, but I dug the weed, the beats, and the wordplay. And it remains my (admittedly self-serving) thesis that thousands of young Americans[4] of all ethnicities shared my sensibilities, and that hip-hop culture helped normalize perceptions of marijuana during this era.

Around that same time, Craig, a "hard-smokin'" junior in high school, had started his own rap group. The band had some success, opening for well-known acts like Aceyalone and Hieroglyphics. The underground rap scene introduced Craig to a treasure trove of black-market contacts; plenty

3 All lyrics for this song on the web say "smoking weed and bamboo," but I'm pretty sure Biggie meant Bambu rolling papers, so I'm going with that.

4 The trend of increased marijuana usage in the early- to mid-nineties also occurred in almost every European country, with statistics showing a generalized peak in usage around 1998. Whether this counteracts my hip-hop theory, or shows the wide reach of American hip-hop culture, remains unclear, and I don't foresee any academic research clearing this up anytime soon.

of hip-hop cats were funding their artistic dreams by flipping ganja. He started bringing in bigger loads, from a grower in Oakland. At twenty-one, when he gave up on his rap career, dealing became his default occupation. "I was like, if I'm not getting paid at twenty-one, fuck that. It's all cliché and trendy to say, 'Oh, I'm a rapper.' I didn't wanna do that. That's when I got out of the rap shit."

Craig claims he wasn't moving pounds and making real revenue, just selling to close friends on some "support-your-habit type shit." After a few years, he moved to New York City to work gigs in television production, mainly for hip-hop videos and music-oriented TV shows. He quickly became familiar with New York's unique weed delivery services.

Over the course of a decade I spent a few thousand dollars on these delivery services. Here's how the system works. A friend gives you a number. (They're not hard to come by; there are thousands of them.) You call the number, leave a message or a page, and someone calls back. Some of the services are mom-and-pop operations, but many are sophisticated, with full-time dispatchers, client databases, and an infantry of bike-riding delivery guys. The first conversation is awkward, citing the person who referred you and then fumbling for non-incriminating words to set up a delivery. They usually respond with some thinly veiled code, like, "How many CDs do you want?" CDs, or some similar term, means how much the delivery guy should bring, in terms of dollars. Once you specify the amount, the operator says the guy will be there in like forty-five minutes, which means he will arrive at some unknown point within the next four hours.

In that time your apartment becomes a jail cell. After calling friends you haven't talked to in months and re-alphabetizing your bookshelves, you realize how much you need to do *outside* your apartment, and how supremely lame it is that you would gladly wait six hours if that's how long it takes "G" to show up. And his name will be "G," or something similarly cryptic and inane, and he will almost definitely be male. I have only had two delivery girls in my decade-long NYC pot-smoking tenure, and I was attracted to both in the way that young men are drawn to even remotely cute female bartenders. But male or female, a dealer will tell you his real name about as quickly as a stripper will admit that her name's not actually Fantasia but Esther Koslowski.

Craig realized the weed delivery services were making a killing at his TV production gigs. "And I was like, Oh man. I can get that type of chronic. And way cheaper, you know what I'm sayin'?" He weighed the amount of pot in a few NYC fifty-dollar delivery containers, which usually come in plastic, transparent cubes. They ranged from 1.3 to 2 ounces, averaging around 1.8 ounces. (Let the record show that fifty bucks is an extortionate price to pay for such a small portion, even with the convenience of delivery.) Craig realized he could sell over two ounces for the same price and still make solid profit. He explains that this was when kind buds were really expensive, "before the medical shit in California" decreased the price per pound by over a thousand dollars.

He picks up the pound of weed sitting on the table. "I'd say like two years ago, some Sour Diesel like this . . . you could sell this for probably six G's. Now you fuckin' sell it for like forty-eight."

Craig hands me the blunt, which we're consuming at a pace languid enough to defy physics. I do my slowest version of puff-puff-give. Craig says that, with his middle-class clientele, you'd think he'd be making more money than his 'hood counterparts, but the opposite is true. "Because they servin' to way more people, and they all sellin' twenties anyway. So you're breakin' it down, and makin' mad loot."

"But it takes a lot of time to deal all that," I say.

"Yeah, but they got fools that just be on the block like all day. They got people, they doin' it just like crack."

Craig continues on about this, something about "the main dude frontin' them," but Dr. Dre's "Forgot About Dre" is playing loud in the background, and I'm beyond high, and he's mumbling something fierce, so I can't make it out.

I nod anyway. "So could you like roll me through a standard . . ." I hesitate here, nervous that I'm getting into dicey territory. ". . . like in the beginning, does your shipment come in the mail? Or do you have to go get it?"

Back before 9/11, Craig says, he would just have it sent—signature waived—to his apartment in Houston. He'd come back from class, and half a pound would be sitting on his porch. Or the apartment complex would hold it for him. "But this is way before like fuckin' electronic. Now if they see a package from San Francisco, they know what's up. I mean, they got their own game, where they make money off it, you know what I'm sayin?"

"How so?" I ask. "You mean like they confiscate it and make money off of it?"

"Yep," he says. "Yowp. They confiscate it, like, the fuckin' feds or the postal police."

Craig says he has only gotten his shipment snatched once. It was over the holidays, at his mom's house in Mississippi. The feds came to the door and said there was a package for Craig. He claimed he didn't know the sender and wasn't expecting a package.

"And they're like, 'Yeah, it's comin' from California.' And they just took it. They left me with all like the boxes and shit. They just took the weed. And they were like, 'Oh if this happens again, you might get in trouble.' Like, 'We're the feds and you might get arrested.'"

Craig says, to his knowledge, most of the weed coming into New York these days is coming through the mail. And most of that is coming from California, because it's the best quality for the cheapest price. The outdoor grows have such incredible yields, and the only American region where you can grow high-volume, high-quality outdoor pot is in northern California.

According to U.S. government officials, Craig is onto something. Weed shipments are indeed on the rise. Between 2007 and 2010, the U.S. Postal Inspection Service claims seizures of marijuana parcels increased more than 400 percent. Inspectors uncovered more than 8,500 pounds of marijuana in 2007. That jumped to 43,500 pounds in 2009, while the number of inspectors remained relatively constant. They found weed concealed inside a variety of items—including packaged food, stereo amplifiers, and microwave ovens. Inspectors have responded by using ZIP code targeting. They track which inspectors find the most drugs, then send inspectors from other centers to help out in those locales. Of the 3,621 parcels intercepted nationwide in 2009, 75 percent originated from Texas, New Mexico, Arizona, and California.

"A lotta people be tied in," Craig explains. "To a mailbox. Tied in with the DHL person. Payin' off the FedEx person. You know what I'm sayin'?"

"Right," I say.

"Just make sure your shit's airtight and shit," he says. "All the game is, is gettin' your shit intercepted."

"It happens," I say.

"Yeah, it happens . . . And that's charged to the game."

This gets me thinking: Thank God *my* package arrived intact, because I don't have a game to charge it to. Before we left Buddha Cheese's place on The Hill, he hooked me and Bilal up with a few generous bags of ganja and a couple pucks of hash. Between that and the goods we got from Puck we were properly loaded up, so we had to decide what to do when we flew home. Or I should say *I* had to—Bilal just packed it in his checked luggage.[5]

I took The Mikey's advice and packed mine in a box like a care package—with some fruit, candy, and a T-shirt—and sent it to myself in Brooklyn via USPS, next-day air, signature waived. The woman at the post office seemed puzzled that my sending address was right next door, but she didn't question me. After a nervy few days of waiting, the payoff was well worth it. In fact it made me feel foolish for having spent all that money over the years on delivery service weed. I could have saved thousands just by befriending one grower in Cali.

"I'm wondering," I say. "When people are getting big bulk, are they having it shipped to them? Or like, do you think it happens differently with different people? Some people drive it . . . ?"

Craig shrugs. "I mean, there are people . . . I mean, the California drive is a *long* drive. A lotta people just do the mail."

Craig says he realizes that one of his biggest assets in the game is his ability to deal with a wide variety of people. Over the years he's become

5 When we picked up Bilal's bags in New York, there was a Transportation Security Administration (TSA) "Notice of Baggage Inspection" certificate inside; remarkably, all his weed was intact. I was reminded of this, in December 2011, when a rapper from Indiana named Freddie Gibbs tweeted about a handwritten note on his TSA Baggage Inspection certificate, amid luggage which was full of weed. "C'mon, son," the note said. This happened just two months after a TSA inspector was fired for writing "Get your freak on, girl" on an inspection note for a bag with a woman's dildo in it.

buddies with hippie growers in Humboldt, black growers in Oakland, "white, country-ass" dealers in Houston, wealthy black distributors in L.A., rappers all over the country, and pan-ethnic female teachers buying eighths in Brooklyn. He went to art school and speaks eloquently (if slowly) on many subjects, but he can also talk the talk of 'hood hustlers. His disposition is ultra-mellow, but he's a big dude, and street-smart enough to not get played.

He says even in the weed game, the recession has cut out the middle class. Either people are buying serious weight, or they're just buying eighths. He used to sell quarter pounds or "QPs" frequently, and that'd be a nice chunk of change. "Cats used to buy ounces all the time. Now, fools are all about fifty bags or eighths. That hurts a little. It would be cool—a QP here, a QP there. Now it's either a little or a lot."

In the current climate, Craig says he earns his easiest buck brokering deals. Those transactions make the best use of his broad network of friends while exposing him to the least risk. By introducing West Coast growers to East Coast distributors, he can avoid contact with cash and herb and just have his commission wired into his bank account. "And both of those worlds, like the fuckin' world up in Humboldt, would be all like fuckin' Nazi'd out, but there's a drug dealer in Atlanta. And the drug dealer in Atlanta wants the connect up in Humboldt. So I'm like an intermediary type. You know what I'm sayin'?"

On the East Coast distributor side of the game, Craig says he knows two types of hustlers: the 'hood rich, and the entrepreneurs. The 'hood rich guys have ambition. They've seen who commands respect and gets women in their neighborhoods, and just about every hip-hop song they've ever listened to has confirmed what they already knew: It's about the dollar bills. So they hustle, stack paper, and get respect. But their game stops there.

"A lot of these cats don't know shit," Craig explains. "They don't get taught shit in fuckin' school. They don't teach you about real estate, or buying property, or fuckin' loans. So they have no idea. And it's not like they have family members that tell 'em. So they spend their money on cars."

But there are other dealers, Craig says, who use their weed proceeds as seed money for bigger things. One of his buddies—who just got out of jail and is on house arrest—is a sort of role model to Craig. He made millions off delivery services. He invested in two hip, successful Manhattan nightclubs. He has the type of attorneys who can magically turn major drug charges into a few months of jail and a year of house arrest.

"You got smart cats, they got lawyers and they have financial advisors." Craig exhales a plume of blue weed smoke for emphasis. "You know? And they'll talk to their lawyers about what they can talk to their financial advisors about. They'll set up shit."

Craig is somewhere in the middle. He limits his involvement in illegal activity, because he's a chill guy and doesn't want to deal with the heat. But he is shrewd enough to understand that the next-level game is about how you launder that money. Craig knows guys who have used their proceeds to start clothing lines and record labels. He wants to penetrate the entrepreneurial side of things, but he hasn't conjured up the initiative to fully set up shit.

"It's like I don't wanna just be looked at as the bud dude," he says. "You know what I'm sayin'? Because a lot of people find that out. It's like, I do other shit too, you know."

One of his projects has been a documentary on indie underground hip-hop. He's been doing interviews and editing footage for over seven years. I know from various friends how labor-intensive filmmaking is, and I'm not convinced it's the best enterprise for someone with Craig's demeanor and cough syrup habit.

"So you went to art school," I say. "You were in a hip-hop band. Now you're working on a hip-hop documentary. Do you think weed makes you more creative?"

"I know it does for some people. But I don't buy that shit. I don't think it does for me. When I used to write raps, I thought I was better when I wasn't stoned."

"And do you think it's addictive?" I ask. "Have you ever been addicted to weed?"

"Mmm," he mumbles, the blunt dangling from his fingers. "Nah, 'cause I can chill on it. I think it's more of a mind thing. I smoke Swishers and I think the nicotine in that, that's what be causin' it. And the oral fixation type thing." Craig murmurs something incoherent about "muhfuckin' stop," then gathers himself to finish the thought. "And it's like I need to smoke, but I'm not gonna die. You know what I'm sayin'? I'm not gonna be fiendin' and break into my mom's house and pawn shit to buy weed."

"You ain't gonna be suckin' dicks for blunts," I say.

"Yeah, exactly."

"Well, personally, I do think I've had periods when I was kinda addicted," I say. "But that was more periods when I was kinda depressed. What about, do you think weed is a gateway drug?"

"Oh, hell no."

"No," I say. "Do you do other drugs?"

"Well, I graduated high school in 1997. And everybody was doin' acid, weed, 'shrooms. I never did acid, coke, none of that. I don't think it's a gateway. I did pop pills and shit. I pop Xanax and shit, not Oxys—I'm not like that. But I like chill pills, the anxiety pills . . ."

"Klonopin," I say.

"Yeah, Klonopins are good. They get you right. They creepers, yo. My homeboy, he's got these disintegrators, like candy." He raises his voice. "Hey Gary, you got one of those disintegrators for my boy?"

Craig's roommate, Gary, an Indian American kid who rarely leaves the computer monitor in his room, walks out with what looks like a piece of candy.

Gary looks at Craig and laughs. "You're the one who wants one of these." He hands it to me.

"Wow," I say. "Thank you."

"Yeah, they disintegrate in your mouth," Craig says. "Like candy flavor and shit."

"Cool."

"Yeah, I never smoked cigarettes. I don't really drink. Weed keeps me from drinking . . . alcohol."

I nod, while wrestling internally with Craig's apparent contradictions. He says he's not a marijuana addict but he chain-smokes blunts. He doesn't think pot is a gateway, yet he knows Klonopins will get you right. He says he doesn't drink booze, but he never mentions the contents of his ever-present Styrofoam cup. One minute he'll be making a cogent point; the next he'll drift off and seem to dissociate from reality. A few months before this interview, I saw him on the street. He shot me a pregnant look, made small talk, then admitted that he thought I was some actor he recognized from a TV show. I wonder if the dealing lifestyle takes a bigger toll on Craig's psyche than he lets on, and if blunts and lean are a means of numbing himself to that.

"So then . . ." I pause, trying to think of something to keep the conversational ball in the air. "What do you think about the whole legalization thing?" I ask.

"I'm pro, bro. I'm pro-advocate, for legalization. And for decriminalization. It would be easier for me, 'cause I feel like I'm just a criminal. Fuckin', an innocent criminal, like that Ben Harper song." He laughs. "I'm definitely pro-legalization. People are just so fuckin' retarded. People are just so programmed, like robot machines."

Craig continues with this theme, but the mumbling is so heavy I miss several sentences.

"Right," I say.

"But everyone's just fucking drones. Wake up, go to work, turn on the TV, go to sleep, drink at the bar. Every fuckin' single day. You know what I'm sayin? It's like that machine. That rat race. I think if more people smoked, people would be like, 'What? Why do we have to work five days a week? Is it really needed, for us to work five days a week?'" Craig thinks for a second then continues. "I think there would just be a lot more questioning of authority. But I'm really into that. Like bull-riding marauder . . ."

I'm not sure he actually says "bull-riding marauder," but this is what I hear. Smoking a full blunt of Sour Diesel hasn't helped my focus. Craig says weed affects everyone differently—some get creative, some get sleepy. But he found it interesting, he adds, that many of the indie hip-hop artists he talked to for his documentary don't smoke weed. "They can't get their shit done. Or it's like, Why am I smoking? Or like, the money. You know what I'm sayin'?"

Craig looks at me, and then stubs the blunt out in an ashtray. "That's what's really a trip."

CHAPTER NINE
SOMETHING POPPED IN MY BRAIN

I'm in the basement of my parents' house. My kitchen supplies have been haphazardly tossed into garbage bags; pan handles jut through the plastic like curious giraffes. Boxes of books are stacked in rows against the wall. A garbage bag next to a single bed is stuffed to the breaking point with sweaters. Three lampshades, indefinitely separated from their lamp companions, are stacked on top of a filing cabinet. A computer monitor is reclining on the couch next to a tennis racket and a tire pump. Crates are overflowing with knickknacks—pens and candles and outdated electronic equipment. My toiletry bottles huddle against each other on a desktop like herded cattle. These are all my worldly possessions.

"Can you believe this shit?" I say.

"I know," my friend Bryce says. "It's crazy."

This is, for all intents and purposes, my new bedroom. A more civilized room is reserved for me upstairs, but I don't feel comfortable there yet. I prefer to be underground. After two more torturous weeks of failed attempts to reestablish something resembling love, or even *like*, with Ida in our ill-fated Brooklyn apartment, I have conceded defeat. I realized that my revelation a few weeks prior, while under the influence of DMT in Puck's living room, applied to my relationship: Just step out of the ring.

On the verge of a total meltdown, I called my father and said I have to get out of here now. He flew to New York and we packed all of this stuff into a U-Haul over a period of twenty-four hours, then drove it here, to this house, this basement. So now I'm sitting on the couch that was, just six months prior, the centerpiece of my living room in Brooklyn. Across from me is one of my oldest friends. I have asked Bryce to come over not just because his presence comforts me, but because he has one of the most complicated relationships to marijuana of anyone I've ever known.

My own pot habit has become a once-a-day ritualized coping mechanism, with mixed results. The routine has been to sneak around the side of the house around noon, smoke the one-hitter, walk it back to my bedroom hiding spot, then go on a run. I know this sounds counterintuitive, since most people associate getting high with chilling out. But for me, smoking before exercise has been a source of joy and solace for years. I used to smoke daily before going to shoot hoops when I first moved to New York, and later, before Rollerblade basketball games in the East Village. I smoked before league soccer games, and once charted my statistics, both high (where I scored more goals but made careless, costly errors) and not-high (better defense, more precise passing).

Now, on good days, my high runs serve the purpose of staving off emotional collapse. While running, with my iPod providing the soundtrack, I am afforded the fleeting delusion of control over my life. My literal forward progress seems suggestive of psychological progress. On more vulnerable days, getting high has an effect I've rarely experienced before: Instead of calming me, it pushes me deeper inside the pain, exposing frayed nerves in a way I would never allow when I'm sober.

This should come as no surprise, as I know that pot amplifies whatever you're feeling. But it's like the instantaneous flip of a brain switch: Within minutes after smoking, all emotional walls crumble at once, and I'm enveloped by sadness. I think about Ida and how she's not the person I thought she was, and about how maybe I'm not either, and about how betrayed I feel, and how betrayed she probably feels, and about how much I miss my New York friends, and about what the fuck am I doing in my parents' basement in southern Indiana at the age of thirty-eight. And I just start sobbing. Twice in the past week, I have started my high runs with wet, swollen eyes. But there is also an element of healing to this ritual, like a cathartic session with a shrink. It helps me delve into deeper wells of melancholy, and I'm hoping to find some answers there.

I ask Bryce if he's ready to tell me his story. He keeps blinking in a way that exposes his discomfort. I explain that what's most important to me is to understand people's life stories, how they got to where they are now, and how marijuana affected that story. I know it might be difficult for him, but I think it would be best if we start at the beginning.

"Yeah," he says. "Okay."

"So do you remember the first time you smoked pot?"

"Let's see here. Hold on, let me . . . yeah. The first time I did was April 29th, 1992."

"Wow, very specific," I say. "So what happened?"

"Okay." Bryce looks down at his hands in silence for several seconds. Then he looks up and says he was a senior in high school. He and three friends were at his house, smoking from a pipe. After the first few hits, he didn't feel anything. So then he took three more big hits.

"And all of a sudden, I stood up, and it just hit me like a freight train. And I felt like this light went off in my head. This red flash. And uh, it just really disoriented me. I felt like I had died."

"Can you explain what you mean?" I ask. "You felt like you had died?"

"Yeah. It was like, all of a sudden reality seemed so much different. How can I put it? I just felt like something really changed. And it seemed like, I could see everything, and talk to people, but it seemed surreal. Like I was in some other world."

The feeling overwhelmed him so thoroughly that he had to go outside. He walked for an hour or two; he wasn't sure. Time no longer made sense. At first it felt good to get away and be alone, but then he started to feel an evil presence. He couldn't stop his mind from focusing on all the evil in the world. When he got back from the walk, he called his brother, who was at a nearby college. While he waited for his brother to come save him from himself, he watched television. But instead of tuning into *Seinfeld* or some other lighthearted fare from that era, he watched coverage of the L.A. riots. The Rodney King verdict had been handed down earlier that afternoon.

"So at the same time that I was feeling that there was just evil everywhere, I was watching the L.A. riots on TV. And there was a black guy pulling a trucker out of his truck and just beating the crap out of him. They showed it on TV. It was filmed. It was kind of like anarchy. It was just real scary."

Bryce clears his throat and pauses for an exceptionally long time. Once he gathers himself, he explains that, at the time, he was taking a class on religious literature. He was interested in spirituality, trying to figure out what the world was all about. This was a curiosity we shared as kids.

I remember a bizarre Sunday where we had been playing tennis and instead of returning one of his shots, I let it hit the fence. "What are we doing here?" I asked. We both agreed that being dead serious about hitting a ball over a net was absurd. We laid down our rackets and went for a walk. Then that also seemed pointless, so we just sat in the grass and said nothing. The rest of the day was one long, wandering existential crisis. We were thirteen years old.

Five years later, after getting high for the first time, something in Bryce's THC-drenched brain sent him into a much deeper spiritual malaise. His brother calmed him down a bit, and he took the next day off school. But it didn't go away. "One of my first reactions was . . . I was a big sinner. I was just this terrible person, and I needed to be saved by God. So I went to talk to a minister about it. He was just a really good guy, and he was kind of reassuring and nice to me and just telling me that, you know, that God loves me. And he's forgiving, and all that."

The next Sunday Bryce went to church. He started going weekly and praying two to three hours a day. He still felt anxious though, like he couldn't say the prayers enough. He wasn't convinced that they were getting through to God. Bryce explains that this was the first real emergence of what was eventually diagnosed as obsessive-compulsive disorder (OCD). He had had a few symptoms before, like touching things a certain amount of times.

"And uh," Bryce says. "But uhhh. So the praying started, and going to church. The term for that is *scrupulosity*."

"Is what?" I ask.

"Scrupulosity. Which is a form of OCD. Where people are over-concerned with morals and religious things."

"Okay," I say. "So did you get the sense that this whole thing was triggered by when you smoked pot that first time?"

"Oh, absolutely."

"Did you feel like your brain chemistry, it shifted or something that day?"

"Yeah," Bryce says. "Another way to describe when I said a light went off in my head. The best way to describe it is that I feel like something popped in my brain. It was like this loud noise in my head."

"Wow."

"But definitely, I felt, like, some sort of brain chemistry shift. I felt like it was altered. And you know, triggering my latent OCD. But it was full blown, after that time."

Meanwhile, it was Bryce's senior year. While other kids partied away their final semester, he couldn't recapture his old, socially smooth, athletically dominant self. He was living in his head. He lost all interest in dating. His friends noticed something was different, and he made it clear that he was struggling. "My social interactions totally changed," he says. "I didn't want to drink because I thought it was sinful."

After an edgy summer, Bryce went to college—a respected liberal arts university, several states away. Unlike many of his friends who went to local state schools, he knew no one. Out of loneliness he joined Campus Crusade for Christ. "And they were pretty zealous. And I was pretty easily influenced. And them just saying things like how Christians should behave. And what's acceptable behavior. I started thinking about accepting Christ into my life as my savior."

Bryce was convinced that, if he accepted Christ into his life, all the anxieties would disappear. They didn't. His paranoia increased. He continued to be obsessed with sin. Even the merest thought about sex seemed sinful, and hooking up with girls was out of the question. He grew increasingly isolated. Halfway through the first semester, he dropped out.

Back in Columbus, Bryce was hospitalized. He was diagnosed with depression, anxiety, and obsessive-compulsive disorder. Doctors struggled to find a cocktail of meds that would alleviate his symptoms. They tried half a dozen anti-anxiety medications and several anti-depressants. Because he seemed at times to have lost touch with reality, they even tried an anti-psychotic.

This reminds me of an interview I had with Dr. Bertha K. Madras, a professor of psychobiology at Harvard Medical School. From 2006 to 2008, she served as the Deputy Director for Demand Reduction for the White

House Office National Drug Control Policy (ONDCP), under President George W. Bush.

Dr. Madras steadfastly insists there is a link between marijuana use (especially early in life) and a later onset of schizophrenia and/or psychosis. She cites seven specific studies, the first of which is a study of Swedish soldiers. Because Sweden keeps meticulous records of their military recruits, she says, they are able to trace their progress over a long period. In this case the Swedish study charted nearly twenty-seven thousand soldiers over many years, and found that those "who had initiated marijuana use were twice as likely to develop psychosis and/or schizophrenia later in life," Madras says.

Other studies were conducted in New Zealand, the Netherlands, Israel, Germany, and Great Britain. An article in *Nature Reviews*, by Murray et al., summarized all this data. The results showed that marijuana users were up to three times more likely than non-marijuana users to have an onset of schizophrenia/psychosis symptoms.

Another study claims children and young adults are particularly vulnerable to this marijuana-psychosis link. An article published in *Archives of General Psychiatry* by McGrath et al. says this about prolonged marijuana use by teenagers: "Compared with those who had never used cannabis, young adults who had 6 or more years since first use of cannabis (i.e., who commenced use when around 15 years or younger) were twice as likely to develop a non-affective psychosis." As for already diagnosed schizophrenics who use marijuana, Madras claims evidence shows the drug exacerbates their symptoms.

Dr. Madras concedes that the bar for saying marijuana actually *causes* schizophrenia or psychosis is quite high: "You need evidence that marijuana use precedes the onset of psychotic symptoms. You need evidence that the people who gravitate toward marijuana are not predisposed to psychosis." Still, if the claims of these studies are legitimate, Dr. Madras feels that these psychological hazards have "not been mainstreamed into the population." From her perspective, it is neither "alarmist nor is it a moralistic case . . . it is simply the evidence. Period . . . We would hope that if we have any methods of preventing brain diseases that can persist for a lifetime, we would try to alert the public that this is a risk factor."

Another Harvard professor feels otherwise. Marijuana activist Dr. Lester Grinspoon, the Associate Professor Emeritus of Psychiatry at Harvard Medical School, says he's not convinced about the marijuana-schizophrenia link. During our interview, conducted in his basement office near a poster of the Australian rock band Grinspoon (named in his honor), he said one study in particular raised his eyebrows. It claimed that kids who started using weed at fifteen or sixteen are 40 percent more likely to suffer from schizophrenia. If that were the case, he said, you would expect there to be a distinct uptick of schizophrenia diagnoses since the 1960s, as teen marijuana use has increased significantly over that period. But there hasn't been.

Grinspoon cited another study in which researchers compared home movies of eight-year-old kids—some of whom were later diagnosed with schizophrenia, and others who weren't. Despite the fact that symptoms don't generally surface until adolescence, experts could consistently distinguish which kids would turn out to suffer from schizophrenia. Grinspoon theorized that it wasn't as if kids were "going along fine and suddenly some switch flips. I think it's already there." He thinks the marijuana use is likely not a cause, but an effect. "I have a hunch that for some of these kids, it's an uncomfortable interior. Just as schizophrenics use more alcohol, more cigarettes . . . I wouldn't be surprised if, ultimately, those kids are attracted to something which alters their consciousness, even subtlely. It may be more comfortable than what they have."

Regardless, considering the conflicting research, Bryce's doctors had valid reasons for prescribing him an anti-psychotic. But the meds backfired. "It put me into sort of like a panic," Bryce explains. "It almost *made* me psychotic for like three hours."

"So it basically did the opposite of what it was supposed to do?" I ask. "Right."

After a month in the hospital, Bryce came back home and started working at his uncle's office, an accounting firm. It helped keep his mind occupied. He went to psychotherapy and behavioral therapy three times a week for the next two years and got stabilized on his meds.

As for his biggest hurdle, the OCD, behavioral therapy worked best. The treatment, called "exposure response prevention," is similar to the exposure therapy used to treat phobias. To desensitize him to his OCD regarding germs, doctors made him touch a public bathroom, then not wash his hands for an hour. For his association between sex and sin, they had him look at sexual pictures until their initial sense of wickedness dissipated. Because he was morbidly afraid of swearing aloud, they had him write down the same swear word for forty-five minutes and say it aloud each time.

"And then with my therapist, we realized that going to church and praying was making me much more anxious. And it was basically just a ritual."

After four years of therapy, he was able to dissolve his ties with the church altogether. He began to feel happier, freer. Two years later, in 1998, he decided to attend the OCD Institute in Boston, an affiliate of Harvard Medical School. Bryce learned that everybody had thoughts that couldn't be controlled, but people with OCD fixated on them to the exclusion of all other thoughts. His therapists taught him to just "let the thoughts be there." It might sound simplistically Zen, but for Bryce it was the "master key" to controlling his psyche.

Still, progress came in fits and starts. With the combination of Prozac, an anti-anxiety medication called BuSpar, and lithium, normally used for bipolar disorder, he started coming out of his shell. He got a job in retail and moved out of his parents' house, to an apartment in a nearby city. But then the next obsessive phase kicked in: sexual addiction. It started with phone dating services but soon blossomed into an irrepressible urge to have anonymous encounters with women. The episodes weren't all bad, but he spent a lot of money and felt out of control. "I was wanting to have sexual experiences," Bryce says. "But I just didn't feel comfortable having a relationship . . . I had had such a tough time with my own emotions, I just didn't want to put that on anyone else."

Bryce moved back in with his parents. After another stint at the OCD Institute, his life started to stabilize. He got a job as an accountant's assistant. He bought a house. He started drinking occasionally, one night of binge drinking here and there, perhaps compensating for what he missed out on when he dropped out of college.

In 2006, he decided to try marijuana again. A friend said it might help his anxiety, but his real motivation was to face the demon that had kicked off fourteen years of psychological turmoil. "The pot experience was so scary for me, I wanted to revisit it and face it, and overcome it. In a way I knew that marijuana was inherently not bad. It was just a plant."

The first few times, he would have a few beers before smoking, to lubricate himself. Nothing popped in his brain this time. He was pleasantly surprised to find himself enjoying the positive effects usually associated with marijuana—relaxation, laughter, taking delight in small pleasures. Soon enough, he no longer needed beer. "I found that I really liked it. It made me feel some euphoria, and clarity in my mind. Things would slow down, in my mind."

In early 2007, Bryce started smoking marijuana daily. At the time he was working with adults with developmental disabilities. The job included helping his patients with basic living skills, activities like swimming, dance, and volunteer work. But it also included thankless chores like changing soiled underwear. He found that if he smoked a small bowl of mid-grade ("middies") pot right before he went to work, it put him in the ideal headspace. "I feel like it made me more empathetic. Just kind of relate to what these people were going through. It just made me feel more loving."

Bryce claims that, in contrast to the hazy feeling most people get after smoking weed, he actually thinks more clearly and rationally when he's high. He becomes more creative and doesn't get so caught up in obsessive thoughts or existential dilemmas. In fact the effect is so profound that he no longer considers his marijuana use recreational. "I believe it's medicine for me . . . I don't take my anti-anxiety pills anymore, because of marijuana. I've started to have more balance in my life."

The American workplace, however, doesn't empathize with Bryce's medicinal view of the drug. Since most of his recent jobs have required drug testing, Bryce has started using synthetic urine to mask his marijuana use. "It's more important for me to do what I think is best for myself, than to abide by those rules," he explains. "If I felt like it was an addictive sort of drug, like cocaine, that would really interfere with my work, I wouldn't do it."

There are a multitude of synthetic urine systems out there—most notably, The Whizzinator, complete with strap-on prosthetic penises in colors like White, Latino, and Black. The product Bryce uses has less of an anatomical focus; it consists of a fake urine–filled bottle that he puts in his underwear, which is blanketed by a heating pad. (In an attempt to foil people like Bryce, most drug tests monitor temperature as well.) Bryce says that for one job, they sent him to a doctor's office, where he waited for almost an hour, gushing sweat while hoping the temperature between his legs wouldn't fall too low. "I felt like my balls were about 110 degrees," he says, laughing.

Drug testing in the American workplace is thought to have originated with the 1981 crash of a U.S. Navy plane into an aircraft carrier, after which tests revealed widespread drug abuse among officers. Governmental drug testing expanded in 1986, when President Reagan issued an executive order declaring that "drugs will not be tolerated in the Federal workplace." Testing expanded into the private sector with the Drug-Free Workplace Act of 1988, which stipulated that federal grant recipients and some contractors maintain a drug-free environment. The Society for Human Resource Management estimates that, in 2011, 57 percent of businesses required all job candidates to pass drug tests. As many as fifty million drug tests are administered in the U.S. annually, generating revenue of nearly $1.5 billion. Pot-smokers are the most affected populace, because marijuana is by far the most used illicit drug, with the longest detection window.

Employees like Bryce view drug testing not as an essential weeding-out of problematic job candidates, but as an insulting invasion of personal liberty. Bryce adamantly believes in the efficacy of his current pharmaceutical formula: Prozac and marijuana. And having been friends with him for twenty-five years, I can say he's never been in better form as a human being. He might not be as confident as he was during the early teenage years, but he's more empathetic and thoughtful. And the irony that the substance that instigated his psychological downfall—marijuana—has now led to his rebirth, is not lost on him. The human psyche is a delicate and mysterious thing.

Which isn't to say that he's flawless. The OCD never fully disappears, and his new fixation involves conspiracy theories and New Age consciousness. He believes that 2012, the end of the Mayan calendar, will bring a fundamental, positive change for mankind. He believes 9/11 was an inside job, perpetrated by the U.S. government. He says there's evidence, confirmed by U.S. Army generals, that nuclear weapons are being dismantled by extraterrestrial aircrafts. He thinks the universe is undergoing an upgrade, designed by God.

Who am I to judge his beliefs? All I know is Bryce seems happy, and that makes me happy. His alternative theories rarely intrude on our time together, which often involves a few tokes and then laughter. He hasn't been to a therapist since 2006, the same year he rediscovered the flip side of a plant that had haunted him since 1992. Now he considers those first few attempts to overcome his fear of a plant as the most crucial turning point of his adult life.

"It was really a time where I began to enjoy life again," he says. "I feel like that's one of the main things marijuana does for me. It helped me to enjoy life again."

CHAPTER TEN
WAITING FOR BUDDHA CHEESE

I'm waiting outside Sacramento International Airport. In the three weeks since I left New York, I have been relentlessly plotting to get back to northern California. It's not where I expected this story to go, but it's the first avenue into marijuana culture I've pursued that throbs with energy—all because of America's conflicting legal landscape. I've been sending Buddha Cheese texts about returning to The Hill so that I can understand his world better and maybe even "go on a mission." I have tried to be cool about it—forcing myself to wait to respond to his texts so I don't seem too eager. But once I started fantasizing about getting involved in the underground marijuana game in some way, the anticipation got too heavy. His response confirmed my status as a rank amateur. He said we shouldn't talk any further, until I took precautions.

First, I had to buy a burner phone—one that wasn't registered to my name, with prepaid minutes. Then I had to send him a letter with the new burner number. My only knowledge of burners is from the HBO show *The Wire*, where they are periodically discarded and replaced by dealers to throw off wiretaps and keep different rungs of the drug-dealing hierarchy from being connected to each other. Well I'm no Avon Barksdale, but I bought one and mailed Buddha Cheese the number. Since then we have been texting back and forth in cryptic shady-speak, which is way more thrilling than it probably should be. After struggling for weeks to coordinate plans while Buddha Cheese traversed the country, we finally decided we would both fly into the Bay Area today.

My burner phone beeps. It's a text from Bull. He's here. Just as I'm texting him my terminal number, a customized mid-nineties Dodge Ram date-rape van pulls up and honks. Bull pops out and gives me a man-hug. I toss my bags in the back. Stepping into the van feels like a time warp. Vinyl interior. Dirty shag carpet. So steeped in the stench of ganja that a cop would have to be clueless (or Californian?) to not investigate further after a traffic stop. The front dash is covered with charger cords and a half dozen burner phones. As we drive off, Bull asks me what my plan is on this trip.

"I have no plan," I say.

"Awesome!" Bull says. "You're on our schedule!"

He pulls out a joint the size of his index finger. "It's my duty to introduce you to NorCal with the proper medication."

He says we're supposed to get a foot of snow tonight on The Hill. They are going to set me up in the house. I do a mental fist pump—the house is the fucking Ritz-Carlton compared to the shack up top. I'll be living in relative luxury, with Buddha Cheese. I ask how many people are on The Hill. Just one—a new guy, Chester, a forty-one-year-old Deadhead. They got rid of Armand, the Brazilian organic chef/handler, because he turned out to be as high-maintenance as he was chill. When he demanded more money to cover expenses, The Mikey set him straight. He would be paid as the others were—in weed. A pound per month, and not until after the harvest, which, if you were smart about who you sold it to, could get you up to four grand per pound. Armand couldn't wait that long, so Mikey cut him loose.

"He'll be fine," Bull says. "He can always drive ten packs for a thousand a pop."

"What's a ten pack?" I ask.

"A ten-pound pack of weed," he says. "You get about a hundred bucks a pound for transporting within state lines."

"Oh yeah? How much is it for cross-country?"

"You can make a lot more money that way, because the demand on the East Coast is about the same, but there's less supply. And the transport risks are *much* higher."

On the East Coast, he says, dealers want the quality strains people already know and like—Sour Diesel and OG Kush and all that. But out here in the West, heads are all about what strains are new and fashionable. Chemdog is Bull's favorite. But Chemdog takes six weeks longer to harvest than Blue Dream, which takes six weeks longer to harvest than Train Wreck. Last year, their first year on The Hill, they grew eight different strains, but only Dream and Wreck grew consistently dense nuggets. They yielded almost three and a half pounds of weed per tree; this year they're hoping to get five.

"The Blue Dream is tasty," I say, looking at the joint. "I think this is the stuff that you gave Bilal and I when we were here a month ago. It has a much cleaner high than the stuff we get in New York."

"Yep, that's the organics," Bull says. "Every single product we use is organic. It's smoother to smoke, not as harsh. And the high feels more natural."

Organic growers can't use standard pesticides. One of the best methods for organically patrolling pests is to release ladybugs and praying mantises. Bull says there are so many different varieties of praying mantises around these parts that growers must have been releasing them for years. Because of this symbiotic relationship with marijuana farmers, the mantis population grows unabated. Bull says last year some mantises became semi-pets with names and personalities. They just chill and eat bugs, the stoners of the insect world.

"But ladybugs are great too!" Bull says. "And they're mad cheap, fifteen bucks for like a thousand ladybugs."

Sounds like a bargain, but then it's tough to judge the value of a ladybug. Their specialty is spider mites, which they hoover up with such gusto that, in indoor grows, they sometimes devour the entire mite population and die off themselves. Bull says a trick to keeping ladybugs from flying away is to put them in a plastic bag, fill it with sugar water, shake it up, and release the polka-dotted predators at the base of the plants. This sugar cements their wings to their little insect bodies (thoraxes?), so they only have the run of the garden—a spider-mite buffet. After the first rain or thorough watering, the sugar becomes diluted and the ladybugs can fly away if they so choose.

Bull relights the joint. "We've been thinking about getting animals up on The Hill. Like goats. Or chickens. I wanna get some buffalo. We have an electric fence, so they could just graze at the bottom of the hill."

"Dude," I say. "If you're gonna get animals, get helper monkeys."

Bull laughs. "Right! If we get trained orangutans, they could lift eight hundred pounds. It would be like having a forklift."

"You could outsource all the hard labor to primates."

"Exactly. And they work for bananas." Bull thinks about this. "No, but if we get animals, I want them to be classy and delicious. Like pheasant."

"Oh, I see; you're trying to slaughter them. Yeah, I don't want to eat orangutan. What animals does Mikey want to get?"

"God knows, man," he says.

The way he says this makes me concerned. "Where is The Mikey anyway? Is he flying in tonight, or already up on The Hill?"

"No, he had to take a little detour down to New Orleans. I guess he's got some business down there."

My eyes widen. "You mean he's not here?"

"No," Bull says. "Says he's got business in Louisiana, but it sounds like he found a piece of ass. Not sure when he'll get back. Probably later this week."

Jesus. My posture deflates at the realization that I have naïvely put my faith in a man whose defining characteristic is undependability. As we turn onto State Route 49, the road named after the 1849 Gold Rush that flooded this area with migrants in search of glittering treasure, I realize that my own search has completely jumped the rails.

*　　　　　*　　　　　*

I wake up early the next morning in an unfamiliar attic bedroom, which is now about as close to home as it gets. I walk downstairs, past Buddha Cheese's second-floor bedroom, into the first-floor living room. It's cozy and minimally decorated, with hardwood floors, a nonfunctioning flat-screen TV, an electric furnace/faux fireplace in a stone hearth, and a Danny DeVito–sized wooden Buddha statue. There are Buddhas everywhere—in tapestries, little statuettes littered about, and paintings—revealing a peaceful side to the mind life of Buddha Cheese.

Next to the fireplace, Bull is sprawled out on the same pink fur Bilal and I slept on the month before. Next to him is a massive beanbag, ten feet in circumference and three feet tall, which has been enveloping the tiny body of Isabelle, Bull's recently anointed girlfriend, ever since last night, when she drank too much, vomited, and passed out there.

Despite my best efforts at cartoonish tiptoeing, Bull wakes up and says he needs a pick-me-up. I ask if we have any coffee. "Nope, no coffee machine," he says. "But I've got something even better." He walks into the kitchen and pulls out what looks like a vitamin container. On the cover, in suspiciously unbranded scientific font, it says: "100% Anhydrous Caffeine Powder." He pulls out a bottle of 5-Hour Energy drink, sprinkles a half spoonful of caffeine powder into it, and downs it in one swallow.

These West Coasters and their obscure drugs: DMT, sassafras, caffeine powder. Whatever happened to good old-fashioned cocaine? For Bull at least, uncut caffeine's effects are not unlike that of cocaine: jitteriness and acute logorrhea. Within minutes he's off and running on an unsolicited monologue about growers with guns. "My girlfriend's dad says if she keeps running around on people's property, she's gonna get shot. That's just a bullshit stereotype about growers. Why would they shoot someone when all that's gonna do is bring cops to the property?"

"Good point," I say.

"At the very most, they might shoot above your head to scare you off. I only know of one guy around here who would actually shoot someone, and he would probably just spray some buckshot at your knees."

"That's comforting."

"Actually, I'm pretty sure Isabelle's dad would shoot me if he got the chance. Any man up here with a hot daughter has a gun and isn't afraid to use it."

I'm beginning to wonder if I'm a girly-man, or these people are all savages. In need of a reality check, I call Joaquin, who gave me the entrée into The Mikey's world. I explain the situation—Bull's caffeine powder, his "hot" and, by all outward appearances, pubescent girlfriend, and Mikey's AWOL status.

"I told you The Mikey is the most irresponsible person on the planet, and you're about to find out in the hardest way." He laughs, an I-told-you-so snicker.

*   *   *

At nine o'clock that night, I open my eyes after a long, rum-soaked nap and find myself in total blackness. The only thing emitting any light is my burner phone. I pick it up and see that I've missed a half dozen calls, all from Bull. I call him back.

"Sleeping Beauty is up!" he says.

"What happened?" I ask.

It's a blackout—the snowstorm brought down a power line. Bull says he and Chester fought their way down the hill, using a chainsaw to break up limbs blocking the road, only to find me passed out, with the key inside the house. They threw snowballs at my window, to no avail. From the disappointment in his voice, it's apparent that now my reliability is being called into question.

While using my phone to guide me around the house, I notice I also have three text messages from Buddha Cheese. They are all vaguely optimistic, suggesting that a big adventure awaits us at some unknown point. He thanks me for helping the boys out on The Hill, which I'm not averse to but never volunteered to do. There is neither apology nor explanation for his absence.

Luckily, Bull and I went shopping today, to get me outfitted for the harsh environment. I dig through my shopping bags and find the headlamp, a crucial purchase. I walk downstairs and realize that, magically, even though it's electrically powered, the furnace is still working. I'm tempted to walk up to the shack, which has electricity, humans, canines, and the potential for something resembling sanity. Bull says I can follow the stream up through a neighbor's property to the shack. I walk outside. The scenery is postcard beautiful, a burbling stream lined by twinkling, amorphous pillows of snow. I go outside for a test run. The snow is two feet deep; each step is its own individual challenge. I think about the stories of cougars, and the prospect of a suspicious neighbor spraying buckshot at my knees. Abort mission.

Back inside the dark house, I'm not sure what to do. No TV, no Internet, no electricity. My regular phone is dead, so I've only got the burner and a couple hours on my laptop. I call a few friends. But after twenty minutes my burner dies, and I'm all alone with my thoughts. The house is bursting with weed, including the four pounds I found in Mikey's drawer, but I feel like getting high could put me in a crazy, lonely headspace. I grab a few books and the half-drunk bottle of rum, pull a chair next to the furnace, and start tapping out a journal entry. As I get to the part about Bull's growers-with-guns monologue earlier, it gets me thinking about the link between marijuana and violence.

Most critiques of marijuana today focus on its nonviolent effects—memory loss and lowered ambition, etc. But the original propaganda campaign against weed in America, launched by Harry J. Anslinger, linked the drug to violent behavior. Perhaps his most famous article, "Marijuana: Assassin of Youth," published in *The American Magazine* a few weeks before the Marihuana Tax Act of 1937 passed, followed up the sordid tale of a Chicago woman committing suicide after getting high with a purportedly nonfiction account of a "youth" smoking a "reefer" on the streets of Los Angeles. "Suddenly, for no reason, he decided that someone had threatened to kill him and that his life at that very moment was in danger," it reads. To summarize, the young man sees "the only person in sight," a shoeshine guy, hurries to his apartment, grabs a gun, and kills the man. What's entertaining about this article, beyond the ludicrously fictional narratives masquerading as truth, is the deliberate use of the word "assassin" in the title.

Anslinger was milking the word's rich history, which involves an ancient legend of mountain-based, cannabis-fueled violence. In the congressional hearings for the Marihuana Tax Act, Anslinger began with a conveniently abridged history of the plant. It omitted all positive historical references, like the Chinese including cannabis in the world's oldest pharmacopeia, the Scythians burning hemp seeds during funeral ceremonies, and the early Sanskrit and Hindu names for cannabis with meanings like "leaf of heroes" and "inspiring of mental powers." Instead, Anslinger testified that "the religious and military order or sect of the Assassins were [sic] founded in Persia and the numerous acts of cruelty of this sect were known not only in Asia, but Europe as well." He went on to attribute *assassin's* word origin to hashish, a "confection of hemp leaves 'marijuana.'"

If you look up the etymology of the word *assassin*, it's true you'll often find some variation on the following: from Arabic *hashishiyyin*, "hashish users." A more thorough search reveals that its etymology is disputed, and other possibilities include "follower of Hassan" or "rowdy people." But most sources on the word's backstory will include the contribution of the Venetian merchant-adventurer Marco Polo, who in 1272, while traveling through Persia, happened upon the legend of the "Old Man of the Mountains."

According to Marco Polo, the Old Man of the Mountains was the leader of a renegade Islamic sect whose followers were notorious for their ruthless murders of oppositional leaders. To indoctrinate his disciples, the Old Man of the Mountains gave his acolytes a "certain potion which cast them into deep sleep," after which they awakened "in a place so charming, they deemed that it was Paradise in very truth." These exquisitely maintained gardens included otherworldly flowers, fountains overflowing with milk and honey, and beautiful young virgins (*houris*) wandering around, ready to fulfill any earthly desire. The devotees stayed there for five days, were drugged again, then brought before the Old Man again. He said if they obeyed his orders, that version of paradise would await them, whether they survived his commands or not. Before going into battle, they took the same drug to fortify their courage and remind them of paradise. That drug was believed to be hashish.

But the story is just that: a legend. The Old Man of the Mountains is widely assumed to represent Hasan ibn-Sabah, a Shiite Islamic dissident who founded the Nizari Ismaili sect around 1090. At odds with the mainstream Islam of the time, the Ismailis were considered a dangerous fringe cult. They lived an ascetic existence in a castle called Alamut, in the remote Elburz Mountains of northern Persia. Their Taliban-esque philosophy, known as the New Propaganda, asserted that Islam had become depraved and should return to its true path. This ideology doesn't jibe well with the notion that they were drug-crazed killers. And indeed there is no evidence that the garden-paradise ritual actually existed, or that the drug administered—which was said to induce sleep—was hashish.

One thing about the Ismailis is rarely disputed, though: They were badasses of the highest order. One could even make the claim that they were pioneers of religious terrorism. Hasan ibn-Sabah created six ranks of disciples, the bottom being the *fida'i*, or "devoted ones." These *fida'i* were fearless foot soldiers who would carry out any orders to guarantee entry into paradise. They were so loyal, wrote the thirteenth-century Bishop of Acre, that they would, on Sabah's command, perform a death leap from the castle walls and "shatter their skulls below." Their first known victim was Abu Ali Hasan ibn-Ali, who was assassinated in 1092 by a *fida'i* disguised as a Sufi. He was the first of a string of rulers, officials, and priests who publicly attacked Ismaili dogma and didn't live to regret it.

Hasan ibn-Sabah died in 1124, but the Ismaili reign of terror continued. Their most notorious assassinations occurred several decades later, against the Crusaders. In 1192, Conrad of Montferrat, the German would-be leader of the kingdom of Jerusalem, was murdered in Tyre. The Ismaili *fida'i* who whacked him spent months living among the Crusaders, disguised as Christian monks, before their opportunity arose. The medieval beat reporters of the Crusades took note, and the legend of the Assassins reached new heights. Marco Polo might have scooped the Assassin story, but it was the Crusades chroniclers who cemented the association of the word *assassin* with hash-crazed mountain Arabs who killed their enemies with calculating ruthlessness.

The layered irony of Anslinger's reference to the word *assassin* as marijuana's historical association with brown-skinned foreigners getting high and killing people is that he used a racist, apocryphal legend to legitimize his own racist, apocryphal smear campaign. Adding to this irony is that, these days, most violence attributed to marijuana is a result of the ban that Anslinger spearheaded. This prohibition leads to secret grow operations and surreptitious exchanges of cash among the type of people who are willing to work in the black market, who are also the type of people willing to defend their cash and merchandise with violence.

In states with medical marijuana laws, there is an ongoing debate as to whether the laws increase crime. Accurate statistics on this are tough to come by, because many victims don't report crimes for fear of arousing unwanted attention from law enforcement. The California Police Chiefs Association used press clippings to document fifty-two medical marijuana-related crimes from April 2008 to March 2009. There is plenty of anecdotal evidence of growers and dispensaries being targeted by thieves, but no consensus on whether medical marijuana laws lead to an inordinate uptick in crime. Denver police claimed that the twenty-five robberies and burglaries that targeted medical marijuana there in the last half of 2009 were fewer than what banks or liquor stores suffered. Some law enforcement officials and anti-pot activists claim that medical marijuana laws prove that the drug and the crime are inseparable, and legalization would increase crime rates. Pro-marijuana activists say the opposite: that prohibition is what causes crime, and legalization would be the antidote. Regardless, there are no statistics on how many of these medical marijuana-related crimes are perpetrated by people who are stoned. My guess is that it's relatively few, because armed robbery is a total buzzkill.

*   *   *

Early the next morning, I hear stomping on the porch. Through the kitchen window, I see a man with a helmet. I only know two people around here, and my last waking thought was of assassins, so it's an alarming sight. I approach the kitchen sink in a crouched position, trying to get a closer look at my assailant. His familiarity with the porch eases the tension, and a closer look reveals the never-subtle presence of Bull. Before I can get to the door, he passes me at the frenzied pace of a man with anhydrous caffeine coursing through his veins.

"I called you this morning. You didn't pick up . . . *again*."

"Sorry, man. I must've been asleep."

"Yeah, yeah. I tried to drive down, but there were too many branches in the way, so I just walked."

He takes off his chainsaw helmet and says we have to get into town, get gas and propane and supplies. "Looks like we also have to go see Puck," he says.

"Why's that?" I ask.

"Mikey owes him money. The only cash I know about is the stash here, and that's only thirty, which isn't enough. And of course Mike won't pick up his fucking phone."

"Shocking." I'm hip enough to know that thirty means $30,000. What's not enough for these guys would be plenty for me.

"You see what happens?" Bull asks. "He says he doesn't pay me to make decisions. But then he won't pick up the fucking phone, and I'm forced to make fucking decisions. And that's when I get in trouble. See how he cuts me off at the knees?"

A half hour later, we pull into the same grocery store parking lot where I met up with Buddha Cheese a month prior. Bull roams the lot until we find Puck's van. Puck and Noah step out. They look surprised to see me. We squeeze into the van. Puck's sort of sit-standing in front, looking back at us. Evidently, the dealer-distributor lifestyle involves a lot of waiting around in parking lots. Puck is bugging—the tics and jerks are in overdrive. His hair looks like he's been combing his fingers through it for hours. Noah looks tranquil by juxtaposition, with a tinge of empathetic concern.

"Why are you in such a good mood?" Bull asks Noah. "You look like you just did some DMT."

Noah laughs. "No, man, I just took a nap in the back of the van."

After a pregnant pause, Puck and Bull start talking the talk. I don't understand the details, but it's clear Puck needs money *now*. I assume his urgent tone means he owes somebody. It's a glimpse of the grimy side of the business. Bull beats his keys against the doggie beanbag on the van floor and ticks off his dilemma. He only knows where some money is, and Mikey won't pick up the phone. So we have to wait for Mikey to call back, and then we should be able to help Puck out.

Puck takes a phone call. It doesn't go well. From what I can gather, someone disappeared while transporting a fifty-pack for him. So now he's a couple hundred grand in the hole, and someone's expecting money from him. This phone call confirms that the transporter is officially off the grid. Puck throws his phone against the passenger side door.

"Fuck!" Puck yells. "Fuck fuck fuck fuck fuck!"

We all avoid eye contact, the awkwardness amplified by the contained space. I empathize with Puck. In a way we have the same problems: debt, and waiting for Buddha Cheese. I assume the consequences of his debt could be more visceral, but that assumption is based mainly on movies I've seen, which involve death threats and chopped-off fingers. Puck bursts out of the van, taking his rage into the parking lot. Why won't Mikey just pick up his phone? But it's a rhetorical question, because we all know it's the price of doing business with Buddha Cheese.

*   *   *

The money I need to pay off my debt: I've been sitting on it this whole time. I mean that literally. Back at the house, Bull asks me to get up off the giant beanbag. He unzips the back, and out come stacks of cash. Thirty-seven thousand dollars—almost exactly the amount of my debt. He counts out twenty grand for Puck. I walk up and pretend not to gawk. Creditors and bill collectors calling me hourly, and I've been sitting on my ticket out of it. Not that I would ever have touched it, had I known. But the sight of it deepens my resolve to find a way out of this hole.

"Probably not enough to make him happy," Bull says. "But it's enough to pay the bills."

He takes off, leaving a cool seventeen in the beanbag. I pack my bags for an evening up in the shack. A couple of hours later, he returns with the girlfriend. We make it halfway up The Hill before we run into a tree across the road. He clears branches while I dig out snow. But it's still too much for a 4x4 SUV, and we have no choice but to beach it and grab as much fuel and groceries as we can handle.

I'm happy to see Stash and Gypsy. I'm not a big pet guy, but for the first time I feel like I relate better to dogs than people. I'm even falling for Daisy, the newly arrived mother hen, with her expressive eyes, regal attitude, and injured leg.

"I once knew a dog that ate socks," Chester says, apropos of nothing. "He had socks lining his intestine, had to get surgery."

Chester is a Deadhead who looks and sounds like Count Chocula, with long, straight hair, a stoner's drawl, and a jackhammer laugh. He's clearly done his fair share of acid, but he's been around the block and has a life outside of Buddha Cheese's weed compound. He licenses images from psychedelic artists to be woven into throw blankets, and he has a teenage daughter in Wyoming whom he named after Grateful Dead lyrics.

We listen to West Coast hip-hop, chat, play with the dogs, and smoke a bowl of the butane hash that exploded on my last trip out here. I'm so perma-baked in the presence of Bull that I lack the ability to critically evaluate the hash's quality. Chester cooks fish and veggies. Says he used to be a chef, once made a meal for Mick Jagger. After dinner I notice Isabelle warming herself by the furnace. I walk over because it's cold and I'm curious about her.

"You like that furnace, don't you?"

"Yeah," she says. "I like fire."

"Fire! FIRE!" we both say, in Beavis-and-Butthead speak.

Then she says this: "The biggest thing I ever burned down was a house." She laughs. I don't.

"Well, at least half a house."

"Right."

"It's really the only way to get rid of anything," she adds.

"Burning it?"

She nods.

"Huh," I say. "Never thought of it that way."

*   *   *

It's hard to forget the moment I realize I need to get the fuck out of here. It's the next day, and we have just returned from another long trip down to the SUV, with more fuel and grow supplies. The plod back up the snowy slope feels like a triumph of the human spirit, with several recovery breaks. At the summit we bust into a breathless rendition of the *Rocky* theme song, accompanied by a flourish of weak punches. We pull off our boots and are all sitting there huffing, when Isabelle points to the dog.

"What is Daisy chewing on?" she says.

Chester rushes over. He pulls back Daisy's jaw and holds something up to the light. It's a vial.

"Jesus Christ," Bull says. "That's the acid! Daisy was chewing on the acid!"

"Oh my God," I say. By acid, Bull means liquid LSD.

"That's not good," Chester says. "If she had chewed through that vial, she would have been tripping balls."

Bull admonishes Isabelle, sounding eerily like her father. Chester—a man who I expect has seen a lot in his time—is gobsmacked. I don't care who's responsible. I can't do this anymore. Blackouts, teenage pyromaniacs, kingpins in debt, arctic conditions, pit bulls chewing on acid vials. It's all too much.

I walk outside and call Nigel, pleading for refuge in San Francisco. I call all rental car stations within an hour's drive. One is closed; the other two close within the hour. I speed walk back inside and ask if there's any way we could make it in time. Bull says no. I book one for the next morning.

My tension level is at eleven. I don't know what angina is, but it sounds like what my chest feels like. I don't want to be here with these people anymore. I grab my flask, take a slug of Jack Daniels, and light a cigarette. Looking at the snowcapped triangles on the horizon, I resign myself to the harsh reality: I'm stuck here on this beautiful mountain.

I march back inside, ready for work. Bull and Chester are pouring nutrients into a water-filled trashcan. They add compost tea, the plant equivalent of an über-healthy smoothie. They add SM-90, which "discourages" fungus, root rot, and bug infestations, as well as Roots Excel and Vitamin B1, to promote root growth. Chester rolls up his sleeve, dips his arm into the water, and stirs.

Bull tells Isabelle and me to fill the bottom of the new pots with two inches of soil. We take the teenage plants out of their old cube-shaped trays, flip them over like bad Catholic-school girls, shake some inoculation powder on their rump/roots, and put them into the new pots. We add more soil, then pat it down thoroughly. Chester observes my patting method with clinical disdain: "You have to pat them down *real* good."

Chester waters the plants, covering every millimeter of the top layer of soil evenly. When he's done he tells me to let the water drain out evenly, tilting and rotating the pots constantly, until each one is completely drained. I do my best, but Chester says he's unimpressed with the thoroughness of my draining. I appreciate the attention to detail, but his managerial style doesn't jibe with my personality. Bull mentions how cool it would be if you had a necklace with Bob Marley's image carved into a medallion made of hash.

"Totally," I say.

As soon as we're done, I catch a ride back down the hill with Bull and couldn't be happier to be alone in the cold, dark house.

*   *   *

I'm teetering on the precipice of losing my shit when Bull and Isabelle pick me up the next morning. As we start down the mountain, Bull shoots me a demented cab driver's stare in the rearview.

"So you've been calling outside people on your burner phone, huh?"

I'm caught off guard. "What?"

"That's the whole point of the burner, to only call people in the inner circle. You've made outside calls."

"Oh . . . I . . . yeah, I guess I did call a couple friends during the blackout, because my regular phone died. It was just two friends."

"It doesn't matter who you called. You've compromised the whole team. Now everyone will have to buy new phones."

"Oh. I'm sorry. I . . . I wasn't thinking. It was just pitch black and I was wide awake and sort of bored and . . . my bad."

"Yeah, yeah. We'll deal with it when we get back."

I can't discern if there's an underlying threat there. Even Isabelle seems disappointed at my gaffe. Part of me feels bad. I'm too indiscreet to be a criminal. But then it occurs to me that the only way he could know

I called someone is if he checked my phone while I wasn't around. This counterbalances my guilt, even gets me a little indignant. I can have a slippery moral compass, but I wouldn't fuck with someone else's phone. But then I'm not a drug dealer with piles of cash and weed sitting around. There's good reason for them to be suspicious of me—a writer and an outsider. This thought crystallizes like frost into a half dozen paranoid self-questions. Did Mikey or Puck ask him to check my phone? Do they think I'm not who I say I am, or just careless? Do they think I'm leaving now for some insidious reason? And how far are we from that goddamned rental car joint?

When we get there, I'm in such haste to vamoose I end up leaving my toiletry bag and one of my Chuck Taylors in the truck. As I'm pulling out from the lot, I get a text from Buddha Cheese that's so timely it raises my Spidey senses: "Working my way back! How's it?" I marinate on his word choice a moment, then can't help harrumphing like a fed-up parent. *Working your way back?* What are you, fucking hitchhiking? Either you're on a plane, or in a vehicle of some sort, or you're not. And my guess is you're not. But I'm determined to meet with Mikey, to penetrate the underworld of a major black-market marijuana operation. And I know he doesn't respond well to negativity, so I slide into his fantasy world and write: "Been good my man! Actually popping down to SF for a couple days, gonna roll back up here Weds or Thurs. That work?"

His response: "I should be there around Thursday."

Got it. I'll put that in my calendar.

CHAPTER ELEVEN
GANJA LAND

I've been with Bull a half hour and am already questioning my decision to wait two weeks for this. We are smoking a joint in a gas station parking lot near Sacramento International Airport, and he's telling me about how he accidentally ran over Stash, and how the other dogs witnessed it and are "totally traumatized." I'm feeling traumatized myself. I was just at this airport three days ago, on the same mission impossible we're on today— picking up Buddha Cheese. Thirty minutes after his flight was scheduled to land, despite the fact that I had confirmed its arrival on the status board, he sent me this text: "Shit flight's canceled!" It was like dealing with a kid who thought peekaboo was real—that you could put your hands in front of your eyes and actually disappear.

Bull hands me the joint. Our windows are cracked and I swear the cumulonimbus cloud of smoke surrounding the truck is so thick and dank that everyone within a hundred-foot radius knows what we're up to.

"Actually, I'm surprised there are no cops around," Bull says. He points to an area just beyond the gas pumps. "They're usually right over there. They come and clear the front of the parking lot every twenty minutes . . . fire hazard or some shit."

Why is he telling me this? I decide to change the subject. "So who's up at The Hill these days?"

"Just Chester," he says. "One of the other workers is supposed to be there, but he's afraid to come because he heard northern California has dangerous levels of radioactivity, due to drift from the nuclear meltdown in Japan. Says he's waiting for a conclusive EPA report. You can't make this shit up, man."

"He sounds either paranoid or pretty creative," I say.

"He's both. So many of these guys are lazy, but they're like bad dogs. They will come eventually, and obey, because they need food and shelter."

Comparing people to dogs is an illustrative snapshot of Bull's world-view. I excuse myself to go to the bathroom. Really, I just need some space. After two weeks of relative peace in San Francisco, I have that feeling again—a tightness in the stomach at surrendering control to whatever strange forces and people occupy Buddha Cheese's world.

"So how are the plants doing?" I ask when I return.

"I've been trying to keep the babies alive," Bull says. "You can tell they have spider mites when the leaves turn white and lose their shine. I've been using chrysanthemum oil, pyrethrum fogger, neem oil extract, Azimax, and sesame oil organicide, but the fuckers won't die."

"That sucks," I say. "So when does Mikey land?"

"Like ten minutes ago."

Is it possible? Could he bail again? The real doglike behavior around here is my steadfast refusal to lose hope in Mikey. I'm cautiously optimistic that the recent flood of texts, most of them bikini shots of the Panamanian pole dancer he met, indicates that he now remembers I am a real human being who's waiting for him. The last one allegedly came from the Phoenix airport, which is closer to Cali than New Orleans.

Bull looks at his phone. "He's here."

He turns on the engine and pulls out. Driving through the parking lot, we find ourselves driving head-on toward another truck, one of those no-man's-land deadlocks where road rules don't apply. The other truck veers left. We pass it and notice the driver is Latino.

"A Mexican standoff with an actual Mexican!" Bull shouts. "The irony is so thick!"

We get to the terminal. I've almost lost the capacity to care and am more intellectually curious about whether Buddha Cheese will show. When the automatic door splits and his form emerges, I feel like I'm watching D. B. Cooper. In my mind's eye, he moves in slow motion, making faint glances in each direction before crossing the street. All he's carrying is a tiny backpack with boots tied to it.

He pops into the truck. Bull hands him the joint. He's all wild energy and chatter, as if he never left. "We've been smoking the Jackalope in New Orleans. Everyone fuckin' loves it! Oh, and now we have a hash hookup down there. Have you talked to Roxanne? Crazy bitch owes me money. Everyone else has paid, but she thinks she's an exception to the rule. But that's the nature of the biz . . . people are shady."

After some small talk, Bull turns to Buddha Cheese. "You know, you suck, as a person. Pick up your goddamn phone!"

The Mikey just laughs. We pass a PG & E truck. Pacific Gas and Electric Company (PG & E) is one of the largest natural gas and electrical utilities companies in the nation. They have more than five million electricity customers, covering almost half of the state.

"PG & E takes advantage of all the ganja growers," Mikey says. "If your bill is high, they'll charge extra because they assume you're growing, and there's nothing you can do about it. And if you don't pay for a few months, they won't do anything, because they figure at some point you'll sell your harvest and pay them off."

"Really?" I say.

"Yup. But if you're poor and have a small bill and you don't pay . . . they'll turn off your electricity immediately."

"Huh," I say.

After a few seconds of silence, he turns to me in the backseat. "Hey, sorry it took me so long to get here. It's just, this girl. So hot, man. I think I'm in love!"

*   *   *

The next morning, I wake up to a breakfast of champions: water with 200 milligrams of caffeine powder, five drops of cannabis tincture, and half of Bull's joint. There's no real food to speak of here in the house—most of the groceries I bought either went bad during the blackout or were pillaged by the shack dwellers after I left. Just as I'm starting to get jittery, Mikey walks in with a ham-and-egg sandwich for me.

"Thanks," I say. "Where did you go?"

"Post office. Got a package."

He cuts the box open and starts pulling out the packaging material.

"What is it?" I ask.

"Cash."

"How much?"

"Fifty grand, I hope."

He lets me open it. Beneath bubble wrap and taped brown paper are four vacuum-sealed bundles of twenties held together with rubber bands. Each one has three stacks of twenties an inch thick. Though it smells kind of nasty, that much cash is a sight to behold.

"Man," I say. "I wanna go on a mission."

"Yeah? You wanna bring cash back right now? I don't know this old guy coming from the East Coast, and I know you. You could fly out and drive back."

"How much cash is it?" I ask.

"Four hundred thousand dollars," he says.

"Whoah," I say. "And how much would I make, if I transported that?"

"Three percent. But you'd have to pay for your rental car and all expenses."

I do a mental calculation: Minus expenses, like $11,000. Not bad. And it'd be pretty stress-free to deliver cash. It's not as pungent as weed, and doesn't take up as much space. And driving around with cash isn't technically illegal, is it?

"It's not like they're gonna search your car," Mikey says. "When was the last time you got pulled over and they searched your car?"

"True," I say. "So would you make more transporting money or weed?"

"Weed."

"How do you do it?"

He knows a guy who owns a shipping company. They put it on shipping crates. He just packs it along with legitimate goods and adds official-looking labels. It's business-to-business, goes to a loading dock.

"How much does it cost?"

"Three hundred and fifty per pound," T says. "Hundred-pound minimum."

Thirty-five grand—that's legit money for a five-day journey and some calculated risk. I ask how much he pays for non-truck drivers. He says it's less but won't give me an exact figure. He does mention that he's got a pending transaction, though—a guy up in Humboldt with dozens of pounds, and a guy on the East Coast who can move it.

"And how would it work? I mean, what's your strategy for transporting it?"

"It's easy. I've done it dozens of times. It's easy for me because I look relatively normal. And you, with no tattoos or facial hair—you look extra normal."

The Mikey explains the process. Triple vacuum seal the weed in one-pound portions, to kill the smell. Wipe it down with rubbing alcohol, to get rid of the residue. Put it inside luggage, so it's easy to transfer. Get a full-size rental car with the biggest trunk available. It all goes in the trunk, so a cop needs probable cause to search it. Drive the speed limit and stop when you get tired. Shave and shower for each segment of the drive; smile and say please and thank-you in all interactions. At hotels, either take the bags inside, disable the trunk mechanism, or roll the dice. And divide the trip into segments.

"What do you mean, segments?" I ask.

"So you'd rent from, say, Sacramento, to Salt Lake City airport. There, you pick up another car, so you're not driving clear across the country with California plates, which looks suspicious. And you always have a story. I'm on my way to Salt Lake, to go skiing. I'm on my way to Chicago, to visit my buddy who got tickets to a Bears game. Or whatever . . ."

"But aren't you vulnerable when you're transitioning from car to car?"

"No. You get the rentals at airports, so you drop off one car then just walk the bags to the next rental agency. Everything's normal. You're just a guy at the airport, traveling."

"The only thing that would worry me would be other people, idiots who can't drive. Someone rear-ending me or something."

"Haha! Someone hits you and your trunk pops open, ganja's all over the place . . . You'd be *fucked*!"

Good that I can amuse him so. But the chance of getting into an accident that empties out the trunk is slim. And an accident wouldn't be cause for a search. I say I would consider that kind of mission. I need the money.

Someone calls. When he gets off, Mikey says it was a guy from a dispensary who wants some product. "I sell to dispensaries too, you know. I actually do sell medical marijuana."

He says the market's gotten brutal though. People come out to Cali wanting to grow, but they don't think about selling it. "No one's making money on indoor. You can rent an abandoned house that's already set up for grows . . . for nothing."

I ask why, when he can flip ganja from grower to buyer with minimal work and make solid money, does he put in the colossal effort of setting up these annual outdoor grows.

"Mainly because I love it. But also because there's an even bigger profit. And transporting goods back and forth across the country will catch up to you at some point."

He says he's gonna go shower before we head to the bank. "Not too many guys can have fun doing what I do. They get stressed out. But I love it. I think it's hilarious!" He shouts this last part down from the top of the stairs.

Bull and Chester show up on the porch. I tell Bull the cash showed up.

"I heard. It must have gotten buried beneath all the other packages. I ordered a chainsaw sharpener, ATV parts, a pistol, and a laser sight."

"Wait," I say. "You can order a pistol online?"

"I've been ordering lots of stuff, like books from Amazon. If we have bundles of cash coming in once a week, I want to have legitimate packages coming in too. They know me by sight at the post office now . . . Hey where's Mikey?" Bull asks.

"Taking a shower."

"Ahh, a shower," Bull says wistfully. Now that I look closely, he does look dirty. When Mikey comes down, I sneak away to take a shower, as fast as I can, so as not to rub it in.

When I come back down, Buddha Cheese is on the phone. His lips are pursed, and he's pacing around. "Just send it to this address I gave you. Send it next day air, and don't waive the signature. You got that—it's gotta be *with* signature. We want someone to be responsible for picking it up on this end."

Pause. "No, just send me the money. I collect money—that's what I do." Longer pause.

"Yeah, yeah . . . lots of talking. Less talk. Pay for it, or give it back. I'll fly out there right now and pick it up. I'll send someone. I'll send homeboy, the nice guy."

He looks at me and gives me a wink. Apparently I'm the nice guy.

"Don't tell me what the market's like! I know what the market's like in every corner of the country, 'cause that's what I do."

He must be talking to Roxanne.

"Oh, so you have a stash, but you're just waiting until you get your cash to pay me? Good to know; I'll remember that for next time. . . . Listen, I'm not triple-fronting; that's not how I do business. . . . Yeah, insure it for like a hundred and fifty bucks. Just send it. No more talk. I've got people here, gotta get going. Send it. Bye."

He hangs up and shakes his head. "I'm not playing games with every-body. . . . I'm not double- and triple-fronting[1] . . . And she wants a fucking discount now, after the fact! That's not how it works. We had a deal and that's the deal. No talking on the phone about it afterward . . ."

"Roxanne's like a child," Bull says. "She's a nightmare."

"Yeah she is," Buddha Cheese says. "But she does bring in a hundred grand a month. Haha!"

Mikey says he's ready to go. We've got to make a deposit, fix his iPhone, and pick up a WiFi hub. He grabs a water bottle off the counter.

"This water tastes funny," he says.

I laugh. "Remember, I told you that's got caffeine powder in it."

"He never listens," Bull says.

As we're walking out of the house, Bull is talking out loud to Chester. "Well I'm thinking . . ."

"Don't do that," Mikey says. "No thinking."

We hop in the truck. "So where are we going again?" I ask.

"We're just two normal guys going to the bank," Mikey says. "And depositing a lot of money."

---

1 Fronting means selling marijuana to someone who doesn't have the money to pay up front but will reimburse you when they sell the weed. Double-fronting means doing it twice before being paid, etc.

I wake up to the clatter of Buddha Cheese running up the stairs into my attic guest bedroom. He runs past me and ducks into the crawl space. I hear the scratch and bang of his rummaging, like some varmint trespasser. He pops his head out.

"I need to grab some ganja," he says. "You got a flashlight?"

"I have a headlamp."

The Mikey sloppily tosses the headlamp on his head, the strap all twisted. He turns it on. "Perfect! This is perfect!" He sprints back out with two turkey bags of weed, tosses me the headlamp, and clip-clops down the stairs.

I rub my eyes, put on some shorts, and follow him. He's sitting across from a guy, on the giant beanbag. I pretend not to notice and walk into the kitchen. This must be the guy who he said he was going to interview as a grow manager, to assist Bull. Mikey says the guy is skittish after having done a two-year jail term for overseeing a dozen grows at once. They shake hands. The guy walks out, carrying the two pounds, averting his eyes as he passes me in the kitchen. Mikey says it looks like the guy's in. He gave him the weed as a show of good faith.

Buddha Cheese confessed to me yesterday: He has upped the ante. Now he wants 300 plants. By his own ambitious estimate of five pounds' yield per plant, that would be anywhere from 1,500 pounds to a ton of total yield. His gross would be in the range of $3 million to $4 million, with a profit of $2.5 million. The amount of workers to manage could get ridiculous, especially during harvest time. And Bull can't handle that.

"He can't do four jobs. What am I gonna tell him? He constantly fucks shit up. And *himself.*" Not long ago, Mikey says Bull was trying to lift up a gate on the property, and it hit him in the head. They had to take him to the hospital, which means giving out addresses and other information they'd rather keep confidential.

Mikey says he wants to hire this new guy so he can stop micromanaging all these projects. "I want to spend less time on the details and create opportunities for other people."

"That's what businessmen do when they move up the ladder," I say.

"They delegate responsibility, then manage the people they delegate to."

Mikey takes off for yoga. Two hours later he bounces into the room like Tigger. He hands me some chicken he got at the organic health food co-op, which he calls the "Hairy Patch" because of all the hairy hippie chicks that hang out there.

"I just ripped the hose off the tank at the gas station! Forgot about it totally, drove away. Fully ripped the hose off. Haha!"

My phone rings. I'm still getting thirty calls a day from credit card companies and collection agencies. My strategy is to never pick up unknown calls until I'm capable of paying something. But I found out yesterday some guy in prison for dealing weed has been trying to reach me from an 866 number. I decide to pick up.

"Hello."

"Hello, Alfred? Alfred Nerz?"

Using the first name. Bad sign.

"This is Joyce from Stiles & Johnson, and we're calling about collection for a past due balance . . ."

"Okay, okay," I say. "How much is that?"

"One second," she says. "Please hold."

She's putting *me* on hold? That's amusing. I hang up.

My buddy Palmer calls, on my regular phone. Palmer is a friend from college, a filmmaker.

"Are you deep cover right now?" he asks.

"Yes," I say. "Hold on."

I walk outside to the porch. I'm gun-shy about taking calls after the "burner phone" drama. Will they think I'm making some illicit call, like as an informant, or blabbing crucial info that could be intercepted? But The Mikey, who should probably care the most, seems to care the least.

"Okay," I say. "We're good."

"Where are you?"

"An undisclosed location in Colusa County."

I tell Palmer about Buddha Cheese and the whole environment. When he presses for what we do on any given day, I offer up a recent adventure: We drove to the secluded home of an amiable hippie weed grower named Roland, and his lovely girlfriend, Liza. They greeted us in robes and showed us their basement grow, accessible only by a pool cue rack that doubled as a Scooby-Dooesque secret door. While Buddha Cheese and Roland discussed insecticides and 18/6 light cycles, Liza talked to me about quantum biofeedback machines and pyramid technology. Roland explained that the shrine in their kitchen was dedicated to his spiritual teacher, who as it turns out is a cult leader with a well-documented habit of plying nubile women with amyl nitrate "poppers" before sodomizing them. We smoked a joint and hit up a local hot springs, where it turned out "clothing optional" effectively meant mandatory nudity. When we returned to their place at four in the morning, Roland explained, over a cigarette, that the 9/11 World Trade Center disaster was actually a scam to get the gold out of the banks beneath the towers, as if there was a treasure chest in the tower's basement, guarded by leprechauns.

"Wow." Palmer laughs. "You should have said to him, 'You know, I've heard a lot of theories about what happened on that day, but you're the only one talking real *sense* about it.'"

I mention the calling-outsiders-on-the-burner-phone controversy, and the subsequent reprimands from both Bull and Puck.

"Damn. Don't you just want to be like, 'Easy there, buddy. You're taking this pretty seriously.'"

"Yeah. But then another part of me says the stakes aren't that high for me, and I can't pretend to understand what these guys are feeling . . . because there is a *lot* going on that should stay on the down low."

On cue, The Mikey rushes outside.

"You ready to go on a mission?" he asks. "Puck is already waiting for us, to pick up some cash. Then we'll go grab some pounds off of Roland, and pick up that bug juice he was talking about in the morning."

I cover the phone with my hand. "Yeah, sure. I'm in."

*   *   *

Buddha Cheese and I are driving on I-20, smoking a joint of Lemon Haze. It's so bright out the world looks bleached, and the truck is packed with marijuana and bug juice. The thirteen pounds Mikey bought off Roland this morning are sitting in the way back, in a black trash bag.

I've survived another evening of Buddha Cheese madness: endless driving, hanging out with Puck in a parking lot, and talking about pit bulls, money, women, and weed. With the aid of surreptitious slugs from a bottle of Jameson's, I have endured another night at Roland and Liza's. They were pleasant enough, but their third roommate was a blowhard who wanted to have a formalized roundtable discussion about medical marijuana.

As for my own marijuana use, it doesn't feel like cause for concern, though I'm surrounded by it. I have even begun to turn it down on occasion, because I feel no pressing desire to get high, and refusing a joint no longer seems like a tipoff for uncoolness or snitch potential. Drinking is the only thing that numbs me to the foreign surroundings, the incessant motion, and the psychological barrage of sadness and negativity from the breakup. It worries me that alcohol is the only reliable means for stifling my anxiousness. But in this environment, it seems best to stick with whatever works.

We have just come from a quaint grow store, where a local man has struck upon a formula for organic pesticide that kills spider mites without harming plants. It's so popular the inventor's daughter apologized for not having enough supply to fill Mikey's hefty order. She has created a new label and a marketing strategy to gain wider distribution. Regardless of where you stand on the legalization issue, there is no denying that California's medical marijuana laws boost local economies. And some of the primary benefactors are old-timer garden gurus who probably don't smoke at all.

I'm driving so Mikey can do his phone thing. He stubs the joint out and tries to describe the local scene to a buddy who's considering coming out to join the Green Rush.

"As far as jobs go, it's a beautiful and safe environment out here. Nothing like out there. You can do grows out here, to a certain extent. The laws are wonderful."

The Lemon Haze high adds a sparkle to the flat farmland and gives the buttes in the distance a dreamlike quality. I make a mental note: I feel serene. In Buddha Cheese's world, being in motion is more relaxing than staying put, where you're a sitting duck for taxing conversation and the plague of rumination. Behind me I see red flashing lights. I look at my speedometer: seventy-one miles per hour. Damn. The calm never lasts. I nudge Mikey with my elbow. He looks at me and shrugs. I motion behind us with my thumb.

"Okay I'm gonna have to call you back," he says. "I'm gonna have to call you back."

He hangs up. "You're getting pulled over?" The wail of a siren answers his question. "Well, pull over."

I gesture at the two roaches sitting next to the cup holder.

Buddha Cheese sighs. "Shit." He grabs the roaches and puts them beneath his seat. "It's cool. Grab your stuff."

I don't know what stuff he's talking about. The truck's deceleration sounds like a jet coming to a halt on the runway. For the first time, I notice ambient New Agey music coming from the CD player.

The cop walks up. "Hello."

"Hello, sir," I say.

"I'm working with a radar today, and I got you going seventy. I need to see your license. Speed limit is fifty-five through here."

"All right."

"Could I see your registration, please?"

Mikey shuffles through the glove compartment. "Let's see . . ."

"Is this a rental?" the cop asks.

"No," Mikey says. "It's my friend's."

"Oh-kay," says the cop, with a tinge of exasperation.

"And . . . it's probably not in that stuff," Mikey says, getting flustered. "You know what? Let me call him and see where the registration is."

The cop is waiting around awkwardly. He points to the sun visor. "A lot of times it's up here."

"Okay." Mikey laughs nervously. This is ridiculous—a traffic cop giving two stoned guys advice on where to find their own vehicle's documents.

"I see a bunch of stuff above it," the officer says.

"Ah. What's that?" Mikey folds out a piece of paper, then shakes his head and keeps searching.

"Or above your head to the right, there's some more stuff," the cop says. "We'll find it yet."

"Is this it?" Mikey says. "Nope. This is a Nissan thing. And this is some other stuff, right here."

I resist the urge to laugh.

The officer points at the obvious place—the glove compartment. "Wouldn't be in there?"

"No, not there. All right. Let me give him a call."

"All right. That'll work."

The officer walks back to run my license. My record's clean; I'm not worried about that. What does concern me—beyond the lack of registration or proof of insurance in a car that's not even ours—is the smell. We just finished a skunky joint. I have read blog posts about whether or not you should chew and swallow your joint at a moment like this. According to the Internet (which everyone knows is never wrong), the answer is yes, as long as you don't have too much herb.[2] If you don't get caught with buds on your chin, shirt, or teeth, you don't have to worry about getting super-high, at least not for an hour or two.[3] But in this case, with thirteen pounds in the back, swallowing two joints would be pointless. And it's not even in a trunk, so the cop wouldn't need probable cause to search it.

2 Several pro athletes have unsuccessfully tried the swallow method. Two months before this episode, former Tampa Bay Devil Rays baseball player Elijah Dukes got caught trying to eat marijuana at a traffic stop, because of the weed flakes on his shirt. Five months from now, former NBA player Samaki Walker will get busted trying to do the same thing, only with a whopping ten grams of marijuana. It's always worth a try, if you have less than, say, a half a gram. But remember, it's like chewing saltines without water. And brush off your shirt, for Christ's sake.

3 Contrary to popular belief, it's actually a myth that dried marijuana buds must be heated to activate the cannabinoids. Heating weed does increase potency by converting a less potent form of THC through decarboxylation. But eating raw, dried cannabis buds can result in a fairly strong high, though it will take a while to kick in.

Mikey insists he can carry nineteen pounds with a medical marijuana recommendation, but the chances he actually has this document—on him, or at all—seems slim.

Though this may sound hypocritical (since I'm being pulled over after smoking a joint), I have never had problems with smoking affecting my driving. If anything I am usually more cautious, an effect that has been supported by several studies. One of the many arguments against marijuana is that it impairs psychomotor coordination and driving ability, but studies show there is no conclusive evidence that weed contributes substantially to traffic accidents.

In the countless studies of driving simulation, on-road performance, and crash culpability that have explored the effect of marijuana use on driving, the research has consistently shown negligible negative effects. A 1993 study by the Department of Transportation (DOT) concluded that among all drugs—both legal and illegal—used by people before driving, "marijuana may be among the least harmful." In fact, according to the book *Marijuana Myths, Marijuana Facts,* three studies concluded that stoned drivers were not only less culpable than alcohol-positive drivers, but sober drivers as well.

But a thorough look at the research doesn't suggest people drive *better* stoned than sober. The most common impairments are those suggested by a 2000 United Kingdom Department of Environment, Transport and the Regions study. They ultimately concluded that marijuana use didn't increase the risk of accidents, but certain perceptual changes did affect driving performance. These changes were: 1) an increased variability in lane position, 2) slightly longer decision-making times, and 3) a more cautious driving style.

One consistent finding about high drivers is that, because they know they're impaired, they compensate with increased focus and care. This is the opposite of alcohol's effect, which causes drivers to take more risks. In fact alcohol has led to many erroneous conclusions about marijuana's involvement in crashes. Studies in the United States, Australia, and Canada have found THC in the bloodstream of from 3 percent to 11 percent of fatally injured drivers. But in 70 to 90 percent of these cases, alcohol was detected as well.

Still some studies show marijuana may debilitate inexperienced drivers and inexperienced marijuana users. One rather unscientific bit of evidence comes from a buddy of mine who lives outside Denver, who says that ever since the medical marijuana laws went into effect there, the driving is noticeably worse. He claims multiple cases of people forgetting turn signals, driving at a snail's pace, and even randomly stopping on country roads. The only rational cause in his view is the proliferation of medical marijuana patients.[4] This phenomenon could be supported by a 1985 study, which showed that the most salient impairment experienced by drivers who used marijuana was the effect on "divided attention." If I am guilty of anything at this moment, it's that: I was thinking about the picturesque mountains and my own serenity, as opposed to the speed limit.

I take a whiff but am too inured by the stink of ganja to discern if it's flagrant. I roll down the back windows and wait for a drawn-out beat, and then roll them back up.

"The wind should help," Mikey says. "Oh, and where should we say we're heading? Green Canyon?"

"Yeah."

"Where would that form be?" Mikey opens the glove compartment again, then shuts it and calls his buddy, the truck's owner. Apparently the guy mailed it; Mikey just never put it in the car.

I shrug. "Well, we'll see what happens."

Mikey says we should get our backstory straight. "So we went to the hot springs . . ."

"We went to the hot springs. Now we're going home." I look at him. "What am I doing out here, from Brooklyn?"

"You're a writer."

---

4 For much of 2011 and 2012, Colorado legislators tried—unsuccessfully—to pass a bill that would make it illegal to drive with a certain amount of THC in your system (more than five nanograms of THC per milliliter of blood). Supporters say the measure would send a message to stoned drivers. Opponents say the limit is too low and would lead to convictions of sober drivers who had smoked hours, or even days, before driving.

"Right." The truth as alibi—what a novel concept.

The officer approaches the car.

"I got him on the phone," Mikey says. "He mailed it to me, and I haven't put it in the car yet."

"You have *nothing* for this car?"

"No."

"Do you have the insurance information?"

"I don't. I can call him back."

"By California law it says you have to have proof of insurance at all times. There's nothing in this car to offer insurance?"

"He mailed me a little . . . two cards . . . like two little things, a folded-up Geico thing, I believe. Or something. I opened the mail, and it's at the house."

"All right. Well, there's nothing I can do about that," he says while walking away.

"He's a nice guy," I say. "He doesn't even want to deal with this."

"Yeah. He's just gonna write a ticket."

"My bad," I say.

Mikey quiets to a whisper. "My bad for smoking, with all that shit in the car. You know?"

Mikey rustles a few more papers before giving up. It occurs to me that, his attention span being what it is, Buddha Cheese shouldn't be trusted on this search. I reach over and grab a handful of papers from the glove compartment. The third paper I see is the registration. I hand it to Mikey, who leans out the window.

"This is it, officer! We found it! We found the, uh, registration."

We are such idiots—so proud just to conjure up one small flash of competence. From the look on the officer's face when he grabs the registration, he almost feels bad for us.

Mikey looks at me. "Dude, when he pulled us over, you just tapped on my arm. You were so calm, like . . ." He reenacts my subtle elbow nudge. "I was like . . . oh . . . yeah, gotta go, bye, haha!"

The officer steps up while we're laughing.

"Okay. All right. I'll hand you this back. What is your hair color and weight?"

"Sure. It's . . . I guess like brown. And blue eyes."

"Your *weight*," he says.

Mikey giggles.

"Sorry. It's 170."

"Okay. That'll work. All right, you gotta slow down a little bit. That's a little fast. Speed limit's fifty-five; you're going seventy on the radar."

"Yup. My bad. That's my fault."

"Sign in that red box right there. You have any questions at all?"

"It's so beautiful, and such a straight road, you know?" Mikey says, snickering.

"I know, it is." Now the cop is laughing too. "Hard to go slow, I understand."

"No," Mikey says. "But that's why we *should* be going slow."

"That's right. You should be enjoying it, right? Where you guys headed?"

"We just came from Harbin Hot Springs, and we're going to . . . we're going to Yuba City."

"Oh, very good. It's nice up there. All right, you guys have a safe trip."

"Thanks. Have a good one."

He walks away.

"I love when cops seem reluctant and slightly guilty," I say.

"I know—love the cops around here, right?" The Mikey says. "Let's go grab some lunch."

*　　　　　　*　　　　　　*

It's the next afternoon, and I'm at a local hardware store, checking items off the shopping list written out by Buddha Cheese. He wants to ship six pounds to an East Coast buddy, so supplies are needed. I have bought a fifteen-gallon bin, Gorilla tape, a Sharpie marker, a box, and insulating foam sealant. Now I'm looking for something resembling a "circuit board" to add to the package, which would make vacuum-packed weed look like organic packing material. Mikey claimed this would be easy—we'd just rip something out of an old computer—but so far no old computers or sacrificable electronic products have surfaced on The Hill. I spot a cheap radio in the shape of a shrunken boom box and make an executive decision: This is our circuit board.

My phone rings. It's Bill Budd, my buddy from Denver who originally turned me on to ganja, back in our junior hockey days together. I am prepared for our usual nonsensical banter, but it's clear from his tone this is a serious call.

"She's leaving me," he says.

I put down the radio and step outside. Bill explains that his girlfriend, Dani, wrote a letter to him about the things that are missing from their relationship. She feels he's not moving forward, spiritually or career-wise, in a way that feels like they're rising up together. Dani thinks he needs to answer some deeper questions within himself.

"And part of it," he adds, "is about how I smoke too much weed."

This makes me think about the classical knock on pot—that it breeds apathy and discourages ambition. It's such a prominent critique that the term "amotivational syndrome" is almost exclusively attributed to cannabis use. Though psychologists don't seem to agree that this syndrome actually exists, it certainly does in the mind of prohibitionists. And there is empirical evidence that some potheads struggle to maintain a satisfying level of achievement during regular use. I am reminded of a line by the comedian Bill Hicks: "They tell you that pot smoking makes you unmotivated. Lie! When you're high, you can do everything you normally do just as well. You just realize it's not worth the fucking effort."

In the past I have wondered if smoking weed has lessened my productivity. And I say this with deep reservations, because I have always fancied myself a motivated stoner, one who smokes before long runs, soccer games, trips to the museum, and marathon cleaning and writing sessions. But I've also noticed at times, while high, the sense that even the smallest tasks—taking a shower, cleaning my room, going shopping—seem like an insuperable burden. There were several years in my mid-twenties where

I was flooded by inspirational ideas but came up woefully short in the execution department.

And I know my buddy Bill feels frustrated by his job. He has a vague desire to branch out and do his own thing but an inability to pin down just what that thing is. I know part of the reason Bill sometimes smokes a bowl in the car on the way to work is his subconscious desire to numb his psyche to the fact that he's capable of doing more than his job demands of him. This dilemma isn't limited to stoners, but it may be exacerbated by a habit that leads to a hazy contentment with the status quo. Its essence was neatly articulated by Terryn Buxton, a budtender at Harborside and one of the more nuanced characters from the TV show *Weed Wars*, who said, "I'm much better at thinking about things I'd like to do than actually accomplishing those things."

CHAPTER TWELVE

BAD THINGS HAPPEN
AT CHRISTMASTIME

I'm sitting where I was told to sit—table six. I'm not wearing what I was told to not wear—no khakis, flip-flops, or white T-shirts. The only possessions I have on me are two bills—a twenty and a ten, maxing out the thirty-dollar limit allowed. No cameras or phones or wallets or pens. They even took my ID. All I got in return was a cheap pencil and a few sheets of paper, which sit on the desk before me.

I look to the left, out the window. There is a walled-in outdoor visiting area, which is empty. The tables are concrete and blocky; they look sad. Beyond them, there are no trees, no vegetation at all.

I pivot my head. Right in front of me, at table eight, is a Latino family. The man is an inmate. You can tell by the uniform: khakis and a white T-shirt. He has a mustache and a cute little brown girl in his arms with two fingers in her mouth. The man looks ecstatic, like he's really drinking this in. To their left is a short, brown-skinned woman who is clearly the girl's mother. She leans into her man awkwardly, like proximity might make up for lost time.

Above the Latino family is a sign that reads KIDS' ROOM—MAXIMUM OCCUPANCY 15. It appears to be empty, and this is no surprise. It's tiny and looks asphyxiating, with a heavy industrial door. It seems designed to scare kids out of a life of crime by creating a microcosm of the prison experience. The wall to my far right is a mural—an aquatic scene, blue with frolicking dolphins. I'd like to think it was created by inmates who were imagining more uplifting circumstances.

I'm taking a day off from the Buddha Cheese experience to visit, of all places, a federal prison. The drive down from The Hill took five hours, plenty of time to consider the possibility that Buddha Cheese could easily end up at a place like Taft Correctional Institution. After exiting the interstate and zipping through endless orange groves, the prison complex appeared like a mirage in the middle of a wide, dusty field—nine blocky buildings in a circular formation, surrounded by fence and loops of barbed wire.

I'm here to see inmate number 56784-113. I'd like to say he's the friend of a friend, but he's more like the friend of an acquaintance. On the phone he has been charming and funny, but scarce on details. His name is Sanjay, and he's in for a weed charge. He joked that his sentence was an "adult time-out," but seemed wistful about "rotting away in the desert." He said to send a book if I could, and that he sometimes purchases random magazine subscriptions just to hear his name called at the three o'clock distribution of mail. When you visit, don't wear a hoodie, he said, or colors affiliated with gangs, or even tight-fitting clothes. He joked that I definitely shouldn't wear a "man-kini."

All I know about this minimum-security prison is three of its inmates: Michael Milken, the junk-bond king; Dale Schafer, a medical marijuana martyr; and Tommy Chong. The more sedate half of the stoner comedy duo Cheech & Chong was rounded up in 2003 as part of Operation Pipe Dreams. According to Chong he was having a dream about a gang of naked women beating on his door, preparing for a sexual attack, when his wife awakened him and said someone was beating on the door. DEA agents with automatic weapons flooded the house, rummaging through rooms and yelling, "Clear!" Though they seized a pound of weed, they had no interest in that. All they wanted was computers and evidence that Chong was financing and promoting a company called Nice Dreams, which was started by his son, Paris. The company sold bongs.

Chong was so convinced the raid was a charade that he asked to take a shit in the middle of it. He was wrong. After costly legal wrangling, Chong pled guilty to one count of "conspiring to sell and distribute drug paraphernalia," in exchange for the non-prosecution of his wife and son. The sentence: nine months in prison, a $20,000 fine, forfeiture of $103,514, and the loss of all merchandise seized during the raid of the warehouse. Of the fifty-five people targeted in Operation Pipe Dreams, Chong was the only one without a prior conviction to receive jail time. The media had been invited to the raid, leading to widespread allegations that the DEA had used Chong as a publicity coup. The estimated cost of the operation—which occurred almost simultaneously with the launch of the Iraq War—was

$12 million, and involved over two thousand law enforcement officers.[1]

I see a man walk through the security checkpoint and turn toward me. This must be Sanjay. He is about six feet tall, with a fit physique and shaved hair, wearing neatly pressed pants and shirt. He looks like a more handsome, Indian version of Sacha Baron Cohen. If you saw him on the outside, you'd think, *What a sharp guy.* We smile and shake hands. It's awkward, because we feel like we sort of do and don't know each other.

"Nice to finally meet you," I say.

"You too, bro."

He starts with small talk, saying it's not that bad here. They even have a tennis court, though it took two years to accumulate enough seniority to get court time. I broach the subject of why he's in here and then cough up an absurd thought.

"Just wondering: Do you smoke weed?"

"I used to!" he says, laughing.

He launches into his story. Like Tommy Chong, Sanjay says he grew up in western Canada—Vancouver, where growing and smoking pot was just part of the culture. "It wasn't really a gangsta scene," he says. "It was more civilized and normal."

Lots of Chinese dudes were moving weed. The Asian gangs, or Northern Triads, had a solid footing in the marijuana trade. He's half-Chinese, half-Indian, so he was familiar with the environment.

A big thing growing up in Vancouver, he says, was shipping weed to the States. It was the Clinton era, and the exchange rate was favorable. Sanjay knew a dozen crews that were going down into the States each month. There were a variety of ways to smuggle. One was "Commando," or basically just walking over the border with weed in a backpack. The border was vast, and certain outposts of wilderness couldn't be monitored. There

---

1 In 2006, Chong published *The I Chong: Meditations from the Joint,* a sort of spiritual treatise about his life and his experiences at Taft Correctional Institution.

were tunnels. In fact there's a Canadian guy here, one of his buddies, who built a tunnel beneath his house.

Canadian weed smugglers are renowned for their creativity. They've been known to load up kayaks and transverse rural rivers, or zip across the border on snowmobiles. They've hidden weed in horse trailers and mobile homes. They have floated hollowed-out logs down the river, filled with waterproof contraband and GPS systems. One of the most publicized smuggling cases involved a Canadian extreme mountain-biking star named Samuel Lindsay-Brown, who flew nearly five hundred pounds of weed over the border in a helicopter—through fog and pelting rain—only to get caught by DEA agents in the Colville National Forest, north of Spokane. Five days later Lindsay-Brown hanged himself in his jail cell.

The most common smuggling method, according to Sanjay, is semi trucks. Lots of Asians own trucking companies, he says. It's a good deal for the truckers, because they're getting paid anyway, and they can play dumb about the cargo if they get caught. The operation was: Weed goes down, coke comes back up. Back then everyone wanted B.C. Bud, because it was the highest quality. Things have changed now, Sanjay says. The government is more conservative, the American marijuana is better, and the dollar is weak. "Now it's just come down and buy coke."

Sanjay says he studied marketing at the University of Hawaii. Brains run in the family; his sister went to Harvard and became a high-powered lawyer. But Sanjay was more laid-back. When he first came to L.A., he planned to keep it mellow.

"At first, I was happy with my truck and a surfboard," he says. "Then I learned to pop bottles and buy expensive watches."

He says anyone who makes it in the distribution game has a "come-up story," in which they started taking bigger risks to make bigger profits. In his case it was a matter of upping the size of shipments and embracing cocaine trafficking, which was more dangerous than moving ganja. One of the side effects of marijuana prohibition, it seems, is that the gateway theory applies to weed dealers as well, in that it can lead to dealing riskier drugs. Sanjay seems reluctant to mention coke as part of his operation, because he only got busted on marijuana charges. But cocaine has a much higher profit margin and was obviously part of his come-up story.

While "shopping" for bulk purchases of quality herb around Vancouver, Sanjay ran into a Chinese kid he knew from elementary school. The guy explained that he had just taken over the business of an old, retired Triad gangster. Sanjay established his old buddy as his Vancouver connection, and started setting up storage units in L.A., as well as distribution points in Chicago, Wisconsin, and Miami.

The money instantly started rolling in, but laundering it took some ingenuity. Sanjay befriended an attorney who put cash in an escrow account. They'd make a fake deal that would "fall through," and the attorney would shift the money for a fee. Sanjay once bought a million-dollar yacht, emptied out the hulls, and filled them with cash. He then invited a bevy of hotties to party with him on the boat all the way down to Costa Rica, where he set up an offshore bank account. "The best tool at any port of entry is women," he says. "If your ratio of hot women to men is high, you get waved right through."

One part of Sanjay's cash problem required less creativity: spending it. He owned a yacht and a fleet of luxury cars—a Rolls-Royce Phantom, a Ferrari, a couple of Mercedes. He had a $15 million mansion in Malibu and multiple properties in Miami, including a mansion on Hibiscus Island. He owned two L.A. nightclubs, a coffee bean company, and a steakhouse. One weekend, he rented a G5 jet just to impress his heiress girlfriend and party with friends, spending $90,000 in Cabo San Lucas over a long weekend.

Sanjay fell into a crowd that mingled with the Hollywood socialite scene. He helped Dennis Rodman open his club. He became buddies with Rohan Marley, son of Bob and the baby daddy of Lauryn Hill's kids. He popped bottles with Nicole Richie and found himself dating *American Pie* actress and professional partier Tara Reid for six months. She had no idea what he did for a living. But she was a clean freak, so there were some eyebrow-raising moments. "She would be like, 'Hey, why is there a million dollars in cash in the closet?'"

No one knew what Sanjay did for a living, and no one cared, as long as the money flowed. When he drove his daughter to school in a Ferrari, other parents were respectful to the point of obsequiousness. One of his favorite parts of the gig was making up what he did for a living.

"I'd be like, 'I was adopted by Steven Spielberg,'" he says, snickering.

"Or I'd say, 'I'm the heir to Indian oil money.' And they'd be like, 'Wait, India has oil?' I'd say, 'Not yet. Still drilling.'"

Sanjay belts out laughing. Like Buddha Cheese, a big part of his modus operandi is pulling one over on the world—getting paid a boatload to live a life of what feels like harmless mischief. But there is a certain superciliousness to his worldview, a superiority complex toward conventional nine-to-fivers. While squares are commuting and pinching pennies, Sanjay and Buddha Cheese have amassed quick wealth by having the balls to take risks, because they have no qualms bucking the conventional moral code.

When things are going well, you could make the case that they're onto something. But as his laughter wanes, I notice Sanjay looking around the prison visitation room wistfully. This is where you end up when the system catches up with you. I recall from our phone conversations that one of the perks of a visit is you get to eat from the vending machines. I ask if he wants something. An Italian sub, he says, if it's not sold out. I ask if he has a second choice, since inmates aren't allowed into the vending area.

"Whatever. It's not as if there's any real *good* options." He grins. "You'd be amazed at how quickly your standards drop. I used to go to my own restaurant, and they'd wait to kill the fish so I could see that it was totally fresh."

As we dig into our sandwiches, I tell Sanjay that all the glamour sounds fantastic, but I'm also interested in the dark side of his story.

He says a lot of the glamour is empty anyway. "L.A. is such a fake world. Lakers and fakers, man. It's actually kind of a shitty-ass fucking scene."

Most of the darker drama involves associates and money. One of his partners, who owed him a bundle, went on vacation and ended up dead. Most of Sanjay's holdings were in this guy's name, but none of it was documented. It was all handshake contracts.

"So were you able to reestablish those holdings?" I ask.

"Yeah," he says. "By *force*."

He laughs, more hesitantly this time. Clearly, Sanjay has a side that's not just handsome playboy drug smuggler. He's capable of getting grimy if the situation calls for it. He casually mentions having had an underling visit someone to dangle him over a banister by his ankles. Then there was a Mexican guy, a coke-dealing associate, who had his finger cut off while being tortured. Sanjay also did business with a guy from the ghetto, whom he called "Diamond in the Rough."

"Anything we did, we would weigh the risk and the reward. So if a guy steals fifty thousand dollars, we would have to make a decision. Should we make a ruckus, or walk away? Me, I'd generally walk away. But my boy Diamond in the Rough, he'd go after the guy on principle."

The worst associates were the sloppy ones. It was one such slacker who got him busted. The Slacker had kids, so Sanjay had a soft spot for him. After returning from a winter vacation in Hawaii, Sanjay asked The Slacker to go pick up some cash from a storage space. The Slacker had a reputation for losing his cell phone, so against his better instincts, Sanjay went to check on him.

"Bad things happen at Christmastime," Sanjay says. "In Asian cultures you try not to work much in December and January, leading up to the Chinese New Year."

At the storage spot, cars were everywhere. Sanjay's instinct was to flee, but he thought maybe they were getting robbed. Just as he was about to take off, a crew of armed undercover cops filed out. He started to back up, but he was surrounded. Turned out the cops had tracked The Slacker because he had been moonlighting as a supplier to medical marijuana dispensaries. The officers asked Sanjay what his relationship was to The Slacker. "I don't know that guy at all," he said.

But Sanjay was driving a $400,000 Mercedes SLR McLaren. The cops were justifiably suspicious. They found $1.1 million in the storage unit and a receipt in The Slacker's car with Sanjay's name on it. Sanjay knew he was screwed. "Now keep in mind, I'm a single father, so I start thinking about my daughter. She's at home with the nanny, and I know one thing for sure: She needs to be able to leave the country."

Sanjay signed papers allowing them to search his home, in hopes of being able to get his four-year-old daughter back to Canada. (Why this compromise seemed necessary isn't exactly clear.) They went back to his apartment and found his computer, with a document detailing his transactions. The officers asked if he wanted to make a deal. Sanjay said he only had $1 million now, but if they waited a couple weeks, he could get them $3.5 million. The cops, who were part of a local task force, said it was a deal.

"And I'm thinking, if I can get out of this with my passport and no sentence, I'm good. I can walk into the sunset, you know?"

It didn't work out like that. They promised him immunity. At the next meeting with the task force, they said if he gave a "statement of involvement," they would tear it up afterward and he would be free to go. Sanjay was suspicious but agreed to show them a spreadsheet detailing all his transactions. "I basically had a little wand, and was giving a PowerPoint presentation," he says, laughing. "But in the end, they did us dirty."

When he arrived at the next meeting with the task force, there was a female DEA agent in the room. "They explained to me that they made a deal that was beyond what this woman would accept."

Sanjay names the agent and calls her a "dirty, dirty bitch." In the end he claims the officers found no drugs. Before he gave the statement in exchange for what he thought was a deal to have the charges dropped, they had nothing on him. But the statement showed more than $40 million in transactions over a period of six months.

"Jesus, Sanjay," I say. "That was a lot of cheddar you were moving."

"Yeah, well there were like three of us." He flashes an impish grin. "So anyway I'm still thinkin' I'm gonna run. But then I got denied bail three times."

He says they got him for conspiracy to distribute ten thousand kilos (eleven tons) of marijuana. He needed a good federal attorney, which was harder to find than a state one. Because he had money, lawyers came in waves, at a rate of three per day. The first one he chose had too high of a caseload: "He was supposed to be a beast, but he turned out to be a dump truck." Meanwhile, Sanjay's partner, who owed him $3.5 million, disappeared. "That was no big surprise. There's always that risk. If the money comes back to you, it's a good spin of the roulette wheel."

For a heavy fee, Sanjay secured celebrity lawyer Donald Re, who had defended John DeLorean and Snoop Dogg. Re started filing dozens of motions for dismissal. The feds fought back with a strategy known as "diesel therapy," transferring Sanjay repeatedly from tough prisons to even tougher prisons. The hardest time he served was at San Bernadino County Correctional Facility. There were seventy people to a room, with three toilets and one shower. The only thing shielding Sanjay from violence was some friends from the Mongols bike gang, who used to hang out at the club he owned in Hollywood.

"The thing is, with the feds, if you go to court and waste their time and money, your sentence gets increased. And they have a 98 percent conviction rate . . . so people almost never go to court."

The feds offered seventeen years. Sanjay told Donald Re to keep fighting. The feds kept pushing back the court date. When the big day finally came, a year and a half after Sanjay's arrest, the prosecutor didn't show up. She had apparently suffered a nervous breakdown. They sent a fill-in instead, who wasn't happy with the situation. "I've got four powerful attorneys ready to eat this guy alive," Sanjay says.

After some negotiation the feds finally agreed to give him a "phone count," or criminal use of a phone device to facilitate a drug transaction. The sentence would be two to four years. The judge maxed him out at four years, plus a massive fine. "I tried to fight the fine," Sanjay says. "But they caught me on tape selling a Rolls-Royce, a Ferrari, and a boat. And the court saw all my high-powered lawyers and was like, 'How's he paying for you guys?'" Sanjay laughs. "And my lawyers said, 'We took all his money!'"

Though Sanjay seems miffed by this sentence, it strikes me as shockingly lenient for a kingpin of his magnitude. To give a sense of how money shapes justice, and how arbitrary marijuana-related sentencing can be in America, I offer the example of one of Sanjay's fellow Taft inmates,

Dale Schafer. Schafer and his wife, Mollie Fry, a doctor, opened a medical marijuana dispensary after Fry started using the drug to alleviate complications from chemotherapy. Despite operating the business within California state law, Schafer and Fry had their home raided by the feds, who confiscated thirty-four plants. But the feds insisted that, since they had grown more than one hundred plants cumulatively over five years, their case satisfied the requirements for a mandatory minimum five-year sentence. The upshot: Sanjay, who moved literally *tons* of weed and cocaine with no pretense at following any laws, is serving a year less than Dale Schafer.

I ask Sanjay what it's like in here. He says he wakes up daily at 5:00 A.M., and works out for three hours with a couple of buddies. There are no weights, so they have to devise their own workout. "They took the weights away the last time there was a riot in here."

His prison life doesn't sound too harrowing. After the workout Sanjay cooks lunch with a buddy. He takes a Spanish course three times a week. He works on business ideas for when he gets out. He plays tennis and has two basketball games per week. He loves running, and logs twenty-five miles a week. He looks youthful and vivacious, almost like an athlete in training. I ask how old he is.

"I'm thirty-two," Sanjay says. "With a lot of gray hair, man."

He lets out his big laugh. Considering the tranquil atmosphere in here, it almost seems too loud, like he's overcompensating for the glum surroundings. One of the major privations, Sanjay insists, is that they just banned smoking, which used to be one of the highlights of his day. Taft was the last federal prison to still allow smoking. The problem was, a lot of federal prisoners have long sentences, and prisons don't want to absorb the health care costs due to smoking-related illnesses. But at the same time, he says, cigarettes used to be a huge moneymaker for the prison system.

And by the prison system, he doesn't mean the federal government's Bureau of Prisons. Taft Correctional Institution, like an increasing number of prisons, is privately owned by an "outsourced correctional services" company called the GEO Group. As the War on Drugs led to a swell in prison populations during the early 1980s, overcrowding and rising costs became problematic for local, state, and federal governments. In 1984, the modern privatized prison industry was born, when the Corrections Corporation of America (CCA) was awarded a contract to take over a facility in Tennessee. GEO Group was founded that same year. In 1997, GEO became the first contract recipient from the Bureau of Prisons—for Taft Correctional Institution. Today, GEO has grown to become the second-biggest company in the industry (behind CCA), with over 20,000 employees managing 114 correctional facilities that include 80,000 beds.

While GEO spent $220,000 on lobbying in 2011, the real lobbying power of the prison industrial complex is best exemplified by CCA, which has spent roughly a million dollars per year lobbying Congress for stricter laws since Obama took office in 2008. CCA's lobbying expenditures peaked in 2005, during the second Bush administration, at more than $4 million. That same year, in its annual report, CCA unabashedly expressed fiscal concern at the prospect of fewer incarcerations, writing that "the demand for our facilities and services could be adversely affected by the relaxation of enforcement efforts" as well as "the decriminalization of certain activities that are currently proscribed by our criminal laws." It added that "any changes with respect to drugs and controlled substances or illegal immigration could affect the number of persons arrested, convicted, and sentenced, thereby potentially reducing demand for correctional facilities to house them." Spending millions to maintain and even increase America's prison population strikes me as soulless to the point of ghoulishness. I would think even rabid anti-drug folks might agree.

But private prison corporations like CCA have some allies in the fight to keep packing jails with drug offenders. Among the best-financed opponents of Proposition 19 were California's police unions, which paid nearly $400,000 to a lobbyist named John Lovell to help defeat the measure. Another powerful group is the prison guard unions. In 2008, the California Correctional Peace Officers Association spent over a million bucks to crush a measure that would have reduced sentences and parole times for nonviolent drug offenders.

Sanjay claims it's not just the prison guard unions that are corrupt and avaricious, but the guards themselves.

"If you have money in here, you can get anything . . . from cell phones to . . ." Sanjay leans toward me and lowers his voice. "Pussy."

"You can get pussy in here?" I ask. "How?"

"From the women correction officers. Not that any of them are supermodels. But if you're that hard up, well . . . At first, I was like, no way. But now, some of the female officers are starting to look pretty good!"

Sanjay says his time at Taft has been relatively easy, because he has money. There is a limit to how much inmates can spend at the prison store, but he purchases the accounts of two other prisoners each month, which triples his limit. With all the groceries he gets, he and his (mainly British Columbia–based Asian) buddies have a dinner party every Sunday night.

"I got a guy who does my dishes, for seven dollars and fifty cents a month. I've got a guy I pay for a locker, 'cause I have too much shit. That's another seven dollars and fifty cents a month. And I have a guy who does my laundry for ten bucks a month. Shit is cheap, man! You don't have to lift a finger in here."

Sanjay doesn't even do his own job. He technically works as an orderly, but he pays another inmate to do his job—for seventeen bucks a week, which is his salary. I laugh. "So you just pay this guy what you would otherwise get if you did your job?"

"Yep," he says. "Classic, right?"

I ask why, if he can get laid in an all-male prison, he can't get cigarettes. Sanjay says you can but the consequences aren't worth it, because you lose your "good time." Inmates get fifty-four days off their sentence each year if they don't get into trouble.

"The main problem is all the in-house rats." Sanjay says that, not long ago, he got investigated for assault. An inmate got his ass kicked, and the prison staff group known as Special Investigative Services (SIS) claimed Sanjay financed the hit. That doesn't seem entirely out of character, though he of course denies it.

"SIS can make your life hell," Sanjay explains. "They put me in the shoe for two and a half months."

"What's the shoe?" I ask.

"SHU Special Housing Unit," he says. "It's isolation, basically."

"Is that pretty hellish?"

"I've gotten used to it. I'd had it before. I spend a lot of time reading. It's basically just time by yourself. A *lot* of time by yourself."

He laughs, but in a way that you know it's not that funny. An alarm keeps going off, every fifteen minutes. It adds tension to what is probably the least edgy environment in the prison. That said, just stepping into a place like this—with so many fortifications and so much barbed wire—is distressing for any freedom-loving soul.

"Time slows down in solitary. Then you get out, and it's weird to be so relieved, because you're still in prison. And it's like, 'Woo hoo! I'm out!'"

More strained laughter. That's pretty bleak.

"You have to be really down low about everything around here. There are snitches everywhere. Especially with me, because I'm a minority, so I stick out like a sore thumb."

Sanjay explains that you come to prison with "your jacket," or your prison record, preceding you. People know what you're in for, and if you have money, or violent tendencies, or powerful connections. To keep fellow inmates from exploiting your weak spots, most people stay with their race on the inside. The blacks watch television together. The Latinos play soccer together. The Aryan guys play basketball together. At Taft there are only ten Indians, and they keep it tight. A few of his fellow Indian inmates are from B.C., a couple even from his neighborhood. Three of them are in on cocaine charges. Another one got busted with four hundred kilos of heroin. "This guy's like the Godfather back home."

He says Taft isn't as hardcore as some other prisons, because most of the inmates aren't lifers with nothing to lose. Many of them will be deported after their sentence. It's predominantly Mexicans, Colombians, Jamaicans, some Africans, and some Canadians. One of the best perks,

Sanjay says, after taking a sip of his vanilla coffee, is that prison is a great networking venue.

"The amount of contacts you make in here is just stupid." He smiles. "How else would I get to meet Pablo Escobar's right-hand man?"

CHAPTER THIRTEEN
ACKNOWLEDGING THE DOG

Now that I've got some perspective on the consequences of being a black-market weed distributor, I need a reminder that some people are in the marijuana game for something more meaningful than profit. To that end, I find myself sitting in the living room of a modest home in Orange County, California. A woman who looks too young to be a mother of three—an attractive Latina with a camouflage baseball cap, pigtails, and an orange, weed-themed "Chronic Fatigue" T-shirt—is telling me about the pharmacist whose drugs changed her son's life.

"Kyle Kushman is a grower," she says with pride. "And he's right up there with Ed Rosenthal. He grows veganically, and he just sort of fell into my circle and never left."

Veganic growing, it turns out, is Kushman's signature technique. It basically means no animal products are involved in the growing process—primary among them being poop, as fertilizer. Kushman uses only composted, liquid plant matter to feed his weed. The end result, allegedly, is ultraclean ganja that lacks the impure plant residues created by animal wastes. But Mieko Hester Perez doesn't concern herself with all that; she only cares about the bottom line.

"All I know is this . . ." She flashes the no-nonsense look of a protective mother. "When Joey finished his brownie that Kyle made veganically, all his symptoms were gone."

"And what are the symptoms?" I ask.

"You'll hear him," Mieko says.

On cue, as if they've rehearsed this for my benefit, is an urgent sound, a loud bleat that's not immediately recognizable as originating from a human source.

"YEEEE!"

"Is that him?" I ask.

Mieko nods. "Yeah. Joey has a long history of aggression. He has a long history of behavioral issues. He's a wreck."

To my right, a huge flat-screen TV starts playing the Looney Tunes theme. If I didn't know better, I'd think Mieko is a multimedia genius playing an elaborate prank on me.

"When you talk about autism and severe autism, he fits the bill," Mieko says. "He doesn't talk. He doesn't walk. And he's mad because he can't communicate."

"YEE!"

I bolt upright on the couch. Joey might not be able to communicate verbally, but the kid's got a set of lungs on him.

"YEEEEE!"

"School me a little bit," I say. "How early did you first start noticing symptoms?"

"When I look back, I think it has to do with who I am. I've been in the legal field for over fifteen years. I do legal research. When I realized something was wrong, it was after a cocktail shot he received."

"Cocktail shot?" I ask.

"It's called an MMR shot. Measles, mumps, and rubella. At the time it was legally pushed. But he had some type of allergic reaction."

"YEE!"

"And my conversations with certain doctors," Mieko says. "I realized that the bonding agent for this particular cocktail was a very damaging and toxic concoction."

"DEE! DEEEE!"

"So wait, do you think the shot actually spurred this on him? Like, you think he wasn't autistic before?"

"I have no comment. None. Because the reality of it, is he's here now. And I could beat my head, and go on a Jenny McCarthy rampage . . ."

"DAYYYYEEEE!"

"But it's not gonna be productive for my son," Mieko says.

"Right. But there's something in you . . ."

"There's a lot. I have a very blunt side. I can tell you what happened to my son."

"DAYEE! DAYYEEEEEE! DAYEEEE!"

"That's it," Mieko says. "And there's a few other thousand parents who have the same story."

Now there's barking. In taps a white Pomeranian that looks like someone put a normal-size dog in the dryer. The combination of his barks, Joey's blurts, and the "What's up, docs?" from the TV make for a mind-jangling cacophony.

"And if the government doesn't want to admit to a bad batch of vaccine, well . . ." Mieko shakes her head. "RFK Jr. called it the vaccine cover-up. It's phenomenal."

The controversial link between autism and vaccinations has been boiling for more than a decade now. In 1998, a British doctor named Andrew Wakefield published an article in the medical journal the *Lancet*. It concluded—based on a study of only a dozen kids—that there was a connection between the MMR vaccine and autism. It was later discovered that Wakefield had conflicts of interest, including his own alternative vaccine patent, and ten of the twelve coauthors of the study removed their name from it and published a retraction. Subsequent studies by the Centers for Disease Control and Prevention and the American Academy of Pediatrics, among others, all found no link between the vaccine and autism.

But plenty of parents continued to insist they had empirical evidence of the autism-vaccination link. All it took were some high-profile media moments to keep the controversy raging. In 2005, Robert F. Kennedy, Jr. wrote an expose for *Rolling Stone* and *Salon*, claiming that thimerosal, a mercury-based preservative in certain vaccines, caused autism.[1] In 2008, on the *Oprah Winfrey Show*, actress Jenny McCarthy said that, as her pediatrician was poised to administer the MMR shot to her (now autistic) son, she told him she had a bad feeling. She had heard this was the "autism shot." The doctor dismissed her concerns and administered it anyway. "And soon thereafter—boom—the soul's gone from his eyes," McCarthy told Oprah.

"STAYYYYYEEE!"

Joey's plangent wails startle me every time, but for Mieko, they have almost become background noise. "I think that's one of the reasons I started my foundation," she says. "It's how my grandmother raised me. It's about the community awareness, to be a real citizen in a community."

---

1 In 2011, *Salon* retracted the article, based largely on the research from Seth Mnookin's book, *The Panic Virus*.

There's a knock at the door.

"Come in," Mieko says.

A man peeks his head in. "I'm here to fix your washer and dryer."

Mieko looks at me and smiles. "Time out!"

Mieko and the repairman walk into the utility room, off to my right. I sit on the couch and watch Looney Tunes. Bugs Bunny's talking shit again. The dog barks in what sounds like a Spanish accent, rolling the r's in his "arrrf." I scan the room. The aesthetic is Spanish-tinged and spooky, but in an upbeat way. Above the TV are eight colorful, bejeweled crosses of varying designs and sizes. A sign above the utility room door says, CHAMPIONS ARE MADE WHEN NO ONE IS LOOKING. Beside that is a shelf with framed photos of the family and three skeleton figurines in flamboyant flamenco attire.

I scan farther left to the entryway that must lead to Joey's room. Below a black-and-white print of some sort of skeleton conquistador, I spot a knee. The knee moves into the entryway. There is an arm now, a red shirt, and then a whole kid. He is sitting in Indian position, scooting sideways along the floor like a crab. He gets to the center of the entryway and stops, body angled in my direction, as if to frame himself by way of introduction. He bobs up and down, glances down to his left, shoots me a glance, jerks his head back to the right, and rocks a few times. Then he puts his hands in his lap, sits up perfectly straight, and stares at me. I stare back. I consider saying hello, but it seems like it would come off as condescending, so I say nothing.

This is Joey. I know a bit about him from my research. He is twelve years old and has severe autism. I know that, two years ago, he refused to eat for weeks, until he got down to forty-six pounds. The doctor said he had weeks to live. Mieko's idea to consider cannabis was conceived through pure maternal pragmatism: Weed gives you the munchies, and she had to get Joey to eat. She knew it had increased the appetites of chemotherapy patients. So after some research, Mieko called a dozen doctors. Only one got back to her. He agreed to give her a recommendation. Mieko started feeding Joey pot brownies. And the kid started eating.

Now here he is, all 112 pounds of him, staring at me. With round cheeks, olive skin, and curly black hair, Joey's kind of handsome. There's something magnetic about him. It's more than the tics and sounds. He has a look like he understands something you don't, as if he draws from a deeper reservoir of pain. Plus, his T-shirt is way cooler than mine—red with drippy psychedelic cartoon creatures on it.

The Pomeranian puffball tap dances in, and a teenage girl appears behind Joey. I'm relieved to know how to handle this social interaction.

"Hi," I say. "I'm Ryan."

"Hi," she says.

"What's your name?" I ask.

"Rebecca."

We make small talk. She has a combination of teen girl shyness and the early-onset maturity of someone who regularly deals with adult issues at home. Mieko has mentioned that, if something ever happened to her, Rebecca is "equipped to make legal decisions" regarding Joey. As we talk Joey starts to crab-walk past us, past the television, toward the utility room. It's as if he's irritated that we haven't included him in the conversation.

"I guess he wants to check on the progress with that washing machine," I say.

"Yeah," Rebecca says. "But also there's two other boxes of toys in there."

"Oh. I see."

I'm amazed at how fast Joey gets around with this seated slide technique. Within a minute he's in the utility room. Rebecca and I follow him. The repairman is telling Mieko she needs to go out and buy an extension for the washer's drain hose. In a vain attempt to seem manly, I ask what size the hose should be, or whether they're all the same.

"Yeah, are they standard?" Mieko asks.

"The width is standard," the repairman says. "The length is not."

"I say that about all my men," Mieko says.

I start cackling. The repairman either doesn't get it, or doesn't think it's funny. Rebecca and I step inside and watch Joey. He's extracting toys from a box and placing them around himself on the floor.

"He has a circle of trust, I guess," says Rebecca.

This strikes me as a potentially profound insight. "What does that mean, circle of trust?" I ask.

"He's putting the toys in a circle around him."

"Oh. I see. He puts them in a circle."

"Circle of trust," she says.

She says she spends a lot of time with Joey. He looks up from his circle of trust and belts out something incomprehensible at his sister. Like Mieko she seems to be an "autism whisperer," at least when it comes to her brother. I'm baffled.

"Is he talking to you?" I ask.

"Yeah," she says. "He's saying, 'Get my shit.'"

*   *   *

I spend the rest of the day with Mieko, doing what a single mother of three does: errands. Much of it is spent driving around in her bright yellow Hummer. Mieko explains that Joey actually picked this vehicle out. By which she means: When they arrived at the car lot, he got into this Hummer and wouldn't get out.

Mieko tells me her story in fragments, punctuated by tasks. En route to the gas station, I learn that she's the co-owner of a corporate compliance firm. I learn that there are several law enforcement officers in her family, including an uncle who's an LAPD narcotics captain. I'm surprised to discover she is Republican, just as, while interviewing Mieko on *Fox & Friends*, Steve Doocy was surprised to hear she was pro-life. I find out she had Rebecca and Joey at twenty-five, "that age where you think you want to get married but actually don't." I learn that their father is no longer a part of their life, and that she got sole legal custody of both kids, which is no small feat in California.

While grabbing lunch at one of those sushi-on-a-conveyor-belt restaurants, I get Joey's story. Mieko speaks of him in terms of before and after cannabis. Before the cannabis, Joey didn't eat. Now he does. Before, he never engaged people, not even his siblings. Now he does. He used to not be affected by music. But one day, after munching on a marijuana edible, he moved in rhythm to music for the first time, which brought Mieko to tears. Now he watches TV. He smiles. And in a breakthrough no one could have predicted, he *acknowledges the dog*. Their old dog, a pit bull, had no idea what to do with Joey, because he was neither afraid nor affectionate. Now Joey smiles when the Pomeranian puffball nestles into his lap.

Before the cannabis Joey had extreme anger issues. He threw toys around the house until there was broken glass everywhere. One day at school, he started pulling his teacher's hair, screaming and yelling, until they had to stage an emergency intervention and escort him out of the building. Before the cannabis Joey's teachers had a behavioral plan set in place for the inevitability of his outbursts. Last year, a year into his medicinal use of marijuana, they removed that behavioral plan.

On the way to Home Depot, Mieko takes a moment to break some heavy news: Joey was recently diagnosed with Duchenne muscular dystrophy, which is terminal. The condition is characterized by rapid muscle deterioration, difficulty walking and breathing, and ultimately, death. Because the combination of severe autism and Duchenne muscular dystrophy is rare, some of the best doctors in the country have volunteered to take on Joey's case. Mieko says some of the doctors claim marijuana has likely been helping his symptoms with both diagnoses. But Joey can no longer feed himself, and most victims die of cardiac or respiratory failure before the age of twenty. After hearing the diagnosis, Mieko says she spent thirty-seven days in a row at home. Her son is living on borrowed time.

*   *   *

Back at Mieko's place, after a full day of listening while traversing Orange County, I pull off the highlight of my day: Joey smiles at me. I don't know why he does it. But I smile at him from the couch and try to transmit positive energy in his direction, and I sense that he reflects that energy back at me.

"I got a smile out of him," I tell Rebecca. "It's gotta be interesting, some of the things that intrigue him."

"Yeah," Rebecca says. "Right now, it's all about the cards, and my phone charger."

"DEE!" Joey says. "Deh. DEH!"

Mieko walks into the room. "We go places, and he won't let go of my credit cards. And he won't lose them . . . Everybody's panicking, and I'm like, 'Dude. He's not letting them go.'"

Mieko sees that Joey is distressed. He's making heavy jerks now and seems agitated.

"What's up?" she asks. "Where do you wanna go?"

"DEEEEE! DEEEEE!"

"He wants my glasses," Mieko says.

"How can you tell from what he says?" I ask.

"I don't know," Mieko says.

"He's sort of predictable," Rebecca chimes in.

"He is?" I ask. "Maybe for you guys. Not for me."

"Joey, do you want this?" Mieko asks. "No, you want glasses."

"DEEEE! DIIIYUUUUH!"

"Rebecca, do you have some glasses that you could give him?"

"Uhh," says Rebecca.

Mieko leans down into Joey. "Do you want some water?"

"*DEEEEEEEE!*"

Even I'm perceptive enough to understand that Joey's level of distress is directly proportional to the pitch and volume of his yawps. It must be maddening to know exactly what you want but be incapable of communicating it.

"What else, Joey?" Mieko asks. "What else do you see?"

Joey is scooting frantically across the floor now.

"He's moving fast," I say. "He's gonna come grab . . . something."

Trying to determine what Joey wants at any given moment is a telling microcosm for the bewilderment doctors seem to feel in the face of battling autism. As Mieko says, "There's not a doctor to this day that's an autism expert." No one really understands what the hell is happening in the autistic brain, and the doctors who have gotten closest still don't know what to do about it. The best resource is probably whoever spends the most time with a specific autistic person. It's all trial and error, like: Last time he acted like this, he wanted my keys. Or: When I gave him Ritalin, he got aggressive and anti-social. Or: When I gave him a pot brownie, he mellowed out and became more engaging. Mieko says her doctor admits that she gets her most perspicacious insights from parents like Mieko, which she in turn shares with others at conferences.

This universal ignorance about the disease seems justification enough for Mieko's organization, The Unconventional Foundation for Autism (UF4A), which promotes treatments like aquatic therapy. She says the organization's original purpose was to create a resource for frustrated parents of autistic kids. And it has worked; Mieko gets hundreds of emails per month. Having worked in law offices for fifteen years, her main contribution is teaching parents how to write persuasive letters to politicians, doctors, and school officials in non-compassionate states. Mieko kept Joey's secret meds to herself for a year, compiling documentation and before-and-after photos, before she finally decided to go public on a San Francisco news show.

"But the everyday parent who doesn't have the arsenal I have, they need to be discreet," she says. "It's a game where you could lose your child, through child protective services, or through not doing what I did. This is America. But this isn't that free world. So chill out. Play the game. Or risk losing your family."

"GOO-GUH-DEE," Joey says. "GOO-GUH. GOO-GUH-DOO."

"That's considered stimming," Mieko explains. "It's when he has a lot of stimulation. When he's stimming, that's sensory overload."

Stimming is short for the self-stimulatory behaviors such as flapping, rocking, spinning, or repeating sounds. Almost all autistic people stim, but then so do most non-autistic people. If you've ever tapped your fingers, paced, or bitten your nails, that's stimming. Like the rest of us, autistic people stim to manage anxiety, fear, or anger, and to handle overwhelming sensory input—too much noise or light, for example.

"DEEE! DEEEEE!"

"I'll give him a granola bar," Mieko says. "The funny part about these granola bars is . . ."

She's interrupted by piercing shrieks. "DEEEE! DAYYYYY! DOE!"

Mieko walks off into the kitchen and comes back with a granola bar.

"Joe. Open. Hey."

"DAY!"

"Hey. Joe. Joe. Hey, buddy. You're just gonna follow Rebecca. Your toys are in there. Open. Joey."

After cajoling Joey into taking a bite, Mieko looks over at me. "These granola bars are gluten-free and casein-free, with raisins, almonds. They're made by someone in Chicago."

Though Mieko is refreshingly forthcoming about her situation, there are still plenty of secrets. I have gleaned that *High Times* writer and grower Kyle Kushman, along with his collaborator Shiloh Massive, are among her core cannabis growers. But they are part of a larger collective that includes a well-known but unmentionable European grower, as well as an anonymous baker from Chicago, who uses the raw buds to bake edibles that won't harm Joey's delicate system. Mieko won't comment on how the marijuana is shipped or transported to the baker in Chicago. And though Mieko claims Joey only takes his medicine—usually in the form of brownies, cookies, or granola bars—once or twice a week, I suspect from our conversations that he gets doses more frequently than that.

"You're getting the best of the best," I say. "I don't know if I can ask, but does the baker send the granola bars? How does he get them here?"

"I can't even tell you that."

Mieko is trying to feed Joey, but his resistance is fierce. If Joey is cognizant that these snacks contain helpful medicine, he's not letting on.

"DEEEE! DAYYYYY! DOE!"

"Joe," she says, leaning over with the granola bar near his mouth. "Open. Hey."

He reluctantly accepts a bite from a cannabis treat that weed connoisseurs would pay top dollar for. One obvious benefit of Mieko's status—which she clearly relishes—is being able to rub shoulders with the semi-celebrities of the cannabis world, and even the world at large. There are photos in the house of her with Lester Grinspoon, Ed Rosenthal, and Snoop Dogg. She once did an interview with pro-pot talk-show veteran (and multiple sclerosis patient) Montel Williams. When she went on *Good Morning America* to talk about Joey, she says Diane Sawyer and Robin Roberts pulled her to the side before the interview for a "girl talk." One element of this phenomenon is the fifteen-minutes-of-fame celebrity fascination that now often accompanies media attention. On the other side is all the serendipitous ways in which the world aligns itself with your plight when you have the courage to take that plight public.

"All the resources I have, I don't even need to go to the library anymore," Mieko says. "I just pick up the phone and call Ed Rosenthal. I just need to speak to Jorge Cervantes. Oh, Dr. Shackelford? I have his cell number."

"That's amazing."

"And Dr. Melamede. Our conversations with Dr. Melamede are hilarious."

I nod and smile. I've chatted with the eccentric Dr. Robert Melamede, a former biology professor and current CEO of Cannabis Science, Inc., who claims that cannabinoids kill cancer cells. Melamede is among a handful of cannabis-as-cancer-cure promoters, along with Rick Simpson, a man from Nova Scotia who claims his hemp oil medicine cured his own cancer and that of many others.[2]

On the flip side of Mieko's elite squad of consultants and benefactors, the publicity has also led to some paranoia. She describes what she calls "a *Pelican Brief* moment," referring to the John Grisham legal thriller and the movie from which it was adapted. Apparently, at the same Starbucks where we just got lattes, Mieko once conducted an interview during which a woman seated nearby kept watching her. Before she left the woman handed Mieko a letter. It contained the name of a doctor who agreed with

---

2 In June of 2012, Tommy Chong will reveal that he has prostate cancer, and that he started experiencing symptoms while incarcerated at Taft Correctional Institution. He claims to be using hemp oil as part of his treatment.

her cannabis-autism views, but who was afraid to come out on the subject. This strikes me as a positive development—as opposed to the murderous thugs who pursued Julia Roberts in the movie—but Mieko seems freaked out that this woman knew where she was. She says she has started Facebook-ing her location, in case something happens to her. She jokes that she might need more life insurance, adding that her lawyer is in a good position to keep up her fight if she's not around.

"Because I know what I'm doing is risky," she says. "I'm leading a revolution. I know what I'm doing is very threatening to certain people and certain agencies. But what about the kids?"

Her ultimate goal is to get autism placed on the list of commissions for current compassion bills, in states with medical marijuana laws.

"This kid, he's given me a life," Mieko says.

"That's right, Joey," I say, trying to include him.

"How does one kid who doesn't even speak make such a huge impact? His voice is the loudest in the cannabis movement right now, when it comes to legitimizing it for medical purposes."

"Speaking of his voice, do you *really* understand the sounds that he makes?"

Mieko explains that it's not always easy, but he has breakthroughs, like when he started saying *mom*. She claims it happened nine months into his cannabis treatments. The last time she had heard her son call her "mom" was when he was eighteen months old, before his last set of immunizations. But because cannabis "blocks his sensories," she claims, Joey is able to be almost social, and he called Mieko *mom*.

"That's it, for me. That's all I ever wanted. Everything else after that is icing on the cake. And that's all these other parents want. We know that we have children diagnosed with autism. We don't expect for him to get up and start walking, and have a regular life. We only want the little things. Did he smile today?"

"He did smile," I say.

"Okay," Mieko says. "Then I'm good."

CHAPTER FOURTEEN
IT'S ALL HAPPENING

In the end, my field trip doesn't redirect me to the path of righteousness. The cautionary tale of my prison visit has been somewhat offset by my experience with an autistic medical marijuana patient and his warrior-activist mother. On the return trip to The Hill, the combined effect of these visits fills me with a vague desire to get more personally involved in the marijuana game, to do something bold, something that makes a statement.

And now, just a few days later, Sanjay and Joey already feel light-years away. I find myself completely absorbed in the Buddha Cheese Experience. It involves constant motion and a distorted sense of time, for which a passed joint is the perfect accompaniment. In the three days since I returned from Taft Correctional Institution, we have driven over a thousand miles through ten counties. We have had vegan lunch at a peacock-filled monastery and an extravagant dinner in one of Napa Valley's finest restaurants. We have shipped six pounds of weed through the U.S. mail[1] and bought five more pounds in a Whole Foods parking lot from a woman zonked on Ecstasy. We have partied like Vikings in Sebastopol. We have nearly died in Buddha Cheese's monster truck when all but one lug nut was shaved off the front right tire, and been forced to rent a car. We have picked up girls at night and dropped them off at their vineyard bungalows in the morning. We have awakened at 4:00 A.M. in an unfamiliar living room and hitchhiked to our hotel by bribing a newspaper deliverywoman with a bag of herb. We have not only our own theme song,[2] but an actual theme—"It's all happening!"— which is Buddha Cheese's response to all questions about plans or destinations.

Now we are four hours into our most brazen mission yet. We are driving to Humboldt County, where Buddha Cheese plans to purchase dozens of pounds of marijuana. Though this has not been confirmed verbally, it seems to be understood that I will be the one to transport this contraband across the country. I am procrastinating confronting this

---

1   For the sender's address, we created a fictional name at a real coffeehouse, so if the package gets returned, some barista will get the most confusing gift of his life.

2   "I Got 5 on It," by the Oakland-based rap duo Luniz. I have discovered, almost two decades after the song came out, that the chorus means *I'll go halfsies on a dimebag of weed.*

reality in the shallow hope that some happenstance on our journey will simplify my decision.

All we see from the rental car is tree trunks the size of Volkswagens, which only begin to suggest what lies above. Riding shotgun is a new member of our band of misfits, B-Nice, a handsome if somewhat reptilian-looking Southern gentleman whose chosen trade is "wine broker," but who claims he's been homeless for nine months and was thus recruited by The Mikey to come learn the ganja game.

"Says here, the world's tallest tree," B-Nice says, squinting at his iPhone, "is a three-hundred-and-eighty-foot redwood in Humboldt known as 'Hyperion.'"

All three counties in the Emerald Triangle—Mendocino, Trinity, and Humboldt—have sizable grower populations. But for decades, long before the passage of Prop 215 advanced the weed-growing trend across California, the word *Humboldt* has been synonymous with high-grade cannabis cultivation in America. In college I remember splurging on some "Humboldt herb" (though it was probably grown in a Hartford basement), and thinking I had purchased the ganja equivalent of Jamaican Blue Mountain coffee. While cannabis-filled counties like Lake and Mendocino are closer to civilization, Humboldt's remoteness lends it the myth of a wild frontier where weed alone is king: Marijuana agriculture is among the only viable industries, and the growers there have never been, and never will be, stopped.

In the late sixties, a migration of countercultural types known as "back-to-the-landers" began to reach as far north as Humboldt, where land was cheap. Because of its remoteness and ideal growing climate, many of these "hippie-billies" began cultivating marijuana to support their self-sustaining lifestyle and purchase their land. Before long, as industries like timber and fishing began to dissipate, marijuana agriculture became the focus of the local economy.

These days, despite DEA helicopter swarms during the harvest months, most growers within the Humboldt County legal limits will rarely be harassed by local or federal officials. But there are plenty of ambitious megagrowers who have come to hide behind the Redwood Curtain, and their paranoia is easily confirmed. A regional radio station, KMUD, has been known to air warnings regarding the whereabouts of law enforcement on their way to raid marijuana gardens. Another common enemy of local growers is thieves, and Humboldt growers have gained a reputation for guarding their crops by whatever means necessary.[3]

I've been nursing the mental image of a secluded farm filled with dogs and guns, so I'm dismayed when we pull into an unremarkable middle-class neighborhood just outside Eureka. But the guy who answers the door doesn't disappoint. He's got a mop of hair and a beard so unkempt it looks unintentional, like he just keeps forgetting to buy a razor.

The house is mid-sized, nicely furnished, decorated with aboriginal art and photos of the bearded guy (who I'll call Jim) from his travels abroad. Buddha Cheese doesn't introduce me and B-Nice, and Jim barely acknowledges our presence. He says he just bought forty 400–watt bulbs for nurturing his plants in the vegetative state, which suggests he's planning a considerable grow.

"Forty of 'em!" Mikey laughs. "What are you using for a generator? The big military generator?"

"Yeah."

They chatter about lights, grow stores, greenhouses. As with any business transaction, it's poor form to immediately launch into the details of the deal. I sense they're not even listening to each other, just pushing toward the inevitable, and putting on a show for me and B-Nice.

"My neighbor has like a hundred-foot greenhouse," Mikey says. "And they have eighty lights in there now."

"Really?"

"Dude, at night, it's ridiculous," Mikey says. "From miles away you can just see this fucking glow."

After a pronounced pause, there is a sudden, tacit understanding that they're ready to do business. Jim pops off the couch. They walk away from

3 Many of these tensions faced by local growers are broached in the 2008 movie *Humboldt County*.

us, into the kitchen, where they speak in whispers. Jim comes back out and drops an industrial garbage bag on the floor.

"That's all Mr. Nice," he says.

"Niiiice," says Mikey. He breaks apart a bud and does the sniff test. "Suh-weeet!"

Jim brings out more bags—some Green Crack, Snowcap, and assorted Kushes. It's an assortment of outdoor weed so exceptional you could fool unknowing buyers into thinking it was indoor. I've noticed Buddha Cheese adopts the verbal tics of whomever he's negotiating with; in this case, that means more swearing and accentuating his chill side.

"And what about those shitty ones you mentioned?" he asks. "Don't know if you wanna sell those . . ."

"Oh yeah, sure!" Jim says. "Where are they?" He comes back with another six pounds, which on close inspection are a far cry from what many people would consider shitty weed.

They agree on $800 per pound. Buddha Cheese probes for information about how Jim runs his grows. He says he pays grow managers $50,000 a year, and trimmers about $200 a day. "A lot of people say they don't pay that much for trimmers anymore. Like one fifty. I don't know. I don't see trimmers wanting to work for that."

"You get Mexicans that will do it for like a hundred," says Mikey. "But you're probably gonna get robbed too."

They talk about the recent weeklong road closings up here, because of mudslides. Jim says buyers from the Bay Area were freaking out because they couldn't get product. The infrastructure in Humboldt County is notorious—potholes and mudslides are the norm, and 4x4 trucks are an essential investment for locals. Some blame the infrastructure issues on the lack of tax revenue. Most growers only pay taxes on a small percentage of their earnings (if at all), and there are rumors about offshore accounts and vast cash stashes in yards, attics, and basements.

With all the goods tallied, B-Nice and I grab the two Santa Claus–sized bags of weed and head for the door. Feeling the heft of the bag against my shoulder makes my pulse throb at the thought of driving all of this. We toss them in the trunk and salute to Jim, who seems noticeably calmer than when we arrived. Buddha Cheese tosses me the keys. I infer that driving back to The Hill will be a test to see if I can handle the pressure of transporting, but it could just be a matter of Mikey's laziness.

"Okay, what are we doing right now, guys?" Mikey says, as soon as the door closes. "We're going across the 299 to . . . we're going to fucking . . . Tahoe."

"We're going to Tahoe," I say. "We're going skiing. Can you ski this time of year?"

"Yeah, totally."

"Because we wanna go skiing," I say.

"Yeah, we're going skiing," Buddha Cheese says. "I snowboard too, so I'm not sure what I'm gonna do. I'll probably rent though . . . bleh bleh bleh."

We bust out laughing at his improvised pre-enactment.

"We're definitely renting something," B-Nice says. "Because we don't have any equipment with us."

"Right. Maybe we're just coming from the coast. We took the highway up from Napa. We rented a car in Napa . . . "

"Saw the redwoods," I say.

"Saw the redwoods," B-Nice adds. "Had lunch in Humboldt."

"Okay, that will work," says Mikey. "Let's just get in as much driving as we can."

Mikey taps his fingers against the dashboard. "People think the world of drug dealing is all crazy and paranoid. But that was pretty easy, right? Easy peasy."

*   *   *

In typical impulsive Buddha Cheese fashion, he decided immediately upon our return to The Hill that he would be leaving the next day, to go hang out with The Panamanian Poledancer again. Now we are eating lunch at a restaurant in Sacramento, two hours before his plane is set to depart. He turns to me.

"So, you ready for this?"

"For what?" I ask.

"To drive what I got yesterday across the country."

"Really?"

"Yep. I've already got a buyer. He's anxious to get the stuff, as soon as possible. I told Bull, Chester, and B-Nice to drop all other tasks and start vacuum-sealing tomorrow."

I don't immediately respond. Having been wrapped up in Buddha Cheese's world—or Ganja Land, as he calls it—for several weeks, it's hard not to absorb his nonchalance regarding all things marijuana. And I must admit that the six-hour drive back from Humboldt was relatively breezy.

But this would be a *forty*-six-hour drive. And I would be alone. The research I've done isn't that comforting. Most of the articles mentioning marijuana transport involve the exact route I would have to take, unless I want to add twenty hours to the trip and brave country roads, which doubles the likelihood of incidents. One article specifically focuses on I-80, where Utah police officers have been trained to "sniff out" transporters by "gauging their mannerisms" and "looking for inconsistencies in their stories."

Spooked by my prison visit, I checked out the potential fines and sentences for each state I would pass through. The fines would range from $1,000 to a mind-boggling $25,000. The shortest possible sentence—in both Iowa and my home state of Indiana—would be six months. The highest sentence would be Illinois—up to thirty years. The scariest state, though, would be Ohio, where I would get a state *mandatory minimum* sentence of eight years—meaning, the judge would have no choice but to give me eight years.

Jesus. Eight fucking years. My friends and family would be shocked and beyond disappointed. And because I'm not rich like Sanjay, my sentence would probably be served in what they call in the movie *Office Space* a "federal pound-me-in-the-ass prison." Steel bars, shared cells, tattooed sociopaths, sodomy. The misery would be unimaginable. And I have never even sold a bag of weed before. My only marijuana charge was the time

I got caught smoking a bowl in Central Park in 2000, and all they did was take me to jail for a few hours. No fine, no record. If I got caught doing this I could easily be in my mid-forties by the time I got out of the lockup. And I would be an ex-con for the rest of my life.

And yet I have basically known it would come to this. Whatever moral qualms and trepidation I once held about the reckless nature of this journey have all but dissolved in the face of Buddha Cheese's unquestioning confidence that *this is what's happening next*. My anxiety has been replaced by a sense of purpose. I have begun to rationalize the assignment as one of redemption, through which debts will be relieved and the absurd hypocrisies of America's marijuana laws will be subverted. What on paper would have to be considered a rash—if not utterly stupid—course of action has begun to seem like the next logical step, requiring equal parts stoicism and courage.

"Where would I be driving to?" I ask.

"Near Boston."

"How much would I get?"

Buddha Cheese explains his fee policy but says he would give me a little extra. How nice it would be just to not get those badgering phone calls from creditors. I'm confident I can drive safely and cautiously, but you never know what could happen. I know the right answer is *hell no* just as clearly as I know what I'm about to say.

"Okay," I say. "I'm in."

*   *   *

It's April 20th, aka 4/20, the international holiday for celebrating marijuana freedom. On the Colorado University campus in Boulder, a swirling sea of stoned humanity—more than twenty-five thousand people—are passing joints and playing didgeridoos and coughing and hula-hooping and generally turning Norlin Quad into an adult playground.[4] One innovative

4 In 2012, CU officials will effectively shut down the Boulder 420 festivities, closing off Norlin Quad entirely and prohibiting nonstudents from entering the campus.

student has created a hollowed-out watermelon pocked with burning blunts, to be inhaled all at once through a carved-out hole. Forty minutes away, in Denver's Civic Center Park, bare-chested women are having their breasts painted with marijuana leaves while bands play to a crowd of thousands. Fifteen hundred miles away, ten thousand ganja enthusiasts have clogged the streets in front of Vancouver Art Gallery and are lighting up simultaneously to the rhythmic wails of Bob Marley's "Redemption Song." Almost five thousand miles away, at 420 London, thousands of Brits are creating a canopy of smoke that drifts up in clumps above Hyde Park. Weed-centric rallies are taking place all over the planet, some with fiery political rhetoric about the oppressive laws, and all with the more apolitical focus on getting blazed.

I would love to be at any one of them. Instead, I'm at Walmart, checking items off my list for my cross-country journey.

1. New vacuum sealer
2. 20 boxes of vacuum-seal bags (at least)
3. 3 big-ass suitcases
4. Neck support pillow
5. Lumbar support
6. Sharpie marker
7. Packing material

For anyone hip to this sort of thing, the contents of my shopping cart are a dead giveaway to what I've got planned. I feel like I should be wearing a ski mask. After some mental calculations, I drop the entire vacuum-seal display into my cart. As I'm counting the packages, a matronly looking employee walks up.

"What you need, honey? More of them vacuum bags?"

"I think so, yes."

"How many?"

"How many you got?" I ask.

"I'll check the back for you."

After a few minutes, she returns with a dozen more packages. I toss them in the cart next to the luggage. "I expect you've got a lot of vacuum-sealing to do," she says, without any noticeable hint of suspicion.

In the parking lot, while I'm stuffing the loot in the trunk, I notice a young goateed guy getting out of a white truck. Buddha Cheese says all the heads around here have white trucks. Whether it's because they arouse the least suspicion, or because white vehicles have the lowest percentage of accidents statistically, at this point there are so many white trucks around that they have become anonymous by sheer volume.

Sure enough, the goateed guy smirks at me and B-Nice as he walks by. "Hey, you guys need something to put in those vacuum bags?" he asks.

I flash him a big grin. He smiles back.

"Naw man, we're all set," I say. "Thanks, though, and good luck."

*　　　　　*　　　　　*

At the local library, I go to the far end of the computer area and tilt the screen so that it's not visible to anyone behind me. One article on a weed-related website, titled "How to Deal with Police," is particularly helpful. It says that if a cop has a reasonable suspicion that you "have, are engaged in, or are about to engage in criminal activity, they can detain you." A hunch is not considered reasonable suspicion. The officer must have specific, articulable facts regarding your suspiciousness, like, *The car smelled like a reggae concert,* or *he was so nervous his hand was shaking.*

It says there are five places where your presence alone constitutes probable cause for a search: international borders, concerts, sports arenas, someone else's private property, and airports. It advises not to answer any incriminating questions—better to invoke your Fourth, Fifth, or Sixth Amendment rights. If asked to step out of the vehicle, lock your door and roll up your window before stepping out. And the Golden Rule: Don't confess to any wrongdoing or consent to a search. The theme is: do only what you're told, and say as little as possible. And if they turn up the heat, stop talking entirely and lawyer up.

Back at the house, we spend the rest of the night counting loot and vacuum-sealing bags. Chester and Bull start by cutting bags, which B-Nice and I then fill and seal, assembly-line style.

"My mom just texted me to say Happy 4/20," Chester says.

"Your mother-son relationship is different than mine," I say.

Roxanne gives me a lesson in vacuum sealing. I explain that Mikey already taught me, but she insists. The hardest part is transferring the weed from the turkey bags into the vacuum bags. There's a lot of shaking and manipulating, because the vacuum bag opening is so narrow. If the turkey bags get too squirmy, little green balls of goodness spill over the sides and scatter like tumbleweeds. Roxanne shows me her preferred method of transference and stresses that if any buds spill, they must not, under any circumstances, be scooped but instead picked up individually, in a vertical fashion, to minimize exposure to debris. I appreciate the advice at first, but after a while I hear myself thinking, *This ain't open-heart surgery, sugar pop.*

"You gotta get them even, fluff the bottom, like this," she says, and then, "You've got to really crunch down on the bag, so it's compact."

"Mikey said not to do that too much, because it damages the product," I say. "I mean, we don't have to get them *too* compact. It's not like I'm squeezing them into a hollowed-out car door."

Roxanne says she was taught all this by some crazy Slovenians, who had lots of experience and were "totally hardcore." I decide not to mention what Mikey told me about these guys, whom he called "fucking morons." Apparently, they got arrested while transporting, because they were speeding and in a minivan, so the goods weren't even in a trunk. Totally hardcore.

Bull and Chester go outside to smoke a celebratory 4/20 joint; I'm too jittery and on-task to join them. It strikes me that one of the consequences of getting knee-deep into America's illicit marijuana underworld is that being high loses some of its luster. I am understandably tense about this drive, and I just want to get this prep work over with. Packaging pot in this manner is monotonous, but there is something about the ritual that soothes my nerves. Dump, shake, clamp, vacuum, seal, label. Having taken Buddha

Cheese to the airport, I feel like my work here is almost done, and I would be wise to exit stage left. There's no reason to push my luck out here in Ganja Land; the next episode could be the one where we lose that final lug nut . . . or Bull runs *me* over.

"Do you know who Mr. Nice was?" I ask, as I'm labeling a bag *Herr Doktor Nice.*

"No," B-Nice says.

"He was England's biggest cannabis smuggler."

I tell him the story of Howard Marks, the Oxford-educated Welshman who became Britain's most wanted man. Marks was doing what Buddha Cheese does, just on a much grander scale—with boats in international waters carrying up to thirty tons of weed. During the mid-eighties, Marks had forty-three aliases and eighty-nine phone lines. He owned twenty-five companies—both shell and legitimate—that traded internationally. His most famous alias was Donald Nice.

After serving a seven-year prison sentence in Terre Haute, Indiana, Marks wrote *Mr. Nice,* one of the most entertaining books I've read about the marijuana trade. He goes from meeting Pakistani smugglers in Hong Kong luxury hotels to partying with prostitutes in Bangkok to arguing with IRA madmen in rural Ireland, all within a matter of pages. He makes contact with the CIA and the Mafia, and is briefly employed by the same British spy network that James Bond made famous, MI6. He conjures witty banter from stoned conversations he had twenty years prior, which—considering he claims to have smoked twenty joints a day—couldn't possibly be remembered. And he describes involvement in drug networks that seem fictional but, under the circumstances, were likely true, such as: "Between 1975 and 1978, twenty-four loads totaling 55,000 pounds of marijuana had been successfully imported through John F. Kennedy Aiport, New York. They had involved the Mafia, the Yakuza, the Brotherhood of Eternal Love, the Thai army, the Palestine Liberation Organization, the Pakistani armed forces, Nepalese monks, and other individuals from all walks of life. The total profit made by all concerned was $48,000,000."

After finishing the packing, I go outside to smoke a cigarette. Roxanne follows me out and lays out a laundry list of all the things that could go wrong on my drive. I have to always check my turn signals and lights, she says, because that's the excuse cops often use to set up probable cause. Oh, and the biggest tip-off is the trunk riding low. There is no way to keep that from happening. It's gravity; what can you do? It would be best if I had a girl with me, because that looks like legitimate travel. Roxanne is about to tell me the riveting tale of how the Slovenians got caught, when I abruptly cut her off.

"I don't want to hear this," I say. "You're putting bad mojo out into the universe for me. If you can't come with positive vibes, I would prefer you don't talk to me at all."

*   *   *

By 10:00 A.M. the next morning, the trunk is packed to the brim and doesn't seem to be riding low. My luggage is in the backseat; there's nothing I can do about that. I have three packs of American Spirit cigarettes and two large bottles of water. Lumbar support is in place. I'm ready to go.

The only person around for the send-off is B-Nice. He stayed up late packing and drinking and taking faux-gangster photos of us next to the cargo. He walks outside as I'm inspecting the car.

"This is for you, papi."

He holds out his hand. In it lies a quartz crystal the size of my pinkie toe.

"For good luck," he says. "Not that you'll need it. But just in case, I'd recommend keeping that in your pocket, or in the car, for the whole drive."

"Thank you, brother," I say, sincerely touched by the gesture.

"Of course. Keep me posted on your progress."

"I will. I took your and everyone else's number off my phone's contact list, but I wrote them down on a little sheet of paper so I can stay in touch."

"Cool, cool."

"All right then. I guess I'm ready."

"I guess you are. Don't think too much. It's just a nice, long scenic drive."

"Right," I say. "Emphasis on *long*."

We hug.

"All right then," he says. "Godspeed, soldier."

CHAPTER FIFTEEN
DRIVEN MAD

After a pleasant evening's drive last night through Wyoming and Nebraska, today's segment has been pure torment. Just a few hours ago, I suffered through that mind-bending stalking incident with the Nebraska state trooper. After a steak-and-beer lunch, I called my sister. She was having a cheerful Easter dinner with her family, but she seemed to detect the tension in my voice. I explained that I was in Nebraska, driving cross-country from California, and I was worried. I would love to see her and the kids, but I also understood if it would be best to stay in a hotel. She was bewildered by my ambiguity but insisted I drive straight to their home. After that I called my ex in hopes of some kind words from a familiar voice, but that quickly devolved into an argument.

I'm in a foul mood. After having I-80 as my constant companion for more than eighteen hundred miles, we finally parted ways an hour back in Davenport, Iowa. I'm just a couple of hours from my sister's place—much-needed sanctuary and normalcy—when I realize I have to pee, immediately. It's late and dark out, so I've been knocking down Poland Spring and Red Bull and American Spirits, trying to stay alert. But my body is all poison and my bladder is bulging and I'm kind of losing my shit.

For the past few hours it's just been me and trucks—18-wheelers, those goddamned rumbling monsters, which I swear have been using their CBs to gang up on me: flashing their brights for no apparent reason, driving next to each other at the same speed for minutes on end, clogging both lanes and then accelerating when I finally get the chance to pass. As if it's not stressful enough to pass a semi at night when you've got a trunk worth a few hundred thousand dollars.

I record a voice note on my phone, a tirade against trucks. Voice notes have been one of my methods of sanity preservation during the long drive, but there are signs that it's starting to have the opposite effect. Needing to let off some steam, both literally and figuratively, I decide to exit. The last sign said something about Ronald Reagan's hometown so I google it and put it into the GPS. Tampico, Illinois, is fifteen minutes away.

I can't pass up the opportunity to piss on Reagan's birthplace. I feel like I can justify this admittedly juvenile act because, as part of his War on Drugs, the Reagan administration pissed all over federal laws, not to mention the civil liberties of Americans. They did this, first of all, by unabashedly ignoring the Posse Comitatus Act, an 1878 law that forbids U.S. armed forces from engaging in domestic law enforcement. In 1982, Reagan had the law redrafted to meet his needs. Recognizing the inability of civilian law enforcement agencies to curb drug smuggling into the United States by air and sea, Reagan directed the Department of Defense to use naval and air assets to reach beyond American borders.

With help from the Supreme Court, which leaned conservative by his second term largely due to his own appointments, President Reagan also had a hand in pissing on the Constitution. In the 1988 case *Illinois v. Gates*, the Supreme Court overturned the judgments of three separate Illinois courts, which had all ruled that a judge cannot issue a search warrant based on an uncorroborated anonymous tip.[1] This ruling created broad new exceptions to the Fourth Amendment, which forbids unreasonable searches, as well as the Sixth Amendment—the right to confront one's accusers.

But these political acts paled in comparison to the Reagan administration's real anti-drug legacy: packing American prisons with nonviolent offenders. During his eight years in office, Reagan passed a variety of bills delineating new drug crimes, lengthening prison sentences, and allowing property seizures. First-time marijuana offenders could receive a sentence ranging from probation to life imprisonment, as well as the forfeiture of their property and assets. Owning a roach clip or rolling papers became an offense. In the wake of the cocaine overdose of basketball star Len Bias, Reagan passed the Anti-Drug Abuse Act of 1986. It called for twenty-nine new mandatory minimum sentences for drug violations, including those involving marijuana. (Before 1986, there had only been fifty-five mandatory minimum sentences handed down in U.S. history.) The bill also effectively eliminated parole in the federal system, ensuring that prisoners would serve at least 85 percent of their sentences. Two years later the Anti-Drug Abuse Act of 1988, which Reagan called a "new sword and shield" in the drug war, established a federal death penalty for "drug kingpins."

---

1 In this case the search was fruitful, to the tune of 350 pounds of marijuana. But that's not the point.

The primary effect of all this legislation was a massive surge in the American prison population. In 1970, 16 percent of federal prisoners were incarcerated for drug-related crimes. By 1994, this figure was up to 61 percent. In 1984, there were 30,000 drug-related prisoners; by 1991, this population had grown 500 percent, to 150,000. And despite the fact that the real eighties drug epidemics involved cocaine, crack cocaine, and transmitting HIV[2] through contaminated needles, the foremost target of the War on Drugs was marijuana. "When Reagan came into office," says Eric E. Sterling, president of the Criminal Justice Policy Foundation, "marijuana was cheap and plentiful, cocaine was scarce and expensive, and AIDS was unknown. When Reagan left office, pot was expensive and hard to find, cocaine was cheap and plentiful, and AIDS had become a full-blown epidemic he refused to address."

Reagan's defenders will point out that his policies were the result of bipartisan efforts, and that's undeniable. Partially because of powerful, populous voting blocs of anti-drug parent organizations, Democrats and Republicans were locked in a decade-long battle to show who could be the toughest on drugs. Other anti-drug advocates say Reagan-era policies led to a decrease in casual drug use during the eighties. But the federal government commissioned most of the surveys that "measured" these improvements. The more significant statistics show increased drug trade violence, no improvement in addiction rates, and the explosion of crack cocaine as the scourge of America's inner cities. And though Reagan wasn't alone in crafting such harsh anti-drug policies, presidents are responsible for picking their advisers, and Reagan chose some grade-A douche jockeys.

Reagan's first drug czar, Carlton Turner, was quoted in *Time* magazine as saying, "Marijuana leads to homosexuality, the breakdown of the immune system, and therefore to AIDS." He also said marijuana use was directly linked to "the present young-adult generation's involvement in anti-military, anti-nuclear power, anti-big business, anti-authority demonstrations." After federal agents sprayed American marijuana fields with paraquat, an herbicide that is lethal if ingested (and commonly used for suicides

2   Reagan didn't even mention AIDS until 1987, after twenty-five thousand Americans had already died of the disease.

in countries like Samoa and Trinidad), Turner said kids deserved to die if they smoked the poisoned marijuana. Two years later he called for the death penalty for all drug abusers.

The most hypocritical element of Reagan's anti-drug policies is that his administration was simultaneously in cahoots with some of the most notorious drug traffickers in the world. National Security Council staff member Oliver North and his associates knowingly worked with drug smugglers while covertly funding the Contras, an anti-communist mercenary army in Nicaragua whose human rights record was so brutal that Congress strictly forbade military assistance to them. Throughout the eighties, the CIA also funded and trained the mujahideen in Afghanistan—Osama bin Laden among them—to fight against the Soviets. These freedom fighters, as Reagan called them, turned to poppy production to supplement their CIA funds and soon became the world's largest heroin supplier. The Taliban would later rise to power, funded by heroin proceeds and bin Laden's riches. Reagan's policies helped create a monster that—on September 11, 2001—turned against the United States in the most horrific way.

But Ronnie wasn't the only Reagan battling drugs. Nancy's contribution to the War on Drugs was significant and, to be fair, much more positive than that of her husband. In the early 1980s, the First Lady visited Longfellow Elementary School in Oakland. A student asked what she should do if she were offered drugs. "Just say no," Nancy said. Against all odds a movement was born. By 1986, there were more than ten thousand Just Say No clubs in American schools, most of which required children to make pacts not to experiment with drugs.

Mrs. Reagan put in overtime spreading the Just Say No propaganda juggernaut. She became the honorary chairwoman of the Just Say No Foundation and the National Federation for Parents of Drug-Free Youth. She appeared on dozens of talk shows, logged 250,000 miles to visit schools and drug rehab clinics, recorded public service announcements (PSAs), and appeared on TV shows like *Dynasty* and *Diff'rent Strokes*. Some critics said the message was dumbing down a complex problem, and that a proper anti-drug campaign should focus on an array of sociological, psychological, and physiological factors. In the quixotic world in which everyone said no, they claimed, there would be no drug problems. But parents and teachers alike were justifiably satisfied to see a positive movement embraced by kids that steered them away from drugs.

The eighties drug concern movement begat dozens of thriving organizations, including Drug Abuse Resistance Education (D.A.R.E.), which started in 1983 in Los Angeles. D.A.R.E. bills itself as "a police officer–led series of classroom lessons" that teaches kids to resist peer pressure, drugs, and violence. The program has spread to 75 percent of America's school districts, as well as over forty-three countries around the world. Another offshoot was the Partnership for a Drug-Free America (PDFA), which produced anti-drug PSAs, mainly in the form of televised ads. The PDFA first entered the public consciousness in 1987 with its "This Is Your Brain on Drugs" PSA. The ad made the analogy that if your brain were an egg, using drugs would be like frying it. The PDFA followed up with a PSA featuring a father confronting his son in his bedroom after finding a box of unspecified drugs. When the father presses for how he learned to use drugs, the son shouts, "From you, all right! I learned it by watching you!"

Say what you will about the simplistic scare tactics involved, but the fact remains: These campaigns worked. Among young Americans, drug use—especially marijuana use—dropped. According to research conducted by the Institute for Social Research at the University of Michigan, high school seniors using marijuana dropped from 55 percent in 1978 to 36 percent in 1987, and then to a startling 12 percent in 1991.

The anti-drug message penetrated so deeply, in fact, that kids started turning in their drug-using parents. In 1986, there were at least five pub-licized cases of vigilante kids turning their parents in to the police. It all started when a plucky thirteen-year-old named Deanna Young walked into the Tustin Police Department in Orange County, California. Deanna was holding a plastic bag filled with almost $3,000 worth of cocaine, some marijuana, and drug paraphernalia. Her parents were arrested, and Deanna was taken to a shelter for abused children.

Encouraged by press coverage of Deanna's story, other kids started following her lead. An eleven-year-old in L.A. told the school police officer her parents smoked pot and had a plant growing in the backyard. A twelve-year-old in California called the police on her parents, who were arrested for drug possession, and then a thirteen-year-old Indiana boy called the local sheriff, who nabbed the kid's parents on the same charge.

The effect these arrests had on the families involved received less publicity. There weren't many follow-up articles on the damage to these parents' reputations, the inevitable breach of trust between the children and their parents, or how the kids felt about living in shelters. *People* magazine did report that Deanna Young was none too psyched with her reward: being penned up for nine days in a youth facility. "She was insisting on going home from the beginning," her parents' attorney said. "Deanna never understood the sequence of events that would unfold when she did what she did."

If more empirical evidence of the effectiveness of this anti-drug fervor is needed, I offer a confession: These campaigns worked on *me*. All the PSAs and the Just Say No message remain indelibly singed into my consciousness to this day. I was entering my teenage years in the late eighties and the only message I had ever gotten about drugs was that they fried your brain and ruined your life. I was an athlete and doing well in school, so drugs didn't seem worth the costs. In fact the mere thought of taking drugs terrified me. I had visions of trying just one puff of a joint, only to realize that it was "laced" with something that instantly transformed me into a slobbering dimwit.

Perhaps I owe a certain debt to these campaigns, for my fruitful childhood. The only problem was, when I finally did surrender to the temptation of drugs—marijuana in particular—I enjoyed them so thoroughly I felt duped by Just Say No and indignantly vowed to make up for lost time with increased drug experimentation. Apparently I wasn't the only one to feel backlash against the eighties brainwash, because marijuana use among youth rose considerably in the mid-1990s,[3] and perceptions of the drug's harms declined.

3   By 1995, eighteen million Americans claimed to be regular marijuana users, a 20 percent increase from 1985.

Despite my bile toward Reagan's drug policies, I've only been driving five minutes before I'm questioning the wisdom of my decision to piss on his hometown. I really have to go *now*. It's inky black out and I haven't seen a single headlight. If by chance I were to get busted on this side mission, I would feel like such an ass. Illinois has among the most draconian laws of the states I'll pass through—from four to fifteen years in prison and a $25,000 fine—so the stress is heavy. Maybe it would suffice to violate Nancy Reagan's hometown instead. I google it—she's from New York City. Mission accomplished. I've been marking my territory there for years.

*   *   *

Allie wants to talk about the Easter bunny.

Yesterday I was on the verge of a prison bid. Today I'm eating breakfast with my eight-year-old niece, in a pleasant suburb of Chicago, earnestly discussing Easter. For Allie, like most kids, it's less about Christ's resurrection than the mysterious delivery of candy by an oversized rabbit. Sort of like Halloween, but without all the effort.

"Uncle Wyan," Allie says. "Mom says you met the Easter bunny. Is that true?"

"Sure is. He was hopping through our neighborhood, back when I was growing up in Indiana. I think it was the day before Easter. I asked him if I could get my candy in advance."

"What did he say?"

"Not much. Mainly just squeaky sounds. I'm not so sure he speaks English."

Allie shoots me a quizzical look—she's not buying it. I decide to put the ball in her court. "What about you? Have you met the Easter bunny?"

"Uh huh. I met him yesterday."

"Oh yeah? Did you ask him about me?"

"Yeah."

"What did he say?"

"He says you're annoying. And you talk too much."

"Oh, really . . ." I let out a snort of laughter. "I'm gonna have to have a word with him about that."

My ten-year-old niece, Olivia, walks up, holding something behind her back. She flashes her almond eyes and pulls out a lace baggie with a ribbon on it. "Uncle Ryan, I got you an Easter present. I figured you didn't really get to have an Easter, because you were driving. So I made you this."

"Aww, well thank you, Olivia." I open the bag. There is a card and a hand-painted butterfly magnet. It's so sweet—and in such stark contrast to the shady undercurrent of this trip—that I feel my eyes welling up.

"I made it myself," Olivia says.

I bite my lip. "It's beautiful." I stand up and give her a hug.

Olivia bounds out of the room and leaves me to think about the kids. If there is a weak spot in the pro-legalization arsenal, it's the kids. Anti-marijuana activists, when backed into a corner, have been known to pull out such lines as: "What message would legalization send to the children? That it's perfectly okay to smoke your life away?" Or, "Kids are already walking past cigarettes and beer at the corner store, when they go to buy candy. Should we add a section for pot too?"

These arguments are valid. Although I'm not personally ashamed about being a pot smoker, I don't want to be the influence for my nieces or nephew to try marijuana for the first time. My nieces have been asking for weeks what my book is about; I say it's about plants. When I think about them finding that massive stash in the basement, or even reading the lines I'm writing right now, I get uneasy. If I had young children and still smoked pot, I know I wouldn't do it around them. Does this make me a hypocrite? I'd like to think that, as they grew into their teens, I would try to educate my kids about cannabis and its effects, and maybe even pull one of those liberal-parent stunts, when they get old enough, of having them try it in my presence.

According to Dr. Eric Voth, the chairman of the Institute on Global Drug Policy, the notion of deliberately exposing your children to marijuana would be unwise to the point of sheer stupidity. "The human brain doesn't quit maturing until about age twenty-four or so," Dr. Voth told me. "And the average age of initiation to marijuana is around thirteen. You do that, and you're going to increase the likelihood of addiction phenomenally, much less the learning, the cognitive skills problems, and the executive functioning impairment. That worries me as much as anything else."

My most memorable confrontation of kids and marijuana occurred on September 18, 2010, when I attended the twenty-first annual Boston Hempfest, otherwise known as the Boston Freedom Rally. As I walked from the bus station toward Boston Common, I was wondering if I'd gotten the wrong date. It was all baby strollers and tourists. Then I saw a smiley kid with one of those weed T-shirts: a mock Adidas logo, only the leaf is a pot leaf, and the shirt reads, ADDICTED.[4] As I reached the cusp of the hill, I realized I'd entered the rally's suburbs. Younger people, more tattoos. Packs of teenagers sitting in circles, sending up puffs of smoke and looking around suspiciously.

As I approached the other side of the park, I heard loud chants that erased all doubt that I was in the right spot: "ROLL DAT SHIT, SMOKE DAT SHIT! PASS DAT SHIT, DO DAT SHIT!"

Beyond some trees a man was standing on the steps of a pagoda, screaming like a deranged preacher. He seemed pissed, as though not being able to smoke weed in public had really been weighing on him. I found myself hoping none of those families I just passed were in earshot. The closer I got to the side stage, the bolder people were about smoking. Two teenage girls in Rastafarian knitted berets were passing a bowl and coughing. A kid in a Lil Wayne shirt was doing that thing where you puff a blunt with pouted lips like you're smooching it. Counting five conspicuous joints within a twenty-yard radius, I decided to take out my pre-rolled joint and join the party.

But I wasn't entirely comfortable in this setting. If there was a theme, it was youth in revolt. I moved toward the stage. Unfortunately, the screaming man doubled as a talent-challenged hip-hop musician, whose

4   This strikes me as an ill-advised boast for a T-shirt. Or is it a public cry for help? American potheads seem to have an urge to come clean about their habit. You wouldn't see an alcoholic wearing a T-shirt boasting about his addiction, with a Nike swoosh morphing into a bottle of Jack Daniels.

songs revolved around a single salient theme—his inalienable right to get supremely fucking high. Off to my right, I noticed the neon yellow vests of two Boston police officers. They were searching the bags of three kids, the oldest of which looked ten years old. The kids looked terrified. Phone cameras popped out, eager to expose the police overstepping their bounds. I'm no fan of cops myself, but I had no qualms with this particular stop-and-frisk. We don't need pre-adolescents waking-and-baking to *Sesame Street* and a bowl of Cheerios. I stubbed out my joint and walked away.

That's why the what-about-the-kids rally cry is an instant rhetorical victory for anti-marijuana tub-thumpers. Who would actively support children getting high? It's no surprise that studies show frequent marijuana use is detrimental to the growing brains and airways of adolescents. Of course most pro-legalization folks are in favor of age limits, just like with the purchase of alcohol or tobacco. But the counterargument then focuses on how legalization might create a cultural shift in attitude toward marijuana, which would trickle down to kids' perceptions and, ultimately, their consumption.

But the reality of the matter is: Regardless of attitude shifts, marijuana is already widely available to American kids. "Our children have never had greater access to marijuana," claims former Seattle police chief and drug reform activist Norm Stamper. "It's easier for them to score pot than a six-pack of Coors." He's probably right—you don't need a fake ID to buy a dime bag off some floppy-haired stoner from your PE class. And contact with these dealers puts kids in proximity to higher-stakes drugs like ecstasy, LSD, and cocaine, which many weed dealers often sell or are able to access.

Perhaps the best way to study how legalization might affect teenage (and overall) drug use in America is to study the effects, over three decades, of Holland's policies. The de facto legalization of cannabis in the Netherlands, in 1983, did not initially affect the rates of cannabis use. But when the age of legal access was lowered to sixteen years old—which would never happen in the States—usage rates increased, only to decrease again when the age limit was raised to eighteen. For the eighteen-to-twenty age group, regular cannabis use increased from 15 percent in 1984 to 44 percent in 1996. But this statistic isn't conclusive in isolation: From 1992 to 1996, overall cannabis use rose sharply in America and many European countries.[5]

Over the years, evidence suggests the prevalence of cannabis use among Dutch citizens rose and fell moderately with the increase and decline in the number of coffee shops. Extrapolating from the Dutch example, there is some evidence that legalization in America could result in an increase in cannabis use. That said, over the past decade, marijuana use in the Netherlands has hovered at about half that of the United States. In a 2008 World Health Organization survey, 7 percent of Dutch teens had tried marijuana by age fifteen. In the United States, that figure was more than 20 percent.

In terms of teenage marijuana use, one difference between the United States and the Netherlands has recently piqued the interest of researchers. A 2011 report written by UC-Berkeley law professor Robert J. MacCoun and published in the journal *Addiction* found that 71.5 percent of American teenagers said it's very easy to get pot, compared with 41.5 percent in Holland. This seems to contradict the argument that legalization would increase children's access to the drug. Skeptics might point to the proliferation of legalized medical marijuana states as accounting for this high perception of access, but Professor MacCoun says this is inaccurate: "Some people want to point to medical marijuana, but it's not a new story and marijuana has been readily available long before we had medical marijuana in dispensaries."

What's behind this phenomenon? In terms of why American kids have access to black-market weed, we don't know. "For whatever reason, we really have—in this campus market—well-established supply lines into schools," says MacCoun. But as for the fact that Dutch teenagers report less access to marijuana than American teens (who report similar levels of access as teens in European countries with stricter legal policies), there are some insights. First off, the Dutch are stringent about not letting minors into their coffee shops; many shops have been shut down for age-limit

5 And it's all Dr. Dre's fault.

infractions. And since adults can buy their marijuana in coffee shops, there are fewer street dealers, which is where kids usually turn for drugs. It would be naïve to assume that some older siblings aren't copping weed for their younger siblings—as is the case with alcohol in the United States—but the overall effect seems to be less availability.

And what about the gateway drug theory so often spouted by American prohibitionists? By this I mean the argument that marijuana use leads to the use of other drugs, which are especially harmful to children. Marijuana advocates often counter that alcohol is the real gateway drug, but I'm not sure I agree. I might never have felt comfortable trying mushrooms or Ecstasy without having first discovered I liked marijuana's effects, which are more psychedelic than alcohol's. (My exposure to other drugs certainly increased by being around pot smokers and dealers.) But part of my psychological shift involved the fact that marijuana had been vilified as dangerous. Once I tried it and realized it seemed relatively innocuous, I wondered what other "dangerous" illegal drugs I might enjoy.

That said, the drugs that I've explored have not been the "hard," addictive drugs—like cocaine, crystal meth, and heroin—that prohibition- ists usually link to marijuana use. According to Ethan Nadelmann, the Executive Director of the Drug Policy Alliance, the gateway theory is "an ounce of truth embedded in a pound of bull." He told me in an interview that, while most users of cocaine and heroin did in fact use marijuana first, the vast majority of marijuana users don't go on to use—much less get addicted to—those drugs: "The notion that we should try to reduce the number of people getting addicted to heroin by focusing on adolescent use of marijuana is like trying to reduce motorcycle fatalities by discouraging bicycle riding."

As they were debating their drug laws in the late seventies and early eighties, Dutch officials theorized that weed's actual gateway effect was the result of contact with hard drug sellers. Their idea was to separate the soft drug market from the hard drug market and create tighter controls on the former. Professor MacCoun's data suggests that this market separation has "somewhat weakened the link between cannabis use and the use of cocaine or amphetamines." The upshot is that nowadays it's less likely in Holland than in America that the floppy-haired kid in PE class peddles weed, and if he does, it's less likely he's also dealing Ecstasy.

*   *   *

My phone rings. It's Joaquin, the buddy who set me up with Buddha Cheese.

"What's up?" he asks. "You still in Mikey Land?"

"Not anymore. Chicago now. I'm driving across the country in a rental car."

Joaquin laughs. "Let me guess . . . with precious goods?"

"Perhaps." I explain in hazy terms the Omaha trooper incident, and the decision to stash the stuff here in the basement for a night and have some family normalcy.

"Nice, I love it. You know, you're gonna have to frisk your nieces whenever they come out of the basement." Joaquin laughs, then goes into a stern cop voice. "Let me see your hands! Who are you working for?"

We cackle like fiends. I explain that I have to go turn this rental car in for one with an Illinois license plate. He doesn't seem convinced.

"Come on, man. I expect you to slink around Chicago under cover of darkness, slide under someone's car with a flashlight, unscrew the license plate, and put it on your car. You gotta be gangsta like that, kid."

*   *   *

On the road again, with a 2.0 upgrade—a new ride with an Illinois license plate, a trunk big enough to fit my luggage, and a new good-luck charm. This morning when I realized I couldn't find the talisman from B-Nice, I asked Olivia if she had anything in the good luck department. She led me to her bedroom cabinet, which had a dizzying variety of charms. I chose a piece of glittering white rock the size of my thumb.

"That one's definitely good luck," Olivia said. "And if it doesn't work, you could probably sell it for like a dollar."

"I won't sell it," I said, laughing. "I know it has special powers."

And I might need them. Leaving Chicago, it's monsoon conditions and murderous traffic. My windshield wipers even seem panicked. I focus on massaging the brake with the ball of my foot and maintaining immaculate equidistance from cars on all four sides. NPR says it's natural disaster time in the Midwest. Missouri got fifteen inches of rain last night. Tornados are everywhere at once. Yesterday they hit Michigan and Pennsylvania. Today they're going after the Southeast—Arkansas, Alabama, Tennessee, Mississippi, and Virginia. I'm leaving the sanctuary of my family on the third and most destructive day of what will become known as the 2011 Super Outbreak—the largest flare-up of tornadoes ever recorded, with 358 twisters causing 346 deaths from New York to Texas.

You'd think I would have checked the forecast. But really it wouldn't have mattered. Every day spent not driving just notches up the tension. I wouldn't recommend a gig like this if you're trying to quit smoking. As a memento from the good ole Dodge Avenger and a reminder to not get pulled over for littering, I stole its ashtray, which is already filled with butts.

NPR says the world has been turned on its head. The Arab Spring revolts are raging. The people in Syria and Libya are pissed, and soldiers are shooting them for being pissed. The financial editor of the *New York Times* says Bernie Madoff made a career of lying so aggressively about his failures that he transformed them into success. It started back in '62, when Bernie got into a crack for putting his investors' money into some shit stock. When they bottomed out, he borrowed money from his father-in-law and pretended he'd navigated the storm perfectly, which bolstered his reputation as a genius.

I'm suddenly indignant. Fuck driving a plant! *These* are the real criminals. Despotic rulers killing innocent civilians! Gluttonous plutocrats swindling investors out of millions! Nations and global corporations built on lies, and the people having to bear the brunt of it when those lies inevitably crumble into dust.

Not that I've been a fount of honesty myself. As I cross into Indiana, I think about my parents, who live two hundred miles south of here. I have been telling them I'm still in California but will be flying to New York soon.

I mention vague job prospects. When my dad probes, I pull from my ass that some of my old contacts at a PR agency say there's a spot opening up. It's awful when he gets excited, but nothing good can come from telling the truth. A quick Google search reveals what Indiana's marijuana laws would do with a scoundrel like me: from two to eight years in the pen and a $10,000 fine.

*   *   *

On the final day of the drive, I wake up late in my hotel room. Isolation and pressure are bubbling to the surface, exposing vulnerabilities that could lead to my undoing. I remember checking in the night before at 11:00 P.M. but not going to my room. I felt the compulsion to be near people, not for conversation but so the proverbial tree falling in the forest would be heard by someone, to confirm that I'm actually going through this.

I drove to a pub with my loaded car and had just enough drinks to silence the demons. My only interaction was with a young woman who declared she was going to run her hands through my hair because it was her twenty-fifth birthday and she could do what she wanted. On the ride to the hotel I passed a cop and got heart palpitations, knowing I was slipping and couldn't hold out much longer. I got back to my room around 1:00 A.M., only to find it occupied, and nearly got my fingers slammed in the door. After relocating to a different room, I took a series of bizarre still life photos, then watched *The Colbert Report* and wrote down in my journal, "Without absolute morality, it's all hookers and blow," before finally passing out around 4:00 A.M.

A knock at the door jolts me to life. I open it just a crack. It's the maid.

"Will you be checking out?"

"Yes, at twelve."

She looks at her watch. "It's twelve thirty."

Right. The problem is I still don't know my exact destination. I talked to Buddha Cheese yesterday and he promised me a Caribbean vacation when I'm done but wasn't sure where I was headed today. I call him on all his numbers. Finally, after I shower and shave, he texts me from one phone and says to message him on another device. Then he gives me the address of my drop point—eight hours and two states away from the initial destination.

Now that I know where I'm going, the reality of it kicks in hard. Six more hours of driving. Crunch time. I decide to pray. I'm not a religious man, but I have prayed to a (nominally Christian) god since I was a kid. I kneel beside the bed and press my palms together, using the same intro I've used since I was six years old.

"Dear God, Jesus, Mary, and Moses . . ."

I tell them all I know I haven't always done the things I should, and maybe this is one of those times, but I have a good heart and sure would appreciate it if they'd help me through today.

*   *   *

It's more of the same—checking the brake lights and flipping early turn signals, Pizza Hut and Taco Bell, Red Bull and cigarettes—but twice as anxious because I'm approaching the end. Each fill-up costs seventy dollars, and I have a newfound appreciation for the NPR segment on people stocking up on used Toyota Priuses. I wind my way through the mountains of rural Pennsylvania, past Anslinger's hometown, Altoona, and the Penn State campus. Not long after an exit for the Jersey Shore, I get too excited and end up on the wrong interstate for a devastating twenty-five miles.

At 9:00 P.M., I slowly glide into a suburban apartment complex. I scan the parking lot for anything suspicious—curious neighbors on their porch, people walking their dogs, someone sitting in a parked car. All clear. I call my connect. He emerges in the doorway with a smile and a little yapper dog at his feet. He opens the garage door and asks me to back into the driveway. He is a soft-spoken, shabbily dressed white guy. The only tip-off to his occupation is the sparkling black BMW in the garage.

The sense of relief is mutual, though heavily weighted in my direction. He asks me how the trip went and gives me a bottle of water. We count the product in his makeshift basement gym and tally up the total. He sends a text to Buddha Cheese and shakes my hand. Walking back up the stairs, I am overcome by a sublime sense of freedom and satisfaction. I don't care how desperately in debt I get—I will never, ever do this again.

The drop-off is just as I had rehearsed it in my head—anti-climactic. But that's a roll of the dice. This could have turned into a prison memoir. While America flirts with a more lenient approach to this long-maligned plant, the marijuana black market that our laws have created is still unforgiving to the point of brutality.

A few months from now, Louisiana police will approach Buddha Cheese and his Panamanian Poledancer girlfriend in a tony restaurant near Baton Rouge. Following a tip from an informant who has just been busted after buying eighty pounds of marijuana, they will search Buddha Cheese's car and find the exact amount of cash the informant predicted they'd find. Buddha Cheese's lawyers will postpone the trial, but it doesn't look like he'll be able to avoid a jail sentence. Meanwhile, in November of 2011, the woman who replaces Bull as Buddha Cheese's grow manager on The Hill, Gia, will bring three hundred plants to harvest. After trimming the buds with a crew of fifteen employees, and celebrating their accomplishment with an LSD-drenched bacchanal on The Hill, Gia will be tasered by a scruffy employee, who will then steal fifty pounds and flee into the mountains.

I didn't intend to focus so intently on marijuana outlaws in this story, and I certainly didn't plan to become one myself. But it has had the effect of viscerally proving—to me, at least—the absurdity of this prohibition. As long as any aspect of the weed business—cultivation, sales, transportation, or consumption—remains illegal, American marijuana culture will be plagued by theft, paranoia, violence, millions in untaxed revenue, and an average of around 850,000 arrests per year.

Though much of the theft goes unreported, the violence can be attributed to the fact that growers and distributors do business in a cash-fueled black market that's not protected by American law. And the real violence is occurring south of the border, in Mexico, where the drug war has caused an estimated 47,515 deaths in the five years after President Felipe Calderon launched his assault on the cartels, in late 2006. American marijuana sales fuel as much as 60% of the cartels' profit.[6] And it's easy profit, because marijuana grows bountifully in the Sierras, and requires little processing. Due to the standard smuggling constraints of bulk and smell, cartels have also begun to grow weed within the states, in U.S. National Forests from northern California to the North Woods of Wisconsin.

But domestically, the medical marijuana states have begun to cripple America's war against the plant. If medical marijuana laws really are a Trojan Horse by pro-pot activists to inch toward full legalization, the tactic is beginning to work. Colorado and Washington have pioneered the trend of transitioning from medical to recreational legalization, and other states will follow. Meanwhile, the quality of product seeping from medical marijuana states into the non-compassionate states far exceeds the quality of the garbage that's coming over the border. (Most marijuana users, myself included, would never stoop to buy Mexican schwag.) And at a time when people complain that America doesn't make anything anymore, marijuana is one of the products we make at a volume and standard of quality that no other nation can match. With all these growers and dispensaries and patients creating commerce in an otherwise stunted economy, there's no way to backtrack. If the government cracks down hard on the medical marijuana industry, they will simply boost unemployment while raising the price of quality marijuana, creating incentive for growers and distributors to enter the black market and make bigger, untaxed profits.

The battle between the states and the federal government over medical marijuana is morphing into a battle over recreational marijuana. When it reaches a boiling point, simply rescheduling and decriminalizing the drug won't be enough. The most practical solution will be, to many Americans, the unthinkable: full legalization, or the United States of Amsterdam.

And then a *new* battle for the soul of American marijuana culture will begin.

---

6   According to a 1997 estimate by the U.S. drug czar's office.

EPILOGUE
MARIJUANA ANONYMOUS

The scene outside the West Broward Club is so at odds with my expectations that I wonder if I'm in the right place. Teenagers and twentysomethings linger outside the front door, smoking cigarettes and chatting. All the flirting and frenetic chatter brings to mind the scene outside a night club after closing time. I walk inside, following a few other stragglers through a labyrinthine series of corridors, toward a room in the back of the building.

It's packed. There are around a hundred people stuffed into a room the size of a small college lecture hall. Nearly every seat is taken, even the ones lining the walls. Trying to be as inconspicuous as possible, I walk down the central aisle and grab one of the few open seats, near the front.

"Welcome to Marijuana Anonymous," a man says. "My name is Ezekiel, and I'm a pothead."

Ezekiel starts explaining the format of meetings for first-timers. Then, unable to contain his frustration, he suddenly launches into a harangue against all the late arrivers, me included, for the show of disrespect to "the rooms." He says that, in the future, if anyone arrives more than five minutes late, they won't get their papers signed. *Papers?* I don't have papers, and I'm not sure what he's talking about.

A scan of the room clarifies things. The group is as diverse as a street scene in Queens, but they all look young. I have been to a few MA meetings before, in Brooklyn. The average age of the attendees there was around thirty-five. Here, it's closer to twenty. And the look of disinterest on most of their faces, accompanied by the talk of signing papers, adds up to one thing: These people are required to be here because a court mandated it, probably as part of a sentencing for marijuana possession.

Ezekiel asks if there are any first-timers. A dozen people raise their hands. We go around the room, introducing ourselves. I'm relieved that people are just saying their names, and not adding, "And I'm a marijuana addict," afterwards, like they did at my previous meetings.

"I'm Ryan," I say.

"Hi, Ryan," the group groans.

"I'm Beavis," says a kid seated against the wall. No one laughs. The kid keeps a straight face, but he's got a cocky, frat-boy air about him and he's wearing an *A Very Harold & Kumar 3D Christmas* T-shirt. *Smartass.*

Ezekiel asks if anyone has a "burning desire" to speak up about their experiences. A young Latino guy in the front row raises his hand. He says it's been three weeks since he's gotten high, and he feels totally different, in a good way.

"Before, it was like my life was just rolling by," he says.

A man at the front of the room, who seems affiliated with the program but is standing off to the side, steps forward and starts nodding his head.

"I can tell from what you sayin' that weed ain't the only problem. I know you been doin' other shit too, right? I can see it in your eyes . . ."

"Well," the Latino kid says. "Not really."

The room busts out in laughter.

Ezekiel takes over, describing his days of using in what feels like forced, deliberate street-speak; things like, "I used to burn all the time, man—before work, dates, whatever."

A young black kid at the back of the class raises his hand. Ezekiel calls on him.

"Man, I just gotta say that I wanna go burn one *right now*."

More laughter. I'll bet most of these people think being busted for possession is ridiculous, and that the whole concept of marijuana addiction is even more ludicrous. Many marijuana lovers claim the drug is not physically addictive, just psychologically addictive. But according to Dr. Margaret Haney, who has studied hundreds of chronic marijuana users, that's not entirely accurate: "If you look at addiction as the compulsive use of a drug, I feel comfortable saying that marijuana can produce addiction." One major factor in determining dependence (as medical professionals call addiction), Haney says, is whether frequent use produces withdrawal. It does. Marijuana withdrawal is characterized by symptoms that aren't as intense as with heroin or cocaine, but still distinct—irritability, anxiety, restlessness, sleep disruption, and decreased appetite. Some studies show that when frequent users stop smoking, their calorie intake plummets by one thousand calories per day.

I must admit I'm disappointed by this meeting. It's a mockery. I'm not exactly panicked about my marijuana use at the moment, but ever since I've been living down here in my parent's winter bungalow, I've been smoking at least once a day, and always alone. I figured it couldn't hurt to check out one of two MA meetings offered in the state of Florida. My experiences at the Brooklyn MA meetings felt sincere, and I would leave with the real desire to, if not stop, then at least get control of my habit. The attendees were often poly-addicts with other problems, but they took their marijuana dependence just as seriously. I remember the testimony of a guy who spoke at my first meeting. He looked like a lawyer or an accountant, dressed in a button-down shirt and khaki pants. "I grew up in a very conservative Christian household," he said, "which I constantly rebelled against. And drugs were one way for me to do that. So I guess you could say I found my god in pot."

I've often felt my own marijuana habit is the result of a vague spiritual yearning. Sure, there are times when I get high just to enhance a movie, or a meal, or music, or sex. But there are many times, especially when I get high alone, that I feel like I'm looking for something bigger. I want that intense feeling of being alive now, of appreciating the world around me with a child's eyes, if only for an hour or so.

I think many Americans feel the same way. This country has by far the most pot-smokers in the world, with almost forty-four million and counting.[1] Why does America feel the need to get so stoned? Do we just dig the feeling, or is there some deeper cultural phenomenon at play? Is getting high a means of rising above the soulless consumerism that drives us to want more and more due to some deeply felt sense of lack? I don't

---

1   This figure is an extrapolation from the United Nations 2012 World Drugs Report, which estimates that 14.1 percent of the American population—over 311 million people—use marijuana.

know, but I have a sense from my research that marijuana is among the means by which we attempt to fill a societal and spiritual void.

If so, perhaps that's not a bad thing. Cannabis has a rich history of spiritual usage. The world's first documented stoners were the Scythians, who cultivated cannabis for funerals and spiritual rituals in southern Siberia as early as 700 BC. The fifth-century Greek historian Herodotus described the use of Scythian smoking chambers—tents designed to trap the fumes from cannabis placed on burning embers. After peeking their heads into the tent to inhale the vapors, the Scythians got so baked that they would "rise up to dance and betake themselves to singing."

Many of the major religions—Judaism and Christianity excluded—have embraced marijuana at one point or another. The use of hashish for recreational purposes was well established in Arabic Muslim society by the eleventh century. Early Arabic texts used metaphors such as "the bush of understanding," "blissful branches," and "the morsel of thought" to describe the plant's psychoactive qualities. Similarly, the many Sanskrit and Hindu terms for cannabis are the antithesis of negative Western monikers (like *pot*, *weed*, and *dope*)—including words like *virapattra* ("leaf of heroes") and *medhakaritva* ("inspiring of mental power"). The sacred Hindu texts known as the *Vedas* recount how Shiva—the Supreme God of Hinduism—brought cannabis plants down from the Himalayas for the people's use and enjoyment, thus earning his title, "Lord of the Bhang."[2]

The Buddha himself went with a one-hemp-seed-a-day diet while practicing the six steps of asceticism that led to his enlightenment. In 530 AD, Taoist Chinese necromancers drank hemp-ginseng concoctions "to set forward time in order, and reveal future events." And then of course there's the world's most famous weed-based worshippers—the Jamaican Rastafarians—who believe that ganja cleanses the body and mind, heals the soul, exalts the consciousness, facilitates peacefulness and pleasure, and

2   Bhang is a Sanskrit term for the leaves and flowering tops of cannabis. Nowadays, it more commonly refers to a cannabis preparation that's smoked or consumed as a beverage in the Indian subcontinent.

brings them closer to their God, or *Jah*. Many Rastas claim that smoking ganja is a way of reclaiming their African spiritual heritage, since tribes in central and southern Africa have been smoking *dagga* as a religious rite since the eighth century.

One possible explanation for the widespread usage of cannabis for both spiritual and medical means across many cultures is the endocannabinoid system. Humans and animals alike naturally synthesize endogenous cannabinoids, chemical compounds that activate the same receptors as THC, the active ingredient in marijuana. When activated, these receptors, which are clustered in the brain but also found elsewhere in the body, allow both THC and endocannabinoids to bind to the nervous system, triggering reactions that reduce pain and anxiety, while also producing a floaty sense of bliss. Studies have shown a link between increased blood levels of endocannabinoids and the euphoric sensation of post-exercise "runner's high." And though research is still evolving, endocannabinoids are believed to provide many psychological benefits, promoting sharing, humor, creativity, the extinction of old memories, and the ability to cast off limiting patterns of thought and behavior from past situations. These effects suggest that the endocannabinoid system might not just have the ability to heal the body and mind, but also—like the cannabinoids in the marijuana plant—to soothe the human spirit as well.

Marijuana Anonymous, like all twelve-step programs, is hip to the spiritual yearning inherent to addiction, and does its best to replace getting high with belief in a Higher Power. But the atmosphere at this meeting isn't very spiritual. Ezekiel's co-leader is a Latina woman who swears constantly and says, as a former dealer, that her Higher Power used to be money. Now she calls her Higher Power "dude," because otherwise it sounds too much like God, which her Catholic upbringing forced down her throat. I can't relate to this in the slightest.

From what I can see, MA meetings aren't very effective when they're court ordered. It's like punishing an unruly kid by sending him to Sunday school. The only other person I've heard speak who seems to be here voluntarily is a frazzled-looking woman who says she's been off of heroin for fifty days, and that the FBI is after her. Most of these other bored kids are just going through the motions. If drug testing isn't a part of their sentence, my guess is that 90 percent of these people will leave this meeting and go smoke a joint within the hour. Of course, this is better than throwing them in jail for possession. But even better would be to not bust people for possession at all, and save MA as a forum for those genuinely unhappy with their inability to control their marijuana consumption and who willfully choose to fight it.

It's time to hand out the sobriety chips. Ezekiel asks if anyone wants a one-day chip. Though I technically qualify, I opt out, and there are no takers. "Was anyone sober for thirty days?" he asks. Crickets. Sixty days? *Nada.* This is pathetic.

"Okay, does anyone want a ninety-day chip?" Ezekiel asks.

The guy to my immediate left, an Asian kid, raises his hand. Everyone seems shocked that even one person is taking this seriously. I scoot over and let him out. Everyone claps, and I sense that this is the evening's one true moment of universal sincerity.

After we're dismissed—and it feels like just that, class being dismissed, to the relief of all—I try to interview a couple people. It's beyond awkward. I don't know whether to say the truth (that I'm writing a book, which conflicts with the anonymity of the twelve-step ethos) or just casually make conversation. I approach a young white guy and try to reveal as little as possible. Eyeing me warily, he says he's just here because of a possession charge, and thinks it's basically bullshit. Then he excuses himself and walks away.

In the parking lot, I see the Asian guy who got the ninety-day chip. He's way ahead of me, so I have to walk-run through the parking lot to catch him. I decide to be honest this time.

"Excuse me," I say. "I'm sorry to bother you, but I'm writing a book about marijuana, and I was just wondering why it was that you chose to stick with this program and stay sober for ninety days."

He starts to chatter, but his English is poor. I have trouble following him at first. But then he says something that sticks.

"You just do it on your own. You decide to stop, and you do it. It's not meetings. It's just, decide and do it."

"Okay, I see. And can I ask why you decided to do it?"

It takes me a while to get the details. His name is Trong. He grew up in Vietnam. There, he had no money, and barely enough to eat. Then he came here to live with relatives, and got a job at a restaurant. He had money for the first time, and started going out to clubs with friends. They all drank and smoked pot, so he started doing it too. I hadn't considered smoking too much weed as being a First World problem, but of course it is. Marijuana is expensive. Many of us First World-ers have too much disposable income, too much time to fiddle with our smartphones, and too few meaningful, spiritual outlets. I ask why he started coming to meetings. At first I don't think he understands the question, but then he says this:

"My brother, he died. It was heroin."

"Was he in Vietnam?" I ask.

"Yes."

After his brother's death, he says he realized he was just sitting on the couch, getting high and playing video games. He felt like he was wasting his life. He could be using that time to learn new skills and make more money. He used to have no access to money, regardless of what he did, but now his income is in direct relationship to the time he puts into working. Getting high and playing video games is a luxury he can't afford. It's like stealing money from himself.

"So will you ever smoke pot again?" I ask.

"Never," he says. "I never use again."

*   *   *

In a way, this Marijuana Anonymous scene is a useful microcosm for examining the conflicting forces that surround American weed culture today. MA meetings operate under the assumption that the plant is addictive, just like alcohol or heroin, even as the debate over the drug's addictiveness continues. The attendees of this meeting—which is meant to be a voluntary program for people who have lost control of their lives due to marijuana—were actually cynical young people coerced to attend because of a court order. The judge who sent them there is a mouthpiece for the local and state laws of Florida, which differ radically from the laws in other states—eighteen of which now have legalized medical marijuana. Meanwhile, had any of the young adults at this meeting been caught possessing *any* amount of marijuana by federal agents, they wouldn't be so lucky as to attend this meeting; they would have been slapped with a $1000 minimum fine and up to a year in jail. And one of the only people benefitting from this meeting, Trong, is not there by a court order—indeed, is not even an American citizen—and actually claims the meetings aren't as important as making a personal decision about one's marijuana use.

My mind shuffles through all the characters, like Trong, that I've met during my two-year-long investigation into this topic. It's daunting. When you tell people you're writing a book on this subject, *everyone's* got a story. My ninety-year-old aunt said she once took her teenage daughter's marijuana seeds and planted them in her garden, just to see if they would grow. (They did.) While trimming the harvested buds from my buddy's basement grow in Denver, he said not to write about him because the firm he worked for had consulting contracts with the federal government. A wealthy sixty-two-year-old real estate agent responded to the description of my book project by pulling a pipe from her purse and lighting it, in the middle of a south Florida restaurant. A Midwestern corporate executive told me he was cutting down on his alcohol intake but compensating by smoking a bowl at the end of each workday, to take the edge off. A former pothead and father of three told me he woke up one morning, a week after his wife had filed for divorce, and decided to quit weed cold turkey. Anyone who thinks marijuana's place in contemporary American culture is straightforward or insignificant simply hasn't talked to enough people.

The characters who I have described in this story don't exactly simplify the situation. Irv Rosenfeld recently smoked his 120,000th government-provided joint, and remains a thorn in the federal government's side by co-directing The Silver Tour, an organization that educates senior citizens about medical marijuana. Steve DeAngelo is still fighting to keep Harborside Health Center open, despite having federal Complaints of Forfeiture taped to its doors in July. Richard Lee is bankrupt. Oaksterdam University remains open with a scaled-back class schedule, while fifteen thousand of its graduates continue to create new cannabusinesses. But Lee says he'll relinquish ownership of his companies, as he remains fearful of federal drug charges. If the feds decide to add up all the plants his nurseries have grown over thirteen years, and that number is over sixty thousand, he could face the death penalty.

But the tug of war continues, and recently the momentum has taken a historic shift in favor of the pro-legalization advocates. On November 6th, 2012, Colorado and Washington both passed ballot initiatives to legalize recreational marijuana. This was by far the biggest victory for pro-weed folks—and yet, for anyone who has been following the movement's developments, it's not at all surprising. Statistics have been leaning toward legalization nationwide, and unlike the messy state of affairs in California, Colorado has been regulating marijuana with an almost mind-numbing bureaucratic efficiency. When the ballots were all tallied, marijuana was more popular than President Obama in Colorado—by more than fifty thousand votes—even as he won the hotly contested battleground state.

The day after the initiatives passed, Ed Gogek, an addiction psychiatrist and anti–medical marijuana activist from Arizona, wrote an op-ed in the *New York Times* titled "A Bad Trip for Democrats." The essay's contention was that, in many medical marijuana states, most cardholders weren't prescribed the drug for serious illnesses like cancer, but rather for inconsequential maladies like pain. What Gogek failed to realize was that, on some level, *that's the whole point.* As Dr. Lester Grinspoon told me, cannabis is a sui generis substance—a plant that grows in almost any environment, a medicine with a wide array of uses, and a recreational drug with the capacity for abuse. In many cases, there's no way to reliably distinguish between cannabis patients who have diagnosable medical needs and recreational users with alleged "chronic pain." In fact, many of the 94 percent of medical-marijuana users in Colorado that Gogek claims were prescribed weed just for pain actually *do* suffer from pain, the same diagnosis for which doctors would otherwise prescribe addictive painkillers like Percocet. The rest of them might just have a boss who's a pain in the ass. The popularity of medical marijuana among this latter group has served to blur the distinctions between the two sides so thoroughly—and so profitably—that the distinction no longer seems that significant. Doctors prescribe Oxycontin; bartenders serve drinks. Both are legal, and marijuana shares some of the most positive effects of both substances. So why not prescribe weed *and* serve it?

As simple as that sounds, the reality of America's transition toward legalization will be much more complicated. Within hours after Amendment 64 passed, Colorado governor John Hickenlooper, who opposed the measure, warned his constituents that "federal law still says marijuana is an illegal drug, so don't break out the Cheetos or Goldfish too quickly." A few days later, Hickenlooper was on the phone to U.S. Attorney General Eric Holder about the urgent need for the federal government to articulate its position on Amendment 64.

As for Washington State's Initiative 502, analysts had predicted it would succeed because of its 25 percent tax rate, which would help generate an estimated $532 million in new revenue per year. These taxes would be implemented by triple-dipping: One tax when the grower sells it to the processor, another when the processor sells it to the retailer, and yet another when the retailer sells it to the customer. After the measure passed, Seattle-area prosecutors quickly announced plans to dismiss nearly two hundred preexistent cases of marijuana possession against individuals over the age of twenty-one. And yet, right across Puget Sound in Bremerton, a man had just been busted smoking pot inside a parked car near a public park. When the man complained that he had heard on the news that pot was now legal, the officer said the measure hadn't formally gone into effect yet, and that it wouldn't cover smoking weed in public places anyway, then carted the poor stoner off to jail.

The piecemeal legalization of marijuana in America will, in the short term, create as many problems as it solves. As states follow in the footsteps of Colorado and Washington, the federal government will slowly remove its collective head from the sand, only to discover that each facet of production, transportation (within states and across state lines), distribution, and consumption will have to be addressed in minute detail. The pharmaceutical companies will likely respond by promoting their (marginally effective) synthetic forms of medicinal marijuana, while throwing their substantial lobbying dollars behind keeping non-pharmaceutical marijuana at bay.

The corporatization of weed will be quick and decisive. Multinational companies like Starbucks and the major tobacco companies will start battling entrepreneurs for dominion over production sites and cafes. Cannabis tourism will take off, and ancillary businesses from paraphernalia to marijuana-based food companies will surge. As long as taxation doesn't grow too extortionate, prices will go down, and the marijuana black market—including that of the Mexican drug cartels—will dwindle. Extrapolating from the Dutch model, there will initially be a small but measurable spike of usage, as people whose only barrier to trying the drug was its illegality. Some experts fear that America's marketing juggernaut will exacerbate this trend, in the same way that the other two "vice industries"—alcohol and tobacco—relentlessly advertise to heavy users, who compose nearly 80 percent of their profits. But as the novelty of legalization wears off, it's likely that cannabis use will dip and then level off at somewhere near our current level, which is already triple the global average. Regardless, anti-marijuana people will respond by saying that all the negative things they've been contending for years—that the drug harms people's health, ambition, memory, and creates a bad example for children—have been unleashed on a wide scale and are turning the country into a cesspool of depravity.

As the argument heats up, the conflicting research on how marijuana affects us will continue to bolster the viewpoints of both pro- and anti-marijuana activists. There are only a few consistently demonstrable effects of marijuana use that don't cause much controversy on either side of the aisle. The acute effects include increased heart rate and blood pressure, distorted sense of time, and short-term memory loss. Prohibitionists can't cogently argue against marijuana's proven ability to ease pain and nausea, increase appetite, relax muscles, and reduce intraocular pressure. It also seems safe to say that the frequent use of smoked marijuana can lead to chronic bronchitis, and that there is a smorgasbord of reasons why children shouldn't smoke pot.

But the other effects are all dependent on the type of marijuana and the individual using it, and you can pretty much prove whatever you want. I recently heard a respected alcohol-and-drug educator claim that he had firsthand evidence of male marijuana users growing man-breasts due to their habit. Many people say getting high makes them euphoric and imaginative and leads to the most gratifying sexual experiences of their lives; others say it makes them dysphoric and paranoid. Some people get energetic; others fall asleep. Some people get the munchies; others get turned off by food after getting high. Studies show weed might be linked to schizophrenia; others show no link. Marijuana use might cause an addiction similar to alcoholism; it might help cure people from their dependence on alcohol. It might make you a worse driver; it might make you a better one. It might cause cancer; it might cure cancer. If you look hard enough, marijuana can be whatever you want it to be.

As for my personal relationship to weed, I'm more comfortable with it than ever before. At the moment, thanks to a recent run-in with California-based growers who I've met through "research," I have a stash of bananas-quality, organic, outdoor Snow Cap strain—with a citrusy scent and an inspirational sativa high. In the past, the proximity of all this ambrosial greenery would have turned me into a binge-smoker. But ever since that chat with Trong outside the MA meeting, I now go several days at a time without even thinking about it.

If I do smoke, it usually involves writing rituals or mood maintenance. I will drink one cup of coffee with breakfast, write until my brain gets clogged, take a couple hits off the one-hitter or Volcano, and go for a run. These runs in the sun are always invigorating, and I often manage to resolve some personal or writerly dilemma by the time I return home.

I am no longer smoking to calibrate my psyche to "normal" or to ease anxiety. I sometimes find that vacuum-brain takes over in the early evening if I smoke too early, but that's a mild consequence.

Not long ago, my grandfather suffered a heart attack and spent two weeks in hospice, slowly fading into the afterlife. He was ninety-six years old. He had been a coal miner for forty-five years, and smoked cigarettes for thirty-five years, so his longevity was a thing of wonder. After falling and suffering a traumatic brain injury a few years before, he had been gradually deteriorating. I had spent quite a bit of quality time with him over the past few years, so I couldn't complain. But seeing him in that hospice bed was overwhelmingly sad, and stressful to the soul. It drove me to tears every time. So after I visited him, sometimes I came home and smoked a little weed. It didn't magically erase the pain, but it allowed me to bathe in the emotion without being overwhelmed by it. Being high allowed me to transmute that sadness into what I wished I could more readily conjure: feeling blessed that such a wonderful man was my grandfather, and that I got to spend as much time with him as I have.

Seeing a dying relative can also invoke that cliché sensation of wanting to milk every moment out of life. To the extent that marijuana has and continues to allow me to do this, I honor the plant and feel blessed to have discovered it. There are some minor regrets: missed opportunities, years when there could have been a higher correlation between inspiration and execution. There were times when I smoked too frequently, in an attempt to avoid reality, and that is among the reasons I wouldn't want my nieces and nephew to be exposed to marijuana too early. That said, I have known and read about successful, functioning adults who claim pot helped them through adolescent years that might otherwise have been emotionally debilitating.

It's no mystery why Colorado's successful legalization initiative was called the "Regulate Marijuana Like Alcohol Act of 2012." The prohibition of alcohol didn't work; neither has marijuana prohibition. And yet, alcohol's ubiquity in American society is among the most compelling arguments for *not* legalizing marijuana. Just as alcohol's legality hasn't resolved the myriad problems of alcohol use and abuse, so it goes with cannabis.

For marijuana aficionados like me, our relationship with the drug won't be greatly altered by legalization. But it should change how we are perceived by others. Indeed, if nothing else is gained from this book, along with the grander march toward legalization that is now underway, I hope we will begin to engage in a more open discussion about marijuana in America. I hope we weed enthusiasts will no longer have to slink around like naughty children when we purchase or consume this plant. I hope we will be able to come out of the cannabis closet to our parents, our kids, our teachers, and our coworkers. I hope some people will even discover that marijuana use is a meaningful experience that's been missing from their lives, like Kevin Spacey's character in *American Beauty*. But even for those of us who discover that marijuana scratches a certain psychological itch, allowing us to lighten up and laugh and enjoy music and transcend the daily blah for a bit, we will still have to find that delicate balance—our own personal Aristotelian mean of marijuana use—and concede that too much of a good thing can indeed be a bad thing.

CITATIONS

CHAPTER ONE

p. 13   *Nebraska's laws are among*: "State Laws," NORML website. http://norml.org/laws

p. 13   *Airports are one of five locations*: "How to Deal with the Police," The I Love Weed Blog, Jan. 11, 2010. http://iloveweed.net/guides/how-to-deal-with-the-police

p. 17   2010 *was the second-biggest year*: "Marijuana Arrests Driving America's So-Called 'Drug War,' Latest FBI Data Shows," NORML website, Paul Armentato, Sept. 19, 2011. http://blog.norml.org/2011/09/19/marijuana-arrests-driving-americas-so-called-drug-war-latest-fbi-data-shows/

p. 20   *Marijuana is a sensitizer*: William Burroughs, *Naked Lunch: 50th Anniversary Edition* (New York: Grove/Atlantic, 1959), 224.

p. 23   *"Any law disobeyed by more than 100 million Americans"*: "If Marijuana is Legal, Will Addiction Rise?" *The New York Times*, Room for Debate blog, July 19, 2009. http://roomfordebate.blogs.nytimes.com/2009/07/19/if-marijuana-is-legal-will-addiction-rise/

CHAPTER TWO

p. 26   *Marijuana first seeped into*: Martin Booth, *Cannabis: A History* (New York: Picador/St. Martin's Press: 2005), 167.

p. 27   *"I never heard the tune"*: Hoagy Carmichael, *Sometimes I Wonder* (Farrar, Straus and Giroux: New York, 1965), 102.

p. 27   *New Orleans banned marijuana in 1923*: "Reefer Madness Rears Its Ugly Head," Pot Culture blog. http://www.ukcia.org/potculture/20/madness.html

p. 27   *In 1930, President Herbert Hoover*: Humberto Fernandez, Theresa A. Libby, PhD, *Heroin: Its History, Pharmacology, and Treatment* (Hazelden: Center City, MN, 2011).

p. 28   *"bestial demoniacs, filled with"*: Universal News Service, 1936.

p. 28   *chief counsel Herman Oliphant*: Martin Booth, *Cannabis: A History* (New York: Picador/St. Martin's Press, 2005), 185.

p. 29   *"There are 100,000 total marijuana smokers"*: "L.A. Times: The Racism of Marijuana Prohibition," NORML Audio Stash Archive Blog, Sept. 8, 2009. http://stash.norml.org/la-times-the-racism-of-marijuana-prohibition

p. 29   *reached the floor of Congress*: Martin Booth, *Cannabis: A History* (New York: Picador/St. Martin's Press, 2005), 188.

p. 29   *Ted Turner*: "Celebrity Stoners," *Cannabis Culture*, Dana Larson, Jan. 8, 2003. http://www.cannabisculture.com/articles/2606.html

p. 29   *Mike Bloomberg*: "Citizen Mike," *New York*, Meryl Gordon, Apr. 16, 2001.

p. 29   *Steve Jobs*: "Steve Jobs' Pentagon File: Blackmail Fears, Youthful Arrest and LSD Cubes," *Wired*, Kim Zetter, June 11, 2012.

p. 30   *cannabis is valued at $35.8 billion*: "Marijuana Production in the United
        States," *The Bulletin of Cannabis Reform,* Jon Gettman, Dec. 2006, 13. http://
        www.drugscience.org/Archive/bcr2/MJCropReport_2006.pdf

p. 30   *the governors of Washington and Rhode Island*: "2 Governors Asking U.S.
        to Ease Rules on Marijuana to Allow for Its Medical Use," *The New York
        Times,* Michael Cooper, Dec. 1, 2011.

p. 30   *New Jersey officials are nearing*: "N. J. Patients Hopeful the Last Hurdle
        Has Been Cleared for Medical Marijuana," Philly.com website, Jan Hefler,
        Nov. 29, 2012. http://articles.philly.com/2012-11-29/news/35412861_1_
        greenleaf-compassion-center-medical-marijuana-marijuana-sales

p. 30   *nearly five hundred dispensaries*: "Medical Marijuana Rally at Michigan
        Capitol Draws Huge Crowd," Steve Elliot, Sept. 8, 2011. http://www.
        theweedblog.com/medical-marijuana-rally-at-michigan-capitol-draws-
        huge-crowd/

p. 31   *the most popular questions*: Obama Laughs off Pot Legalization at Town
        Hall Meeting," John A. Farrell, *U.S. News and World Report,* Mar. 26, 2009.
        http://www.usnews.com/opinion/blogs/john-farrell/2009/03/26/obama-
        laughs-off-pot-legalization-talk-at-town-hall-meeting

p. 31   *became uncharacteristically tongue-tied*: "Obama Dodges Medical
        Marijuana Question in Minnesota," Raw Story blog, David Edwards, Aug. 15,
        2011. http://www.rawstory.com/rawreplay/2011/08/obama-dodges-medical-
        marijuana-question-in-minnesota/

p. 31   *overseen the arrest of*: "Cuomo Seeks Cut in Frisk Arrests," *The New York
        Times,* Thomas Kaplan, June 4, 2012.

p. 32   *Ray Kelly released a memo in September*: "Police Memo on Marijuana
        Warns against Some Arrests," *The New York Times,* Elizabeth A. Harris,
        Sept. 24, 2011.

p. 32   *New York remained the marijuana arrest capital*: "Marijuana Arrests Rose
        in 2011, Despite Police Directive," *The New York Times* "City Rooms" blog,
        Andy Newman, Feb. 1, 2012, updated 4:20 pm.

p. 32   *American prisons now hold in excess of*: "The Caging of America," *The New
        Yorker,* Adam Gopnik, Jan. 30, 2012.

p. 32   *Since 1980, we have gone*: "Incarceration Nation," *Time,* Fareed Zakaria,
        Apr. 2, 2012. http://www.time.com/time/magazine/rticle/0,9171,2109777-
        1,00.html

p. 32   *Drug convictions rose tenfold*: Ibid.

p. 32   *We now arrest one American*: "The War on Pot: America's $42 Billion
        Annual Boondoggle," *Alternet,* Rob Kampia, Oct. 8, 2007. http://www.
        alternet.org/story/64465/the_war_on_pot%3A_america's_$42_billion_
        annual_boondoggle

p. 32   ***taxpayers an estimated $42 billion***: "Lost Taxes and Other Costs of
Marijuana Laws," *The Bulletin of Cannabis Reform,* Jon Gettman, Sept.
5, 2007, 1. http://www.drugscience.org/Archive/bcr4/Lost%20Taxes%20
and%20Other%20Costs%20of%20Marijuana%20Laws.pdf

CHAPTER FOUR

p. 49   ***more than seven hundred and fifty thousand***: California NORML website,
May 31, 2011. http://www.canorml.org/news/cbcsurvey2011.html

p. 49   ***California grew more than twenty million marijuana plants***: "Marijuana
Production in the United States," *The Bulletin of Cannabis Reform*, Jon Gettman, Dec. 2006, 11. http://www.drugscience.org/Archive/bcr2/MJCropRe-
port_2006.pdf

CHAPTER FIVE

p. 69   ***According to a leading researcher in the field***: "Study: Intelligence, cognition
unaffected by heavy marijuana use," *Harvard Gazette*, William J. Cromie,
October 15, 2001. http://news.harvard.edu/gazette/2001/10.11/marijuana.html

p. 71   ***"Forgetfulness is the catalytic germ"***: From Howard Marks' Foreword to
The God of Hellfire: The Crazy Life and Times of Arthur Brown (SAF Publishing: London, 2006), Polly Marshall.

p. 71   ***"lantern theory of attention"***: *High Times*, Mary Ought Six, Aug. 24, 2009.
http://hightimes.com/activism/ht_admin/5792

CHAPTER SIX

p. 76   ***In the first eight years since Colorado***: "Colorado's Green Rush: Medical
Marijuana," *CNN*, Jim Spellman, Dec. 14, 2009. http://www.cnn.com/2009/
US/12/14/colorado.medical.marijuana/index.html

p. 77   ***Just weeks after her appointment***: "Obama's War on Pot," *Rolling Stone*,
Tim Dickinson, Feb. 16, 2012.

p. 77   ***On October 13, Haag will***: "Mendocino Pot Raid Causes Stir among
California's Medical Marijuana Advocates," *Sacramento Bee*, Peter Hecht,
Last modified Jan. 17, 2012. http://www.sacbee.com/2011/10/30/4017018/
mendocino-pot-raid-causes-stir.html

p. 78   ***estimates the total taxpayer cost***: "While Obama's Thugs Raid Marijuana
School, People Die," *The Huffington Post*, Neill Franklin, April 3, 2012. http://
www.huffingtonpost.com/neill-franklin/oaksterdam-raid_b_1401116.html

p. 78   ***"I think with my legal issues"***: "Richard Lee Leaves Oaksterdam," *High
Times*, Mike Hughes, Apr. 7, 2012. http://hightimes.com/news/mike_
hughes/7616

p. 83   *no increase in the risk of developing*: "Large Study Finds No Link between Marijuana and Lung Cancer," *Scientific American*, David Biello, May 24, 2006. http://www.scientificamerican.com/article.cfm?id=large-study-finds-no-link

p. 83   *marijuana smokers tend to hold smoke*: "Study Finds No Cancer-Marijuana Connection," *The Washington Post*, Marc Kaufman, May 26, 2006.

CHAPTER SEVEN

p. 107   *In Mendocino County, patients used to*: "Local Medical Marijuana Cultivation & Possession Guidelines in California," California NORML website, Updated Oct. 25, 2012. http://www.canorml.org/medical-marijuana/local-growing-limits-in-california

p. 107   *further complicated by a state supreme court*: "Court Strikes Down SB 420 Limits," California NORML website, May 22, 2008. http://www.canorml.org/news/kellyruling.html

CHAPTER EIGHT

p. 117   *told* Rap Pages *magazine in 1995 that*: "DJ Screw: From Cough Syrup to Full-blown Fever," *The Guardian*, Jesse Serwer, Nov. 11, 2010.

p. 118   *50 percent in 1978 to a low of 20 percent*: "Monitoring the Future: National Results on Adolescent Drug Use: Overview of Key Findings, 2008," Johnston, L.D., O'Malley, P.M., Bachman, J.G., Schulenberg, J.E., National Institute on Drug Abuse, 2008, 13.

p. 118   *arrestees increased from 25 percent*: "Monitoring the Marijuana Upsurge With DUF/ADAM Arrestees, Final Report," National Criminal Justice Reference Service, U.S. Dept. of Justice. https://www.ncjrs.gov/pdffiles1/nij/grants/188867.pdf

p. 122   *seizures of marijuana parcels*: "You've Got Mail: Marijuana Shipments Skyrocket," ABC News: The Blotter blog, Drew Sandholm, Mar. 16, 2010. http://abcnews.go.com/Blotter/mail-marijuana-shipments-skyrocket/story?id=10108912#.UI_vcm_A-oY

p. 122   *Of the 3,621 parcels*: Ibid.

CHAPTER TEN

p. 149   *the religious and military order or sect*: "The Marihuana Tax Act of 1937, Transcripts of Congressional Hearings: Additional Statement of H.J. Anslinger, Commissioner of Narcotics," Schaffer Library of Drug Policy website. http://www.druglibrary.org/schaffer/hemp/taxact/t10a.htm

p. 150   *a castle called Alamut*: Martin Booth, *Cannabis: A History* (New York: Picador/St. Martin's Press, 2005), 80.

p. 151 *six ranks of disciples*: Ibid, 81.

p. 152 *The California Police Chiefs Association*: "Medical Marijuana a Frequent Target for Criminals," Associated Press, Mar. 18, 2010.

CHAPTER ELEVEN

p. 173 *former Tampa Bay Devil Rays*: "Report: Elijah Dukes Tried to Eat Bag of Marijuana after Traffic Stop," *Washington Post*, Matt Brooks, Feb. 23, 2012. http://www.washingtonpost.com/blogs/early-lead/post/report-elijah-dukes-tried-to-eat-bag-of-marijuana-after-traffic-stop/2012/02/23/gIQAF1cVVR_blog.html

p. 173 *Samaki Walker will get busted*: "Ex-NBA Lottery Pick Eats Pot during Arrest," *CBS News*, Stephen Smith, Aug. 1, 2011. http://www.cbsnews.com/8301-31751_162-20086281-10391697.html

p. 174 *study by the Department of Transportation*: Marijuana and Driving: A Review of the Scientific Evidence, NORML website. http://norml.org/library/item/marijuana-and-driving-a-review-of-the-scientific-evidence

p. 174 **Studies in the United States, Australia and Canada**: Ibid.

CHAPTER TWELVE

p. 182 *DEA agents with automatic weapons*: Tommy Chong, *The I-Chong: Meditations from the Joint* (Simon Spotlight: New York, 2006), 28.

p. 183 *was $12 million, and involved*: Julie Holland, *The Pot Book: A Complete Guide to Cannabis: Its Role in Medicine, Politics, Science, and Culture* (Park Street Press: Rochester, VT, 2010), 208.

p. 190 *who confiscated thirty-four plants*: "Dale Schafer and Dr. Mollie Fry: Ask President Obama to Grant Clemency for Patients Caught in the Cross Fire," Americans for Safe Access website. http://www.safeaccessnow.org/article.php?id=6394

p. 191 *the modern privatized prison industry*: "Prison Privatization and the Use of Incarceration," Sentencing Project website. http://www.sentencing-project.org/doc/publications/inc_prisonprivatization.pdf

p. 191 *GEO spent $220,000 on lobbying*: Open Secrets website. http://www.opensecrets.org/lobby/clientsum.php?id=D000022003&year=2011

p. 191 *at more than $4 million*: "Private Prisons Profit from Immigration Crackdown, Federal and Local Law Enforcement Partnerships," *The Huffington Post*, Chris Kirkham, June 7, 2012. http://www.huffingtonpost.com/2012/06/07/private-prisons-immigration-federal-law-enforcement_n_1569219.html

p. 190 *demand for our facilities and services*: "The Caging of America,"
The New Yorker, Adam Gopnik, Jan. 30, 2012. http://www.newyorker.com/
arts/critics/atlarge/2012/01/30/120130crat_atlarge_gopnik

p. 190 *to a lobbyist named John Lovell*: "The Top Five Special Interest Groups
Lobbying Marijuana Illegal," Republic Report blog. http://www.republic
report.org/2012/marijuana-lobby-illegal/

CHAPTER FOURTEEN

p. 216 *shortest possible sentence*: "State Laws," NORML blog. http://norml.org/
laws/item/indiana-penalties-2?category_id=858

CHAPTER FIFTEEN

p. 227 *16 percent of federal prisoners*: "Sourcebook of Criminal Justice Statistics,"
University at Albany website, 519. http://www.albany.edu/sourcebook/
pdf/т657.pdf

p. 227 *"the present young-adult generation's"*: "More Reefer Madness," *The Atlantic
Monthly*, Eric Schlosser, April, 1997.

p. 227 *30,000 drug-related prisoners*: "Obama Marijuana Legalization Stance
Rebutted By Failed Drug War," The Huffington Post, Ryan Grim,
Sept. 4, 2012. http://www.huffingtonpost.com/2012/09/04/obama-
marijuana-legalization_n_1852741.html

p. 234 *"It's easier for them"*: "If Marijuana is Legal, Will Addiction Rise?" *The
New York Times*, Room for Debate blog, July 19, 2009. http://roomfordebate.
blogs.nytimes.com/2009/07/19/if-marijuana-is-legal-will-addiction-rise/

p. 234 *from 15 percent in 1984*: "What Americans Need to Know about Marijuana:
Important Facts about Our Nation's Most Misunderstood Illegal Drug,"
National Criminal Justice Reference Service, Office of National Drug
Control Policy, Dept. of Justice, 10. https://www.ncjrs.gov/ondcppubs/
publications/pdf/mj_rev.pdf

p. 235 *"Some people want to point"*: "Going Dutch: Teen Marijuana Use in the
U.S. vs. Netherlands The Full Interview with Cal Professor Robert Mac-
Coun," East Bay Express, David Downs, Sept. 22, 2011. http://www.
eastbayexpress.com/LegalizationNation/archives/2011/09/22/going-
dutch-teen-marijuana-use-in-the-us-vs-netherlands-the-full-interview-
with-cal-professor-robert-maccoun

p. 237 *2011 Super Outbreak*: "Powerful Storms Threaten the Ohio Valley," Rich
Apuzzo, Nov. 1, 2011. http://www.examiner.com/article/powerful-storms-
threaten-the-ohio-valley

p. 241 *estimated 47,515 deaths*: "Mexico Updates Death Toll in Drug War to
47,515, but Critics Dispute the Data," *The New York Times*, Damien Cave,
Jan. 12, 2012.

EPILOGUE

p. 253 *Complaints of Forfeiture taped*: "California medical marijuana operation targeted by feds," *Los Angeles Times*, Joe Mozingo, July 11, 2012. http://articles.latimes.com/2012/jul/11/local/la-me-0712-marijuana-oakland-20120712

p. 254 *estimated $532 million in new revenue*: "Give Pot a Chance," *The New York Times*, The Opinion Pages, Timothy Egan, Nov. 22, 2012. http://opinionator.blogs.nytimes.com/2012/11/22/give-pot-a-chance/

p. 254 *a man had just been busted*: "Prosecutors in Washington Dismiss Dozens of Marijuana Cases in Response to Legalization," Gawker website, Neetzan Zimmerman, Nov. 12, 2012. http://gawker.com/5959810/prosecutors-in-washington-dismiss-dozens-of-marijuana-cases-in-response-to-legalization

p. 255 *extrapolating from the Dutch model*: "What Americans Need to Know about Marijuana: Important Facts about Our Nation's Most Misunderstood Illegal Drug," National Criminal Justice Reference Service, Office of National Drug Control Policy, 10. https://www.ncjrs.gov/ondcppubs/publications/pdf/mj_rev.pdf

p. 255 *increased heart rate and blood pressure*: "Marijuana Use and Its Effects," WebMD website. http://www.webmd.com/mental-health/marijuana-use-and-its-effects

ACKNOWLEDGMENTS

For inspiration, guidance, and near saintly patience, I'm indebted to David Cashion and Alex Glass.

For invaluable editorial insights and support, thanks to Brendan Koerner, Otto Dumpf, Ezra Edelman, Lola Winters, Tristan Patterson, Nicolai von Higuys, Javier Guzman, Nahna Kim, Mbanga Ka, Minh Martin, Justina Rabbithole, and Fred Nerz.

For all variety of support, including but not limited to housing, ideas, laughter, guided tours, interviews, and generous donations of kind buds, thanks to User Experience, George Peele aka Orange Peel Moses, Ahkbar Babar, William the Kidd, Bela Love, Mawiyah Lythcott, Mike Ciserella, Dom the English Gent, Zac Krug, Ethan Nadelmann, Danny Danko, Miss Bliss, Cher Aslor of the Northerly Winds, Erin Janow, Jamie Yoder, Denver ToneAge squad, Rick Riviezzo, Sanam Mahloudji, Team You Better Belize It, Caroline McCloskey, Brittany Morrison, Lester Grinspoon, Bryan Swinton, Ryan Cook, Quentin Mantooth, Warren Edson, David Blatty, Tatiana Tensen, Ida Odolade, Angela Alonzo, Tabatha Conrad, James from Cheeba Chews, Robert Platshorn, Amy Rose, Dave Bienenstock, Eric Voth, Amanda Roth, and of course, the NorCal hustlers—Puck, Bull, Noah, Roxanne, Chester, B-Nice, and Buddha Cheese.

ABOUT THE AUTHOR

Photo by Lindsey Cherry

Alfred Ryan Nerz is a freelance journalist who has written for NPR, *Esquire*, and the History Channel. He is the author of *Eat This Book: A Year of Gorging and Glory on the Competitive Eating Circuit*. Raised in Columbus, Indiana, he has lived in Brooklyn, Berlin, and southwest Florida.